教科書ガイド

三省堂 版

クラウン English Communication Ⅲ

TEXT BOOK GUIDE

文研出版

はじめに

本書は、三省堂発行の高等学校の教科書『CROWN English Communication Ⅲ』で英語を学習するみなさんの予習と演習のために書かれました。

教科書の学習は、教室でみなさんに直接英語を教えられる先生方のご指導によらなくてはなりませんが、英語の勉強は事前に自ら調べたり、また、授業のあとで復習し演習することで、学習した内容を確かなものにすることができます。本書はこうした予習・演習をより効果的に進めることを目的に作られた案内書であり、問題の解答をそのまま与えるものではありません。

本書では、教科書の内容を正しく理解するだけでなく、教科書で扱われる表現を文法の体系からわかりやすく解説し、さらに多くの例題を解くことにより応用力をつけることを目指しました。本書を教科書学習の理解に役立たせるばかりでなく、積極的に英語でコミュニケーションをはかる手がかりとして利用していただければ幸いです。

2024年2月

編集部

本書の構成と学習の進め方

本書では、教科書本文の１セクションを１つの単位として取り上げ、重要項目ごとに解説をつけました。

次のような流れで学習できるように、構成されています。

■教科書本文

教科書本文の１セクションを１単位として転載しています。

セクション分けされていない課は、便宜的にいくつかのまとまりに区切り、それぞれを１単位として転載しています。

■このセクションの内容

そのセクションの概要がつかめているか、空所補充問題で確認できるようになっています。

解答は、次ページのいちばん下に掲載されています。

■解説

教科書本文を理解する上で重要な箇所を取り上げ、構文、文法、および語句や表現の観点からわかりやすく解説しています。

解説が理解できたかどうかをチェックするために、解説のあとに、適宜基本的な演習問題を入れています。解説が理解できているかを確認しましょう。解答は、本書巻末に掲載しています。

■確認問題

次の項目ごとに、段階を踏んで教科書の英語の理解を総合的に確認しましょう。解答は、本書巻末に掲載しています。

語彙

教科書本文に登場した語彙について、空所補充、語形変化、発音・アクセントなど、さまざまな形式の問題を解くことで確認します。

文法・表現

教科書本文で学んだ文法、語法、表現を演習します。

総合

教科書本文を掲載し、空所補充、英文和訳、整序問題など、さまざまな形式の問題を付しました。文法や内容の理解を総合的に確認します。

CONTENTS

Lesson 1 How Language Shapes the Way We Think

教科書p.10　Section 1

①There are many languages spoken in the world. ②Do you think people who speak different languages have different ways of thinking? ③Lera Boroditsky, a professor of cognitive science at the University of California, San Diego, discusses this issue in a talk.

1

④I'll be speaking to you using language. ⑤This is one of these magical abilities that we humans have. ⑥Because of this ability, we're able to transmit our ideas across vast reaches of space and time.

There are about 7,000 languages spoken around the world. ⑦And all the languages differ from one another in all kinds of ways—in sound, vocabulary, and structure. ⑧We may ask the question: Does the language we speak shape the way we think?

⑨Some people would say yes, and others would say no. ⑩The arguments have gone back and forth for thousands of years. ⑪Until recently, there hasn't been any data to help us decide either way. ⑫But now we have scientific data to weigh in on this question.

このセクションの内容

世界中では約（A.　　　　　）の言語が話されていて、すべての言語は、音声、語彙、構造など、あらゆる点で異なっている。ところで、言語が違えば、（B.　　　　　）も異なるのだろうか。これは何千年もの間、議論の的となってきたが、現在の私たちには、それについて検討するための（C.　　　　　）的なデータがある。

① There are many languages spoken in the world.

▶ many languages spoken in ～は「～で話されている多くの言語」。

② Do you think people who speak different languages have different ways of thinking?

▶ people who speak different languagesは「異なる言語を話す人々」。whoは主格の関係代名詞。

▶ different ways of thinkingは「異なる考え方」。文全体で、「使う言語が異なれば、物事に対する見方や考え方が異なると思うか」という質問。

③ Lera Boroditsky, a professor of cognitive science at the University of California, San Diego, discusses this issue in a talk.

▶ a professor ~ San Diegoは、Lera Boroditskyの説明。cognitive scienceは「認知科学」(情報処理の観点から、人間や動物の知的なあり方を探求する学問領域)。

▶ this issue「この問題」とは、②の文で問われている内容を指す。

▶ in a talkは「(ある)講演で」。

④ I'll be speaking to you using language.

▶ will be V-ing(未来進行形)は、「~することにしている、~することになる」と、すでに決まっている予定を表す。

▶ speak to ~は「~に話しかける」。

▶ using languageは「言語を使いながら」の意味で、〈付帯状況〉を表す。

⑤ This is one of these magical abilities that we humans have.

▶ Thisは④のusing languageを指す。

▶ these magical abilities (that) we humans have「私たち人間が持っている不思議な能力」。weとhumansは〈同格〉の関係。

⑥ Because of this ability, we're able to transmit our ideas across vast reaches of space and time.

▶ transmit ~ across ...は「…を超えて~を伝える」。transmitには「~を送(り届け)る、(病気など)を伝染させる、(ニュースなど)を放送する」などの意味もある。名詞形はtransmission。

例 The news was *transmitted* to all of them.
「その知らせは彼ら全員に伝えられた」

▶ vast reaches of space and timeは「空間と時間の広大な範囲[広がり]」(≒ a huge area and time)。reachは通例複数形で「(一面の)広がり」の意味。

⑦ And all the languages differ from one another in all kinds of ways—in sound, vocabulary, and structure.

▶ differ from one anotherは「お互いに異なっている」。

✍ 英文を完成させなさい。

習慣は国によって異なる。

Customs (　　　) (　　　) one country to (　　　).

▶ in all kinds of waysは「あらゆる種類の方法で」→「あらゆる点で」。具体例がダッシュ(—)以下に並べられている。structureは「(文法などの)言語構造」のこと。

このセクションの内容 の答え→ A. 7,000 B. 考え方[思考方法] C. 科学

⑧ We may ask the question: Does the language we speak shape the way we think?

▶ We may ask the question: ～は「私たちは～という質問をする[疑問を持つ]かもしれない」。コロン(：)以下はthe questionの具体的な内容。

▶ the language we speakは「私たちが話す言語」。

▶ shape the way we thinkは「私たちの考え方[思考方法]を形成する」。動詞のshapeには「～を形づくる、～を決定する、～を方向づける」などの意味がある。

⑨ Some people would say yes, and others would say no.

▶ Some people ～, and others (= other people) ... は「～する人たちもいれば、…する人たちもいる」。

✍ 英文を完成させなさい。

高齢者の中には運動が好きな人もいれば、そうでない人もいる。

( ) elderly people like to exercise, and ( ) ( ).

▶ wouldは「～するかもしれない」という〈推量〉を表す。

⑩ The arguments have gone back and forth for thousands of years.

▶ The arguments「その議論」は、⑧の文のコロン(：)以下に述べられた質問に関する議論を指す。

▶ have goneは継続を表す現在完了。go back and forthは「行ったり来たりする」→「定まらない、結論が出ない」。

▶ for thousands of yearsは「数千年の間」。

⑪ Until recently, there hasn't been any data to help us decide either way.

▶ Until recentlyは「最近まで」。

▶ there hasn't been any ～「どんな～もなかった」は継続を表す現在完了。

▶ data to help us decide ～は「私たちが～を決定するのを助けるデータ」で、to以下は〈help + 人 + *do*〉の形。

▶ decide either way「どちらかの方に決定する」とは、「言語が人の考え方[思考方法]を形成するかしないかについての結論を出す」ということ。

⑫ But now we have scientific data to weigh in on this question.

▶ scientific data to *do*は「～するための科学的データ」。

▶ weighには「～をよく考える、～を比較検討する」の意味があり、weigh in on ～で「～について検討する」(≒ give *one's* opinions on ～「～について意見[見解]を述べる」)の意味を表す。

教科書pp.10〜12　Section 2

2

①Let me tell you about some of my favorite examples. ②I'll start with an example from an Aboriginal community in Australia. They are the Kuuk Thaayorre people. In their language, they don't use words like "left" and "right." ③Instead, everything is in cardinal directions: north, south, east, and west. ④You'd say something like, "Move your cup to the north-northeast a little bit." ⑤When you want to say "hello" in their language, you'd say, "Which way are you going?" ⑥And the answer should be, "North-northeast in the far distance. How about you?"

⑦We used to think that humans were worse than other creatures at orientation, but if your language trains you to do it, you can do it.

⑧There are also big differences in how people think about time. Here I have pictures of my grandfather at different ages. ⑨If I ask an English speaker to organize the pictures in time order, she might lay them out from left to right, which indicates that time moves from left to right. But how would the Kuuk Thaayorre do it? They don't use words like "left" and "right." ⑩When facing south, time moves from left to right. When facing north, time moves from right to left. When facing east, time comes towards the body. ⑪What's the pattern? East to west, right? ⑫For them, time doesn't get locked on the body; it gets locked on the landscape. It's a dramatically different way of thinking about time.

このセクションの内容

オーストラリアのアボリジニであるクーク・ターヨレ族には、「左」や「右」という言葉はなく、（A.　　　　　）で表す。また、彼らの（B.　　　　　）の流れに対する考え方も独特で、どちらを向いているかにかかわらず、常に東から西に進む。つまり、時間は（C.　　　　　）にではなく、風景に対応している。

① Let me tell you about some of my favorite examples.

▶〈let + 人 + *do*〉は「(人) に〜させてやる、(人) が〜するのを許す」。Let me tell you about 〜. で「皆さんに〜についてお話ししましょう」の意味。

② I'll start with an example from an Aboriginal community in Australia.

▶ start with ～は「～で[から]始める」、an example from ～は「～に由来する例」。AboriginalはAborigine「オーストラリア先住民」の形容詞形。

③ Instead, everything is in cardinal directions: north, south, east, and west.

▶ Instead「代わりに」は、直前の文の内容を受けて、「『左』や『右』のような言葉を使う代わりに」ということ。

▶ everything is in cardinal directions「すべてのものは基本的な方角に存在する」とはつまり、クーク・ターヨレ族は、どんなものの位置も東西南北の方角で表すということ。

④ You'd say something like, "Move your cup to the north-northeast a little bit."

▶ You'd (= You would) say something like, ～は「～などと言うだろう[言うかもしれない]」。youは一般的な人を指す。

▶ Move your cup to the north-northeast「あなたのカップを北北東に動かしてください」とはつまり、「左」や「右」という言葉を使わずに、方角を使って指示するということ。

▶ a little bitは「少し」(≒ slightly)。*cf.* a little bit of ～「少量の～」

⑤ When you want to say "hello" in their language, you'd say, "Which way are you going?"

▶ 彼らの言語における「こんにちは」という挨拶は、やはり方角を使って、「どちらの方に行くのですか」という言い方になるということ。

⑥ And the answer should be, "North-northeast in the far distance. How about you?"

▶ the answerは、⑤の"Which way are you going?"に対する返事のこと。

▶ should be ～は「たぶん～だろう」という〈可能性・推量〉を表す。

▶ North-northeast in the far distance「ずっと遠くの北北東に(行くところだ)」。in the distanceは「遠くに」(≒ far away)。

▶ How about you?は「あなたはどちらの方角に行くのですか」という意味。

⑦ We used to think that humans were worse than other creatures at orientation, but if your language trains you to do it, you can do it.

▶ used to *do*は「(今は違うが)以前は～していた」。

▶ humans ～ orientationまでがthat節の内容。

▶ be worse than ～ at ...は「…の点で～よりも劣っている」、other creatures

このセクションの内容 の答え→ A. 東西南北[方角] B. 時間 C. (身)体

は「(人間以外の) ほかの生物」。

▶ orientationは、動詞orient「特定の方向に向きを合わせる」の名詞形で、「方角を正しく把握すること」→「方向感覚」を表す。

▶ if your language trains you to do itは無生物主語構文。〈train + 人など + to *do*〉で、「(人など) を～するように訓練する」の意味を表す。もし言語による訓練を受ければ、クーク・ターヨレ族のように方角に鋭くなることができるということ。

✍ 英文を完成させなさい。

彼はその象が芸をするように訓練した。

He (　　　) the elephant (　　　) perform tricks.

⑧ There are also big differences in how people think about time.

▶ in how people think about timeは「時間についての人々の考え方において」。

✍ ほぼ同じ意味を表すように、英文を完成させなさい。

I'm interested in the way they built the robot.

I have interest (　　　) (　　　) they built the robot.

⑨ If I ask an English speaker to organize the pictures in time order, she might lay them out from left to right, which indicates that time moves from left to right.

▶〈ask + 人 + to *do*〉は「(人) に～するように求める」、organize ～ in time orderは「～を時間順に系統立てる[編成する]」。

▶ mightは「～かもしれない」〈可能性・推量〉、lay them (= the pictures) outは「それらを並べる」(≒ put them in order)。

▶〈, which〉は非制限用法の関係代名詞で、直前の内容 (写真を左から右へ並べること) を指す。

▶ indicates that time moves from left to rightは「時間が左から右に進むことを示している」。なお、日本の絵巻物などでは時間は右から左に進むように描かれている。

⑩ When facing south, time moves from left to right.

▶ ここから3つの文は、クーク・ターヨレ族における「時間の流れ」を説明している。「南を向いているとき、時間は左から右に流れる」の意味。

⑪ What's the pattern? East to west, right?

▶ クーク・ターヨレ族における時間の流れには、どんなパターンがあるか。それは「東から西へ」というパターンだということ。

⑫ For them, time doesn't get locked on the body; it gets locked on the landscape.

▶ get locked on ～は「～に固定される」、landscapeは「風景、景観」。

3

①Here's another human trick. ②Suppose I asked you how many penguins you see. ③I know how you'd answer. You'd go, "One, two, three, four, five, six, seven, eight." ④You'd count them. ⑤Having number words in your language opens up the whole world of mathematics. ⑥This little trick gives you a stepping stone into a whole cognitive realm.

Some languages don't have number words. ⑦In fact, people who speak these languages don't count, and they have trouble keeping track of exact quantities. ⑧For example, if I asked you to match a certain number of penguins to the same number of ducks, you would be able to do that by counting. ⑨But folks who don't have that linguistic trick can't do that.

⑩Languages also differ in how they divide up the color spectrum. Some languages have lots of words for colors. ⑪Some have only a couple of words: "light" and "dark." ⑫Languages also differ in where they put boundaries between colors. ⑬For example, in English, *blue* can cover all shades of blue, but in Russian, there isn't a single word. ⑭Instead, Russian speakers have to differentiate between light blue, *goluboy*, and dark blue, *siniy*. ⑮So, Russians have this lifetime of experience of distinguishing these two colors in language.

⑯The difference in how languages categorize the color spectrum has important consequences. ⑰When we test people's ability to perceptually discriminate among these colors, we find that Russian speakers are faster across this linguistic boundary. ⑱For example, when you have colors shifting slowly from light to dark blue, Russian speakers will have a surprised reaction in their brains, whereas English speakers won't.

このセクションの内容

言語によっては（A.　　　　　）を持たないものもあり、そうした言語を話す人は、2つのものが同数かどうか、（B.　　　　　）に把握するのが難しい。また、色についても言語によって異なり、例えば（C.　　　　　）語では「明るい青」と「暗い青」は別の色に分類される。

① Here's another human trick.

▶ Here's ～は「ここに～がある」、human trickは「人間の巧みな芸当[技術]」。

② Suppose I asked you how many penguins you see.

▶ Suppose (that) ～は命令文で、「～だと想像しなさい」→「仮に～だとしたらどうだろう」などの意味を表す。なお、suppose[supposing] ～は接続詞ifの代用としても使われる。

例 *Suppose*[*Supposing*] you were in her place, what would you say?
「あなたが彼女の立場だったら、何と言いますか」

▶ how many以下は間接疑問。

③ I know how you'd answer.

▶ how以下は間接疑問。how you'd answerは「あなたがどのようにして(ペンギンの数を)答えるか」。

④ You'd count them.

▶ countは「～を(1つずつ)数える」。themはpenguinsを指す。

⑤ Having number words in your language opens up the whole world of mathematics.

▶ Having number words in your languageが主語で、「あなたの言語に数を表す語[数字]があること」の意味。

▶ open up ～は「～を広げる」、the whole world of mathematicsは「数学の世界全体」。

⑥ This little trick gives you a stepping stone into a whole cognitive realm.

▶ This little trick「この小さな技術」とはlinguistic trick「言語的技術」(⑨の文)のことで、数字を使って数を数えることを指す。

▶ a stepping stone into ～は「～への足がかり[手段]」。

▶ a whole cognitive realmは「認知領域全体」の意味で、cognitive realmとは、私たちが観察などによって得られる知識や理解のこと。

⑦ In fact, people who speak these languages don't count, and they have trouble keeping track of exact quantities.

▶ In factは「事実、実際、実のところ」。

▶ 前半の文の主語はpeople who ～ languagesで、these languagesは「数字を持たない諸言語」のこと。

▶ have trouble V-ingは「～することが困難だ」。

✍ 次の英文を日本語に直しなさい。

There are a lot of elderly people who have trouble living alone.

______________________________高齢者が大勢いる。

このセクションの内容 の答え→ A. 数を表す語[数字] B. 正確 C. ロシア

▶ keep track of 〜は「〜を把握する」、exact quantitiesは「正確な数量」。

⑧ For example, if I asked you to match a certain number of penguins to the same number of ducks, you would be able to do that by counting.

▶「仮に私が〜するとしたら、あなたは…することができるだろう」という仮定法過去の文。

▶〈ask + 人 + to *do*〉は「(人)に〜するように頼む」。

▶ match 〜 to ... は「〜を…に一致させる」。match a certain number of penguins to the same number of ducksとは、「ある特定の数のペンギンを同じ数のアヒルに一致させる」→「ペンギンとアヒルの数を一致させる」ということ。

▶ by countingは「数を数えることによって」。

⑨ But folks who don't have that linguistic trick can't do that.

▶ 文の主語はfolks (≒ people) who 〜 trick。

▶ that linguistic trick「その言語的技術」とは、数字を使って数を数える技術のこと。

▶ do thatは、⑧の文のペンギンとアヒルの数を一致させること。

⑩ Languages also differ in how they divide up the color spectrum.

▶ differ in 〜は「〜の点で異なる」。

▶ howは先行詞the wayを含む関係副詞で、theyはLanguagesを指す。

▶ divide up 〜は「〜を分ける[分割する]」(≒ split up 〜)、color spectrumは「色のスペクトラム[連続体]」。

⑪ Some have only a couple of words: "light" and "dark."

▶ SomeはSome languagesのこと。

▶ a couple of 〜は「2つの〜、一対の〜」。複数のものについて、「2、3の〜」「いくつかの〜」を表すこともある。

✍ 英文を完成させなさい。

2、3時間したらここを出発しよう。

Let's leave here (　　　) a (　　　) of hours.

⑫ Languages also differ in where they put boundaries between colors.

▶ differ in where 〜 between colorsは「いろいろな色の間のどこに境界線を引くかという点で異なる」。

⑬ For example, in English, *blue* can cover all shades of blue, but in Russian, there isn't a single word.

▶ *blue*は「(英語の) blueという語」。

▶ cover all shades of blueは「あらゆる色合いのblueを含む[カバーする]」で、shades「陰」はここでは「色合い」の意味。

▶ there isn't a single wordは「(blueを表す) 単一の単語がない」。

⑭ **Instead, Russian speakers have to differentiate between light blue, *goluboy*, and dark blue, *siniy*.**

▶ Instead「代わりに」は、「単一の語を使う代わりに」ということ。

▶ differentiate between ～ and ...「～と…とを区別する」。*goluboy*は「明るい青」、*siniy*は「暗い青」を表すロシア語。

✍ 次の英文を日本語に直しなさい。

Can you differentiate between opinion and fact?

---

⑮ **So, Russians have this lifetime of experience of distinguishing these two colors in language.**

▶ have this lifetime of experience of V-ingは「～するという経験を生涯にわたって持つ」、distinguishは「～を区別する」。

⑯ **The difference in how languages categorize the color spectrum has important consequences.**

▶ 文の主語はThe difference ～spectrum「諸言語が色のスペクトラムをどのように分類するかの違い」。

▶ consequenceは「結果」。どのような結果かは、⑰の文に述べられている。

⑰ **When we test people's ability to perceptually discriminate among these colors, we find that Russian speakers are faster across this linguistic boundary.**

▶ ability to *do*は「～する能力」、perceptually discriminate among these colorsは「これらの色(＝青のスペクトラム)を知覚的に識別する」。

▶ faster across this linguistic boundary「この言語的境界を越えて(反応が)より速い」とは、「その変化によりすばやく気付く」ということ。

⑱ **For example, when you have colors shifting slowly from light to dark blue, Russian speakers will have a surprised reaction in their brains, whereas English speakers won't.**

▶ 〈have + O + V-ing〉は「Oに～させる[させておく]」。have colors shifting slowlyで「色をゆっくり[少しずつ]変化させる」の意味。

▶ have a surprised reaction in their brainsは「脳の中で(あっ、色が変わった、と)驚きの反応を示す」。

▶ whereasは「だが一方」(≒ but、while)。

▶ 文末にhave a surprised reaction in their brainsが省略されている。

教科書pp.13～14 Section 4

4

①Languages also differ in how they describe events. ②Take an event like an accident. ③In English, it's fine to say, "She broke the vase." ④In Spanish, you wouldn't say that someone did it; rather, you'd say, "The vase broke," or "The vase broke itself."

⑤Again, this has consequences. ⑥English speakers will remember who did it, because English requires you to specify the actor. ⑦In contrast, Spanish speakers might be less likely to remember who did it, because there's no such requirement.

⑧So far, I've given you a few examples of how language can shape the way we think, and how it does so in a variety of ways.

⑨Now, the beauty of linguistic diversity is that it reveals to us just how ingenious and flexible the human mind is. ⑩We have invented not one cognitive universe, but 7,000—there are 7,000 languages in the world. ⑪The tragic thing is that we're losing so much of this linguistic diversity. ⑫By some estimates, half of the world's languages will be gone in the next hundred years.

⑬I want to leave you with a final thought. ⑭I've told you about how speakers of different languages think differently, and how the language that you speak shapes the way you think. ⑮This gives you the opportunity to ask, "Why do I think the way I do?" "⑯How could I think differently?" "⑰What thoughts do I wish to create?"

Thank you very much.

このセクションの内容

(A.　　　　　　)を説明する方法も、言語によって異なる。世界に7,000もの言語があるということは、人間が7,000もの認識宇宙を発明したということ、つまり、人間の心が独創的で柔軟であることを示している。しかし、言語の(B.　　　　　　)は失われつつあり、100年以内にその(C.　　　　　　)が消滅すると推定されている。

① Languages also differ in how they describe events.

▶ differ in how ～は「～する方法という点で異なる」。theyはLanguagesを指す。

② Take an event like an accident.

▶命令文で、「～を取り上げてみよう」の意味。

▶ like ～は「～のような」、accidentは「事故、偶発的で好ましくない出来事」。*cf.* by accident「偶然、たまたま」

③ In English, it's fine to say, "She broke the vase."

▶ itはto say ～を指す形式主語。it's fine to say, ～は「～と言ってもかまわない[問題ない]」。

④ In Spanish, you wouldn't say that someone did it; rather, you'd say, "The vase broke," or "The vase broke itself."

▶ wouldn't say that ～は「～と言わないだろう」。

▶ someone did itは「誰かがそうした(＝花瓶を割った)」。

▶セミコロン(；)は接続詞の働きをし、2つの関連する文をつないでいる。ratherは「むしろ～」。

▶ The vase broke「花瓶が割れた」、The vase broke itself.「花瓶は自ら壊れた」は、どちらも「人」を主語にしない言い方。

⑤ Again, this has consequences.

▶ Againは「また、やはり」。

▶ this「このこと」は、英語とスペイン語では表現方法が異なることを指す。

▶ consequence「結果」は、「異なる表現方法を使った結果」を指し、どのような結果になるかは、次の⑥と⑦の文に述べられている。

⑥ English speakers will remember who did it, because English requires you to specify the actor.

▶英語という言語の特質を述べた文。who did itは間接疑問で、「誰がそれをしたか」。

▶〈require＋人＋to *do*〉は「(人)に～するように要求する」。

英文を完成させなさい。

その授業では、生徒は3本のレポートを書くことが求められる。

The class (　　　) students (　　　) write three papers.

▶ specify the actorは「行為者を明確に述べる」。英語では、腕が折れた場合でも、She broke her arm.「彼女は腕を折った」のように、行為者を主語にして表現する。

⑦ In contrast, Spanish speakers might be less likely to remember who did it, because there's no such requirement.

このセクションの内容 の答え→　A. 出来事　B. 多様性　C. 半数[半分]

▶ In contrastは「(それとは)対照的に」。

▶ might be less likely to *do*は「あまり～しないかもしれない、～しそうにない」。mightは〈可能性・推量〉を表す。

✍ 英文を完成させなさい。

旅行者はあまりその地域のイベントに参加しないかもしれない。

Tourists might be (　　　) (　　　) to participate in the local event.

▶ such requirement「そのような要求」とは、行為者を明確に述べるという要求[必要性]を指す。

⑧ So far, I've given you a few examples of how language can shape the way we think, and how it does so in a variety of ways.

▶ So farは「今まで(のところで)は、これまでは」。

▶ how language can shape the way we thinkは「言語がどのようにして私たちの考え方[思考方法]を形成し得るのか」。

▶ how it does so in a variety of waysは「それ(＝言語)がどのようにしてさまざまな方法でそうする(＝私たちの考え方を形成する)のか」。

⑨ Now, the beauty of linguistic diversity is that it reveals to us just how ingenious and flexible the human mind is.

▶〈S＋V＋C(＝that節)〉の文。

▶ the beauty of linguistic diversityは「言語の多様性の美しさ[すばらしさ]」。

▶ that節のitはlinguistic diversityを指す。

▶ reveals to us just how ～は「いかに～であるかを私たちに明示する[明らかにしてくれる]」。justは強調を表す。

▶ how以下は間接疑問。ingenious and flexibleは「独創的で柔軟な」。

⑩ We have invented not one cognitive universe, but 7,000 —there are 7,000 languages in the world.

▶ not ～, but ...は「～ではなく…」。

✍ 次の英文を日本語に直しなさい。

Try not to become a man of success but to become a man of value.

＿＿＿＿＿＿＿＿＿＿＿＿＿＿＿＿ 価値のある人間になろうとせよ。

▶ cognitive universe「認識宇宙」とは、「物の見方や考え方」のこと。世界には7,000の言語があるのだから、7,000もの認識宇宙を発明したことになるということ。

⑪ The tragic thing is that we're losing so much of this linguistic diversity.

▶ The tragic thing is that ～は「悲しむべきことは～ということだ、残念なことに～だ」。

▶ so much of ～は「非常に多くの～」。

⑫ By some estimates, half of the world's languages will be gone in the next hundred years.

▶ By some estimatesは「ある推定[見積もり]によると」。

▶ will be goneは「なくなるだろう、失われてしまうだろう」(≒ will be lost)。goneは形容詞で、「存在しない、出発した」などの意味。

✍ 英文を完成させなさい。

社長は明日から1週間、不在になります。

The president will (　　　) (　　　) for a week starting tomorrow.

▶ in the next hundred yearsは「今後100年のうちに」。

⑬ I want to leave you with a final thought.

▶〈leave + 人 + with ～〉は「(人)に～を託す[預ける]」、a final thoughtは「最後の考え」。

▶文全体で、「最後に皆さんに考えてもらいたいことがある」という意味。

⑭ I've told you about how speakers of different languages think differently, and how the language that you speak shapes the way you think.

▶ howで始まる2つの節がaboutの目的語になっている。1つ目のhow ～は「異なる言語を話す人はどのように違う考え方をするのか」(主語はspeakers of different languages)、2つ目のhow ～は「話す言語はどのように考え方[思考方法]を形成するのか」(主語はthe language that you speak)。

⑮ This gives you the opportunity to ask, "Why do I think the way I do?"

▶ This「このこと」は、⑬の文のa final thoughtの内容、つまり⑭の文で述べられた具体的な問いかけを指す。

▶ opportunity to *do*は「～する機会」。

▶ Why do I think the way I do?は「私はなぜ私のやり方で考えるのか」→「私はなぜそのような考え方をするのだろうか」。

⑯ How could I think differently?

▶ couldは〈可能性〉を表す。「私はどうすれば違って考えることができるのか」→「私はどうすれば違った考え方ができるのだろうか」。

⑰ What thoughts do I wish to create?

▶ wish to *do*は「～したいと願う」。文全体で「自分はどんな考えを生み出したいのか」という意味。

確認問題

語彙

1 次の文の意味が通るように、右から単語を選んで(　)内に補いなさい。

(1) I still have enough English (　　　).
(2) The (　　　) of food is good enough at this restaurant.
(3) They are active in the (　　　) of natural science.
(4) He is recognized worldwide as a (　　　) painter.

realm landscape vocabulary quantity

2 第2音節にアクセント(強勢)のある語を3つ選び、記号で答えなさい。

ア　cog-ni-tive　　イ　in-gen-ious　　ウ　mag-i-cal
エ　lin-guis-tic　　オ　dis-tin-guish　　カ　car-di-nal

文法・表現

1 日本語に合うように、(　)内に適切な語を入れなさい。

(1) 性格は人によって異なる。
Personality (　　　) (　　　) person to person.
(2) 原発に賛成の人もいれば、反対の人もいる。
(　　　) people are for nuclear power, and (　　　) are against it.
(3) できることから始めることが大切です。
It's important to (　　　) (　　　) what we can do.
(4) はるか遠くに青い山脈が見えた。
I could see the blue mountains (　　　) (　　　) far (　　　).

2 各組の文がほぼ同じ意味になるように、(　)内に適切な語を入れなさい。

(1) There are some languages that have no words for numbers.
(　　　) (　　　) (　　　) have any words for numbers.
(2) Why do you think in such a way?
Why do you think (　　　) (　　　) (　　　) do?

3 日本語に合うように、(　)内の語句を並べかえなさい。

(1) その問題についての私たちの考え方には、いくらか違いがある。
There're some differences (how / about / we / think / in) the problem.
There're some differences ________________________ the problem.

(2) 私が皆さんに、どの季節が一番好きかとたずねたとしましょう。
Suppose (season / asked / you / the best / what / you / I / like).
Suppose ______________________________.

(3) 今週末は、雨になる可能性はあまりなさそうだ。
It might (likely / be / be / rainy / less / to) this weekend.
It might ______________________________ this weekend.

(4) 最も大切なことは、あなたが決してあきらめないということだ。
The most important thing (never / that / up / you / is / give).
The most important thing ______________________________.

総合

次の文を読んで、あとの問いに答えなさい。

Languages also differ (①) how they divide up the color spectrum. Some languages have lots of words for colors. Some have only a couple of words: "light" and "dark." Languages also differ (①) where they put boundaries between colors. For example, in English, *blue* can cover all shades of blue, but in Russian, there isn't a single word. (②), Russian speakers have to differentiate between light blue, *goluboy*, and dark blue, *siniy*. So, Russians have this lifetime of experience of distinguishing these two colors in language.

③The difference in how languages categorize the color spectrum has important consequences. When we test people's ability to perceptually discriminate among these colors, we find that Russian speakers are faster across ④this linguistic boundary. For example, when you have colors shifting slowly from light to dark blue, Russian speakers will ⑤have a surprised reaction in their brains, whereas English speakers won't.

問1　2つの(①)に共通して入る語を書きなさい。

問2　(②)に適するものを下から選び、記号で答えなさい。
ア So far　イ Again　ウ Instead　エ In fact

問3　下線部③を日本語に直しなさい。

問4　下線部④の内容を具体的に日本語で説明しなさい。

問5　下線部⑤について、ロシア人たちはなぜこのような反応を示すのか、日本語で説明しなさい。

Lesson 2 Weak Robots

教科書p.24 Section 1

①We expect robots to work for us, performing a range of services. They are our servants. ②After all, the word *robot* comes from *robota*, a Slavic word meaning "slave" or "servant." ③But is it possible for us to form a more cooperative relationship with robots?

1

④When we think about robot technology, we often think about autonomous robots which can work independently of human beings. ⑤Space probes which wander across the surface of Mars. ⑥Delivery robots that drop packages right on our doorsteps. ⑦Our vision of the future is a vision of autonomous robots driving our cars, cleaning our houses, cooking our meals. ⑧They might be called "strong" robots, in the sense that they can work without human help.

⑨While we wait for that future, we make do with "weak" robots like the cleaning robot that sweeps our floors. ⑩The little guy is cute but not very smart. ⑪He's always getting tangled up in electrical cords. ⑫In order to help him clean the room without getting into trouble, you might start by picking up things which could be in his way.

⑬The room gets cleaned up. ⑭But when you ask: "Who cleaned this room?" you make an interesting discovery. ⑮The little robot did not clean the room by itself. You did not clean the room by yourself. ⑯The two of you did it together. ⑰The robot cleverly managed to get your cooperation in cleaning the room. ⑱What's interesting about the little cleaning robot is that, for all his weakness, he has become part of your family.

このセクションの内容

人間から（A.　　　　　）して働くことができる自律的な〈強い〉ロボットが活躍する未来を待つ間、私たちは人間の手助けを必要とする〈弱い〉ロボットで間に合わせることが可能だ。例えば、床掃除を行う小型の掃除ロボットは、部屋の掃除をするとき、人間の（B.　　　　　）を巧妙に得る。このロボットの興味深い点は、その（C.　　　　　）にもかかわらず、使用者の家族の一員になるという点だ。

① **We expect robots to work for us, performing a range of services.**

▶ expect ～ to *do* は「～に…することを期待する」、performは「～を行う」、a range of ～は「さまざまな～」、serviceは「奉仕、用役」。

▶ performing ～は、本来必要な意味上の主語robotsが省略された特殊な分詞構文になっている。ふつう、分詞の主語が主節の主語と異なるときには、分詞の前にその主語を置く必要がある。

例 *It* being a holiday, almost all the shops were closed.
「祝日だったので、ほとんどすべての店が閉まっていた」

▶ 文全体で「私たちはロボットに、自分たちのために働いてさまざまな奉仕をしてもらいたいと期待する」や「私たちはロボットに自分たちのために働いてもらうことを期待し、彼らはさまざまな奉仕をしてくれる」などの意味になる。

② **After all, the word *robot* comes from *robota*, a Slavic word meaning "slave" or "servant."**

▶ come from ～は「～に由来する」。slaveとservantに引用符（" "）がついているのは、スラブ語の*robota*が持つ意味を英語で明確に表すため。なお、*robot*はチェコスロバキア（現・チェコ共和国）の作家カレル・チャペックによる造語とされており、1920年発表の戯曲作品中で初めて使用された。

③ **But is it possible for us to form a more cooperative relationship with robots?**

▶〈it is ～ for — to ...〉の疑問文。Is it possible for us to *do* ～?で「私たちは～することが可能か」という意味。

④ **When we think about robot technology, we often think about autonomous robots which can work independently of human beings.**

▶ whichは主格の関係代名詞で、先行詞はautonomous robots。autonomousは「自律的な」。

▶ independently of ～は「～から独立して」（≒ without the help of ～）。

✍ 英文を完成させなさい。

トムは、親元を離れて自活し始めました。

Tom started to live (　　　) (　　　) his parents.

⑤ **Space probes which wander across the surface of Mars.**

▶ whichはSpace probes「宇宙探査機」を先行詞とする主格の関係代名詞。

▶ wander across ～は「～を動き回る」（≒ move around ～）。

▶ 後ろに続く⑥の文と同様、④の文で述べられている「私たちがよく考える

このセクションの内容 の答え→ A. 独立 B. 協力 C. 弱さ

自律的なロボット」の具体例を名詞句で挙げている。

⑥ Delivery robots that drop packages right on our doorsteps.

▶ deliveryは「配達」、packageは「小包」、doorstepは「戸口の上がり段」。

▶ thatは主格の関係代名詞で、先行詞はDelivery robots「配達用ロボット」。

▶ rightは「ちょうど〜、すぐ〜」という意味の副詞。

例 A new café has just opened *right* across the station.
「新しいカフェが駅の真向かいにオープンした」

⑦ Our vision of the future is a vision of autonomous robots driving our cars, cleaning our houses, cooking our meals.

▶ どのような自律的なロボットかを説明するために、driving 〜、cleaning 〜、cooking 〜の３つが並列されている。

⑧ They might be called "strong" robots, in the sense that they can work without human help.

▶ mightは〈可能性・推量〉を表す助動詞。

▶ strongに引用符（" "）がついているのは、そのように呼ばれ得るから。⑨の文の"weak" robotsと呼応している。

▶ in the sense that 〜は「〜という意味で」。このthatは同格節を導き、sense「意味」についてthat以下で具体的に説明する働きをする。

⑨ While we wait for that future, we make do with "weak" robots like the cleaning robot that sweeps our floors.

▶ 文頭のwhileは「〜している間に」という一定の期間を表す接続詞。

▶ make do with 〜は「〜で間に合わせる」（≒ manage by using 〜）。

▶ ２つ目のthatは主格の関係代名詞で、先行詞はthe cleaning robot。

⑩ The little guy is cute but not very smart.

▶ guyは「男、やつ」で、manよりくだけた語。The little guy「その小さなやつ」とは、⑨の文のthe cleaning robotのことで、擬人化して言いかえることで読者により親近感を持たせる意図がある。

⑪ He's always getting tangled up in electrical cords.

▶ He'sはHe isの短縮形。代名詞Heは⑩の文のThe little guy（= the cleaning robot）を指す。

▶ このalwaysは「しょっちゅう〜している、〜してばかりだ」という非難やいら立ちなどを表し、この意味では進行形と共に用いる。

例 She is *always* complaining. 「彼女は不平を言ってばかりだ」

▶ get tangled up in 〜は「〜に巻き込まれる」（≒ get caught up in 〜）。〈get ＋過去分詞〉で「〜される」という受け身を表し、tangle up 〜は「〜をもつれさせる、〜を絡み合わせる」の意味。文全体で「彼は、電気コードに絡まってばかりいる」となる。

⑫ In order to help him clean the room without getting into trouble, you might start by picking up things which could be in his way.

▶in order to *do*は「～するために」、〈help + 人 + *do*〉は「(人)が～するのを助ける」。

▶get into troubleは「厄介なことになる、トラブルに巻き込まれる」(≒ come across a problem)。troubleとは、⑪の文の電気コードに絡まるようなことを指す。withoutがあるので、「(ロボットが)トラブルに巻き込まれないように」ということ。

✍ほぼ同じ意味を表すように、英文を完成させなさい。

We got into trouble.

We came (　　　) a problem.

▶start by V-ing「～することによって始める」とはつまり、「～することから始める」ということ。picking ～ wayがbyの目的語になっている。

▶whichはthingsを先行詞とする主格の関係代名詞。

▶in *one's* wayは「～のじゃまになって(いる)」。

⑬ The room gets cleaned up.

▶⑪の文と同じ〈get + 過去分詞〉「～される」の文。get cleaned upで「(部屋が)掃除される」の意味。

⑭ But when you ask: "Who cleaned this room?" you make an interesting discovery.

▶コロン(:)のあとに具体的な質問を示している。make a discoveryで「発見をする」(≒ discover)の意味。

⑮ The little robot did not clean the room by itself.

▶by *oneself*は「一人で、単独で」。次の文のby yourselfも同様。

⑯ The two of you did it together.

▶did itは話題に挙がった動作を表し、ここではcleaned the roomのこと。

⑰ The robot cleverly managed to get your cooperation in cleaning the room.

▶cleverlyは「賢く、巧妙に」、manage to *do*は「～をなんとかやりとげる」。

⑱ What's interesting about the little cleaning robot is that, for all his weakness, he has become part of your family.

▶What's interesting about ～ is that ...は「～に関して興味深い点は…」の意味で、whatは先行詞を含む関係代名詞。What'sはWhat isの短縮形。

▶for all ～は「～にもかかわらず」(≒ despite)。

2

①Many robot engineers find dependence on humans to be a defect. ②They want to make weak robots stronger, which is to say, more independent of people.

③However, the little episode above suggests that weak robots might help create a positive relationship between robots and humans. ④In fact, Okada Michio, a professor at Toyohashi University of Technology, sees weakness as a virtue. ⑤He is working on robots which are designed *not* to work without human interaction.

⑥Take a wastebasket called *Sociable Trash Box* (STB), for example. ⑦Its job is to see that trash gets picked up. ⑧This weak robot approaches the trash and circles around it helplessly, waiting for someone's assistance. ⑨When people come along and see the robot moving its body as if asking for help, they usually pick up the trash and place it in the basket. ⑩STB bows, as if to say, "Thanks !"

⑪In the conventional way of thinking, a room cleaner that gets tangled up in a cord, or a machine that cannot pick up the trash by itself, is weak or maybe defective. ⑫But from Okada's point of view, this weakness draws out our cooperative spirit. ⑬Far from being dehumanizing, working with a robot like STB can make us more human.

このセクションの内容

〈弱い〉ロボットは、人間とよい（A.　　　　　）を築くかもしれない。岡田美智男教授は、人間と交流なしでは働かないように設計されたロボットを研究している。岡田教授は、弱さこそが私たちの協力的な精神を（B.　　　　　）と言う。このようなロボットとの共同作業により、私たちはより（C.　　　　　）らしくなるかもしれない。

① Many robot engineers find dependence on humans to be a defect.

▶ find 〜 to be ... は「〜が…だと思う」、dependence on 〜は「〜への依存」。

② They want to make weak robots stronger, which is to say, more independent of people.

▶ which is to sayは「つまり」(≒ which means)の意味で、それまでに述べられた内容を言いかえたり、さらに説明を加えたりするときに使われる。このwhichは非制限用法の関係代名詞で、ここでは挿入句になっている。

✍ 英文を完成させなさい。

彼は内気だ、つまり、知らない人と話をするのが得意ではない。

He is shy, (　　　) (　　　) to say, not good at talking to strangers.

▶ independent of ～は「～から独立した」。

③ However, the little episode above suggests that weak robots might help create a positive relationship between robots and humans.

▶ the little episode aboveとは、Section 1にある掃除ロボットについての話を指す。ここでのaboveは副詞で「前述の、上記の」。

▶ mightは「～かもしれない」と〈可能性・推量〉を表す。help createは〈help + *do*〉の形で、「～を築くのを助ける」の意味。

④ In fact, Okada Michio, a professor at Toyohashi University of Technology, sees weakness as a virtue.

▶ Toyohashi University of Technologyは「豊橋技術科学大学」。

▶ see ～ as ... は「～を…と見なす」、virtueは「美徳」。

⑤ He is working on robots which are designed *not* to work without human interaction.

▶ work on ～は「(研究など)に取り組む」。

▶ whichはrobotsを先行詞とする主格の関係代名詞。

▶ be designed to *do*は「～するよう設計されている」。ここでは、toの前に否定語のnotがあるので、「～しないように設計されている」の意味。*not*がイタリック体になっているのは、ロボットの特異な設計を強調するため。

▶ not ～ without ... は二重否定。「人間との交流なしでは働かない」→「働くには必ず人間との交流が必要」という肯定の内容になる。

▶ interactionは「交流、相互作用」。

⑥ Take a wastebasket called *Sociable Trash Box* (STB), for example.

▶ take ～, for exampleは「～を例に取る」、wastebasketは「ゴミ箱」。

⑦ Its job is to see that trash gets picked up.

▶ Its jobとは、⑥の文の*Sociable Trash Box*の仕事のこと。

▶ see that ～は「～を確かめる」、〈get + 過去分詞〉は「～される」。

このセクションの内容 の答え→ A. 関係　B. 引き出す　C. 人間

⑧ **This weak robot approaches the trash and circles around it helplessly, waiting for someone's assistance.**

▶動詞approachesとcircles (around) が並列している。circleは動詞で「(円を描くように)回る」の意味。

▶waiting ～は〈付帯状況〉を表す分詞構文で、「～を待ちながら」の意味。

⑨ **When people come along and see the robot moving its body as if asking for help, they usually pick up the trash and place it in the basket.**

▶come alongは「現れる」(≒appear)。

▶as if ～は「まるで～のように」の意味で、ここでは主語it(= the robot)とbe動詞isが省略されている。ask for ～は「～を求める」。

⑩ **STB bows, as if to say, "Thanks !"**

▶as if to say ～は「～と言うかのように」。as if節内の主語と動詞が省略されている。

✍ 英文を完成させなさい。

メアリーは、「さようなら」と言うかのように私に手を振った。

Mary waved her hand to me, (　　　) (　　　) to say, "Goodbye."

⑪ **In the conventional way of thinking, a room cleaner that gets tangled up in a cord, or a machine that cannot pick up the trash by itself, is weak or maybe defective.**

▶conventionalは「従来の、型にはまった」。

▶a room cleaner that ～とa machine that ～が並列している。thatはどちらも主格の関係代名詞。a room ～ by itselfまでが文全体の主語になる。

▶defectiveは「欠陥のある」。

⑫ **But from Okada's point of view, this weakness draws out our cooperative spirit.**

▶from *one's* point of viewは「～の観点では」、draw out ～は「～を引き出す」(≒bring out ～)。

✍ 次の英文を日本語に直しなさい。

From my point of view, robots are like friends.

________________________ ロボットは友人のような存在だ。

⑬ **Far from being dehumanizing, working with a robot like STB can make us more human.**

▶far from ～は文頭で用いて「～するどころか」の意味。

▶dehumanizeは「～の人間性を奪う」。接頭辞de-は「除去・分離・否定」などの意味を付け加える。*cf.* deactivate「～を不活性化する」

教科書pp.26～27　Section 3

3

①"OK," you may say, "but how about the human-AI interactions we already enjoy? I can talk to my smartphone. ②I ask her a question. She answers. We communicate." ③But is that really communication? ④How often does your smartphone call *you* up?

⑤Okada wants us to think of a more intimate human-robot relationship. ⑥Real communication is not a matter of *me* talking to *you* and *you* talking to *me*, but rather a case of *us* communicating with one another. ⑦Is this sort of communication possible between humans and robots? ⑧Perhaps.

Think of babies. Babies cry for milk. ⑨They show their satisfaction by becoming quiet. ⑩Parents learn to listen to the way their baby cries and watch their baby's reactions. ⑪Although no words are exchanged, a real form of communication exists between them.

⑫Raising an infant involves interaction. ⑬The baby is cared for and gets the milk that it wants. ⑭The parents experience joy in looking after the child. ⑮The baby's helplessness and weakness draw out the parents' love and support. ⑯Could this natural form of communication also take place between humans and robots? ⑰Okada is looking at how such a coexistence might occur.

⑱In order to explore this possibility, Okada and his colleague made *Mako-no-te*, a small one-armed robot which can walk. ⑲When walking hand-in-hand, the robot gives you cues, adjusting the direction and speed by pulling your hand with its arm. ⑳You infer the robot's intentions. ㉑Apparently, just walking with the robot helps you build an interpersonal relationship with it. ㉒A kind of natural form of communication seems to be taking place between the human and the robot.

このセクションの内容

岡田教授は、親と赤ん坊のような本当の（A.　　　　　）が、人間とロボットとの間にも発生し得るかを研究している。この（B.　　　　　）を探るためにつくられたのが「マコのて」だ。散歩をすることで、人間とロボットに（C.　　　　　）が築かれているように思われる。

① **“OK,” you may say, “but how about the human-AI interactions we already enjoy?**

▶ Section 2の最後にある「STBのようなロボットと共に働くことで、私たちはより人間らしくなる」という説に対して予期される反論を示している。

▶ 主語のyouは読者のこと。You may say, “OK, but ～”と主語で始めることもできるが、you may sayをbutの前に挿入することで、but以下の反論に読者の注意が向くようにしている。

▶ human-AIは「人間とAI（の間）の」。

② **I ask her a question. She answers. We communicate.”**

▶ herとSheは直前の文のmy smartphoneを指す。

③ **But is that really communication?**

▶ ①、②の文の反論に対する問いかけ。「それは本当にコミュニケーションと言えるだろうか」という意味。

④ **How often does your smartphone call *you* up?**

▶ How often ～?は頻度をたずねる疑問文。call ～ upは「～に電話する」（≒ give ～ a call）の意味。

⑤ **Okada wants us to think of a more intimate human-robot relationship.**

▶〈want + 人 + to *do*〉は「（人）に～してもらいたい」、intimateは「親密な」。

▶ human-robotは「人間とロボット（の間）の」。

⑥ **Real communication is not a matter of *me* talking to *you* and *you* talking to *me*, but rather a case of *us* communicating with one another.**

▶ not *A* but rather *B*「AでなくむしろB」の構造。ここではa matter ～ to *me*が*A*に相当し、a case ～anotherが*B*に相当する。

▶ *me* talking to *you*は、動名詞talkingの前に目的格の代名詞meを置き、意味上の主語を示している。*you* talking to *me*、*us* communicating with one anotherも同様で、それぞれ*you*と*us*が続く動名詞の意味上の主語。なお、*me*や*you*、*us*がイタリック体になっているのは強調のため。

▶ a case of *us* communicating with one anotherは「私たちが互いに[双方向に]コミュニケーションをとり合う場合」の意味。

⑦ **Is this sort of communication possible between humans and robots?**

▶ this sort of communication「この種のコミュニケーション」とは⑥の文の*us* communicating with one anotherを言いかえたもの。

⑧ **Perhaps.**

このセクションの内容 の答え→ A. コミュニケーション B. 可能性 C. 対人関係

▶⑦の文に対して「おそらく(可能かもしれない)」と1語で答えている。

⑨ They show their satisfaction by becoming quiet.

▶Theyは直前の文のBabiesを指す。

▶satisfactionは「満足(感)」で、satisfy「～を満足させる」の名詞形。

▶by becoming quietは「静かになることによって」。

⑩ Parents learn to listen to the way their baby cries and watch their baby's reactions.

▶learn to *do*は「～の仕方を学ぶ」。andのあとにlearn toが省略されている。親は、赤ん坊の泣き方を聞いたり反応を見たりすることを学ぶということ。

⑪ Although no words are exchanged, a real form of communication exists between them.

▶althoughは「～だけれども」。

▶a real form of communication「コミュニケーションの本当の形」とは、⑥の文の互いにコミュニケーションをとり合うことを言いかえている。

▶themはparents「親」とbabies「赤ん坊」のこと。

⑫ Raising an infant involves interaction.

▶Raising an infant「幼児を育てること」が主語。

▶involveは「～を必要とする」。

⑬ The baby is cared for and gets the milk that it wants.

▶care for ～「～の世話をする」(≒look after～)が受け身で用いられている。

✍ほぼ同じ意味を表すように、英文を完成させなさい。

One of my friends takes care of six cats at home.

One of my friends (　　　) (　　　) six cats at home.

▶the milk that it (=the baby) wantsは「赤ん坊がほしがっているミルク」。

⑭ The parents experience joy in looking after the child.

▶experience joy in ～は「～に喜びを感じる」。

✍次の英文を日本語に直しなさい。

The students experienced joy in helping people in need.

生徒たちは、＿＿＿＿＿＿＿＿＿＿＿＿＿＿＿＿＿＿＿＿＿＿＿＿。

⑮ The baby's helplessness and weakness draw out the parents' love and support.

▶baby'sはhelplessnessとweaknessの2つを修飾している。同様に、parents'はloveとsupportの2つを修飾している。

⑯ Could this natural form of communication also take place between humans and robots?

▶〈可能性・推量〉を表すcouldを用いた疑問文。「～ということはあり得るだろうか」の意味。

▶ this natural form of communicationとは、ここまでに述べられた親と赤ん坊との間に起こるようなコミュニケーションのこと。

▶ take placeは「発生する、起こる」(≒ occur)。

⑰ **Okada is looking at how such a coexistence might occur.**

▶ このlook at 〜は「〜を調べる」の意味。

▶ howは「〜する方法」を表す関係副詞で、先行詞のthe wayを含む。

▶ coexistenceは「共生、共存」。接頭辞co-には「共同の、共通の」という意味がある。*cf.* coauthor「共著者」

⑱ **In order to explore this possibility, Okada and his colleague made *Mako-no-te*, a small one-armed robot which can walk.**

▶ in order to *do*は「〜するために」。

▶ this possibility「この可能性」とは、人とロボットとの間に自然な形のコミュニケーションが起こる可能性のこと。

▶ *Mako-no-te*とa small one-armed robot which can walk「歩くことができる小さな片腕のロボット」は同格の関係。コンマの後ろで*Mako-no-te*がどのようなものかを説明している。

⑲ **When walking hand-in-hand, the robot gives you cues, adjusting the direction and speed by pulling your hand with its arm.**

▶ 接続詞Whenの後ろに主語とbe動詞(the robot and you are)が省略されている。

▶ hand-in-handは「手をつないで」。

▶ give 〜 a cueは「〜に合図を出す」(≒ give 〜 a sign)。

▶ adjustは「〜を調整する」。adjusting 〜は分詞構文で、続いて起こる動作を表す(≒ and adjusts the direction and speed 〜)。

⑳ **You infer the robot's intentions.**

▶ inferは「〜を推測する」、intentionは「意図」の意味。

㉑ **Apparently, just walking with the robot helps you build an interpersonal relationship with it.**

▶ apparentlyは「どうやら〜らしい」。主語はjust walking with the robot。

▶ 〈help + 人 + *do*〉は「(人)が〜するのを助ける[手伝う]」。

▶ interpersonal relationshipは「個人間の関係、対人関係」。

㉒ **A kind of natural form of communication seems to be taking place between the human and the robot.**

▶ a kind of 〜は「〜のようなもの」、seem to 〜は「〜と思われる」。

教科書pp.27～28 Section 4

4

①Okada's concept of weak robots is not just of theoretical interest; it may have a practical implication. ②One of the main concerns in present-day Japan is the rapid growth of its aging population, an increase which means more and more care workers are needed. ③In reality, however, caregivers are in desperately short supply. ④As part of the solution to the problem, the government and private sectors are introducing care robots in nursing homes.

⑤Here are a few examples of robots at work. ⑥One is a back support device which is designed to assist caregivers when they lift and move patients. ⑦Another type of robot provides services such as bringing tea. ⑧These robots satisfy practical needs, easing the burden of caregivers.

⑨But there are other types of robots whose main function is to provide companionship and make the environment more friendly and livable. A robot baby seal is an example. ⑩Not only does it give comfort to the elderly, but it also gives a sense of security. ⑪Perhaps it is in this area that Okada's weak robots have the greatest potential for application.

⑫Professor Okada and his team want us to think of robots as our companions. ⑬They are pointing the way to a future in which people and robots can exist in harmony, learn to treat one another with respect, and, just possibly, enjoy one another's company.

このセクションの内容

〈弱い〉ロボットの概念は、理論上の関心のみならず、(A.　　　　　) な意義を持つ。実際、高齢化社会における介護者不足の問題への解決策として、日本の介護現場ではロボットが導入されている。癒しや (B.　　　　　) を与えてくれるアザラシ型のロボットも導入されており、〈弱い〉ロボットはこの分野において大きな可能性を秘めている。岡田教授らは、私たちがロボットを (C.　　　　　) と見なすことを望んでおり、人々とロボットが調和して共存できる未来への道筋を示している。

① Okada's concept of weak robots is not just of theoretical interest; it may have a practical implication.

▶ conceptは「概念」。ofの前後、Okada's conceptとweak robotsは同格。

▶ of theoretical interestで「理論的な関心をそそる」の意味。〈of＋抽象名詞〉で形容詞と同様の意味になる(of interest ≒ interesting)。

例 This is *of importance*. (≒ This is important.) 「これは重要だ」

▶セミコロン(；)は接続詞の働きをし、ここではnot justに対応して「(単に～ではなくて)むしろ」(≒ but)の意味。

▶ practical implicationは「実用的な意味」。

② One of the main concerns in present-day Japan is the rapid growth of its aging population, an increase which means more and more care workers are needed.

▶ the rapid growth of its aging populationは「その(＝日本の)高齢者の人口の急激な増加」。an increase ～は同格で、さらに詳しく説明している。

▶ more and more ～は「ますます多くの～」の意味。

③ In reality, however, caregivers are in desperately short supply.

▶ in realityは「実際に、現実に」(≒ actually)、in short supplyは「不足して」(≒ insufficient)の意味。

英文を完成させなさい。

その店では労働者が不足している。

Workers are (　　　) short (　　　) at the store.

④ As part of the solution to the problem, the government and private sectors are introducing care robots in nursing homes.

▶ the problemが表しているのは、③の文で述べられている介護者不足の問題。

▶ private sectorは「民間部門」、nursing homeは「介護施設」。

⑤ Here are a few examples of robots at work.

▶ Here is[are] ～は「(これから以下に述べることが) ～である」の意味。

▶ robots at workは「仕事中のロボット」→「作業ロボット」。

⑥ One is a back support device which is designed to assist caregivers when they lift and move patients.

▶ oneはan[one] example of robots at workを表す。

▶ whichはa back support device「腰を支える装置」を先行詞とする主格の関係代名詞。関係代名詞節内でさらに接続詞whenが用いられている。

⑦ Another type of robot provides services such as bringing tea.

▶ anotherを使って、⑥とは別のタイプのロボットを紹介している。

このセクションの内容 の答え→ A. 実用的 B. 安心感 C. 仲間

⑧ These robots satisfy practical needs, easing the burden of caregivers.

▶ easing ～は分詞構文で、主語が２つの動作（satisfy ～と ease ～）を同時に行っていることを表す。easeは「～を和らげる」。

⑨ But there are other types of robots whose main function is to provide companionship and make the environment more friendly and livable.

▶ whoseはother types of robotsを先行詞とする、所有格の関係代名詞。

▶ 関係代名詞節内では、main function「主な機能」が主語、名詞的用法の不定詞が補語になっている。provide ～と make ～が並列の関係になる。

▶ provide companionshipは「仲間付き合いを提供する」。

▶〈make + O + C（形容詞など）〉は「OをCにする」で、ここではCがmore friendly and livable「より親しみやすく生活しやすい」になる。

⑩ Not only does it give comfort to the elderly, but it also gives a sense of security.

▶ not only ～ but also ...「～だけでなく…も」のnot onlyが文頭に置かれ、倒置が起きている。

▶ comfortは「癒し、快適さ」、a sense of securityは「安心感」。

⑪ Perhaps it is in this area that Okada's weak robots have the greatest potential for application.

▶ It is ... (that) ～.の強調構文で、in this areaを強調した文。文全体で、「ひょっとしたら、岡田氏の弱いロボットを応用できる可能性が最もあるのは、まさにこの分野においてかもしれない」の意味。

⑫ Professor Okada and his team want us to think of robots as our companions.

▶ think of ～ as ...は「～を…と見なす」（≒ see ～ as ...）の意味。

⑬ They are pointing the way to a future in which people and robots can exist in harmony, learn to treat one another with respect, and, just possibly, enjoy one another's company.

▶ point the way to ～は「～への道筋を示す」（≒ lead to ～）。

▶ in which ～は〈前置詞＋関係代名詞節〉で、a futureを後ろから修飾している。先行詞はa futureで、whichが前置詞inの目的語になる。

▶ exist ～、learn to ～、enjoy ～の３つの動詞が並列している。

▶ in harmonyは「調和して」。

▶ treat one another with respectは「敬意を持ってお互いを扱う」、enjoy one another's companyは「お互い一緒にいることを楽しむ」。

確認問題

語彙

1 次の文の意味が通るように、( )内の語を適する形にしなさい。

(1) Some people expect that robots will be our (serve) in the near future.
(2) I missed the last train. Could you (possible) drive me home tonight?
(3) The politician announced his (intend) to run in the next election.

2 次の各組でアクセントの位置が同じなら○、異なるなら×を書きなさい。

(1) (vir-tue　de-vice)
(2) (in-ti-mate　com-pan-ion)
(3) (de-liv-er-y　au-ton-o-mous)
(4) (de-fec-tive　de-pend-ence)

文法・表現

1 日本語に合うように、( )内に適切な語を入れなさい。

(1) これらの国々の間で、大きな軍事衝突が起こった。
A huge military conflict (　　　) (　　　) between these countries.
(2) 先生は、まるで「その通り」と言うかのようににっこりうなずいた。
My teacher nodded with a smile, (　　　) (　　　) to say, "You're right."
(3) アルバイト従業員は、ほかの人から独立して働かないように言われた。
Part-time workers were told not to (　　　) (　　　) of others.
(4) 彼の冗談は、それで誰も傷つかないという点ではよいように思える。
His joke seems good in the (　　　) (　　　) it doesn't hurt anyone.
(5) その話し手は、聴衆から同情を引き出そうとした。
The speaker tried to (　　　) (　　　) sympathy from the audience.
(6) 夫婦はちょっとした交通事故に巻き込まれた。
The couple got (　　　) (　　　) in a minor traffic accident.

2 各組の文がほぼ同じ意味になるように、( )内に適切な語を入れなさい。

(1) Masa showed me how he played the musical instrument.
Masa showed me (　　　) (　　　) he played the musical instrument.
(2) In my opinion, artificial intelligence benefits society.
From my (　　　) of (　　　), artificial intelligence benefits society.
(3) Despite my efforts, I failed the math test yesterday.
For (　　　) my efforts, I failed the math test yesterday.

3 日本語に合うように、( )内の語句を並べかえなさい。

(1) 私たちの飼い犬のソラは、ペットではなくむしろ家族の一員だ。
Our dog, Sora, is (rather / a pet / not / of / our family / but / a part).
Our dog, Sora, is ______________________________.

(2) この映画に関して興味深い点は、それが1日で撮影されたということだ。
(this movie / that / is / interesting / what's / about) it was shot in a day.
______________________________ it was shot in a day.

(3) クラス中が、まどかのスピーチがすばらしいものだと思った。
The whole class (to / Madoka's / excellent / speech / be / found).
The whole class ______________________________.

総合

次の文を読んで、あとの問いに答えなさい。

One of the main concerns in present-day Japan is the rapid (①) of its aging population, an increase which means more and more care workers are needed. In reality, however, caregivers are in desperately short supply. As part of the solution to ②the problem, the government and private sectors are introducing care robots in nursing homes.

Here are a few examples of robots at work. One is a back support device which is ③(design) to assist caregivers when they lift and move patients. Another type of robot provides services such as bringing tea. These robots satisfy practical needs, ④(ease) the burden of caregivers.

But there are other types of robots whose main function is to provide (⑤) and make the environment more friendly and livable. A robot baby seal is an example. ⑥Not (comfort / it / only / give / does / the elderly / to), but it also gives a sense of security. ⑦Perhaps it is in this area that Okada's weak robots have the greatest potential for application.

問1 (①)(⑤)に適する語を下から選んで入れなさい。
〔colleague growth companionship defect infant〕

問2 下線部②の内容を具体的に日本語で説明しなさい。

問3 ③、④の( )内の語を適する形にしなさい。

問4 下線部⑥の( )内の語句を並べかえて、英文を完成させなさい。

問5 下線部⑦を日本語に直しなさい。

Lesson 3 Fake News Is Everywhere: Beware!

教科書p.38 Section 1

①Social media has made it possible for us to obtain information for free. ②But there is a pitfall: there's a lot of fake news, or misinformation, on social media. ③How can we cope with it?

1

In March 2020, the Covid-19 epidemic was just beginning. ④In front of a supermarket in Tokyo, more than 20 people were lined up waiting for the store to open. ⑤Paper products such as toilet paper and tissues sold out in five minutes.

⑥During that week, there were over 200,000 Twitter posts mentioning the words "toilet paper," "out of stock" and "shortage." ⑦People thought protective masks were made of paper and worried that the rush to make masks would take up Japan's entire wood supply. ⑧Images of empty store shelves appeared on TV and people were passing on the message: "Following the shortage of sanitizers and masks, toilet paper is running out."

⑨Finally, one shop owner put up a sign reading, "The rumor that there will be shortages of paper products is a lie."

⑩That shop owner was correct: The rumor was fake news. ⑪With a quick search on the Internet, anyone could have found a message from the Japan Paper Association that there was no shortage of toilet paper.

⑫How could the idea of a shortage have spread to so many people so quickly? ⑬The answer: It spread very quickly throughout the country on social media.

このセクションの内容

新型コロナウイルス感染症の（A.　　　　　）が始まりつつあった2020年３月の日本では、トイレットペーパーなどの紙製品がすぐに売り切れた。人々は、マスクが紙でできていると思い、マスク生産の激増により（B.　　　　　）の供給が使い果たされることを心配したのだ。しかし、この（C.　　　　　）はフェイクニュースで、ソーシャルメディアによって国中で急速に広まったものだった。

① Social media has made it possible for us to obtain information for free.

▶ Social media「ソーシャルメディア」は日本でSNSと呼ばれることが多い。

▶ make it possible for ～ to *do*は「～が…することを可能にする」の意味で、itはto以下を指す形式目的語。for usがto ～の意味上の主語。

② But there is a pitfall: there's a lot of fake news, or misinformation, on social media.

▶ pitfallは「(比喩表現として) 落とし穴、間違いやすい点」。コロン (:) 以下で、どのような落とし穴かを具体的に説明している。

▶ 接続詞orは「つまり」の意味で、fake newsをmisinformation「誤報」と言いかえている。

③ How can we cope with it?

▶ cope with ～は「～にうまく対処する」(≒ manage)。

英文を完成させなさい。

私は一人で、その問題にうまく対処せねばならなかった。

I had to (　　　) (　　　) the problem by myself.

▶ このitは、②の文のソーシャルメディア上にフェイクニュースが多数あること、または、フェイクニュースそのものを指す。

④ In front of a supermarket in Tokyo, more than 20 people were lined up waiting for the store to open.

▶ be lined upは「一列で並ぶ」(≒ be standing in a line) の意味。

▶ for the storeは不定詞to openの意味上の主語を表す。

⑤ Paper products such as toilet paper and tissues sold out in five minutes.

▶ such as ～「～のような」で、paper productsの具体例を示している。

⑥ During that week, there were over 200,000 Twitter posts mentioning the words "toilet paper," "out of stock" and "shortage."

▶ mentioningは、Twitter posts「ツイッターの投稿」を後ろから修飾する現在分詞。the wordsの内容が*A*, *B* and *C*と、並列して示されている。

▶ out of stockは「在庫切れで」。*cf.* in stock「在庫があって」

⑦ People thought protective masks were made of paper and worried that the rush to make masks would take up Japan's entire wood supply.

▶ andで、thought ～とworried ～の２つの動作が並列されている。

▶ rushは「需要の激増」、take up ～は「～を使い果たす」(≒ use up ～)。

このセクションの内容 の答え→ A. 流行 B. 木材 C. うわさ

⑧ Images of empty store shelves appeared on TV and people were passing on the message: "Following the shortage of sanitizers and masks, toilet paper is running out."

▶ pass on ～は「～を人に伝える」(≒ tell ～ to someone)。

▶ コロン(：)以下は、the messageの具体的な内容になる。

▶ followingは「～の後で、～に続いて」。Following the shortage of sanitizers and masksで「消毒液やマスクの不足に続いて」の意味。

▶ run outは「尽きる、なくなる」(≒ be used up)。

⑨ Finally, one shop owner put up a sign reading, "The rumor that there will be shortages of paper products is a lie."

▶ a sign reading ～は「～と書いてある掲示」の意味(≒ a sign that says ～)。引用符(" ")を用いて、書かれていた掲示内容を説明している。

▶ 引用符内のthatは同格節を導き、ここではThe rumor「うわさ」の内容をthat以下で示している。引用符内の主語はThe rumor ～ products。

⑩ That shop owner was correct: The rumor was fake news.

▶ That shop ownerとは、⑨の文にあるone shop ownerを指す。

▶ コロン(：)は「つまり～」の意味で、直前の内容を言いかえている。

⑪ With a quick search on the Internet, anyone could have found a message from the Japan Paper Association that there was no shortage of toilet paper.

▶ 仮定法過去完了の文で、過去の事実に反する仮定を表している。with ～は「～があれば、～があったら」、〈could have＋過去分詞〉は「～できただろうに」の意味。if節の代わりにWith ～ Internetが用いられている。

✍ 次の英文を日本語に直しなさい。

With enough money, I could have bought that piano.

____

▶ that以下はa message (from the Japan Paper Association)と同格で、メッセージの内容を説明している。

⑫ How could the idea of a shortage have spread to so many people so quickly?

▶ How could ～?「いったいなぜ～ということがあり得たのだろうか」という疑問文。couldは〈可能性・推量〉を表す。

▶ ここでのofは「～という」の意味で、同格を表す。

⑬ The answer: It spread very quickly throughout the country on social media.

▶ ⑫の問いに対する答えで、その内容がコロン(：)以下で示されている。

教科書pp.39〜40　Section 2

2

①Fake news is not a 21st-century phenomenon, nor is it always dangerous.

②Sometimes fake news is the result of misunderstanding, like the toilet paper scare of 2020. ③Other times, it is a simple mistake, like the day in 1874 when a newspaper reported that America's beloved author, Mark Twain, had died. ④Everyone was saddened, except Mark Twain, who was perfectly fine and traveling in Europe. ⑤Twain sent a telegram: "The reports of my death have been greatly exaggerated."

However, sometimes false news is extremely dangerous. ⑥Consider the Nazi propaganda (official government fake news) that controlled the thinking of millions of Germans in the 1930s and contributed to the massacre of millions of Jews.

⑦Up until the 21st century, fake news spread from person to person or over radio and TV. ⑧But in the current century, it spreads faster and farther and much more dangerously on social media. ⑨In fact, millions of people are exposed to extremely destructive false information on the Internet.

⑩It is a matter of the greatest importance to have a discerning mind in order to identify and reject fake news. But how should we proceed?

このセクションの内容

フェイクニュースは21世紀の（A.　　　　　）ではなく、いつも危険なものというわけでもない。それは、誤解の結果や単純な間違いである場合もある。しかし、フェイクニュースは、1930年代のナチスドイツによる（B.　　　　　）のように、極めて危険なこともある。21世紀以前は、フェイクニュースは人づてに、あるいはラジオやテレビで広まったが、21世紀ではソーシャルメディア上でより速く、より遠くに、そしてより危険に広まる。フェイクニュースを特定して退けるために、（C.　　　　　）を持つことが最も重要だ。

① Fake news is not a 21st-century phenomenon, nor is it always dangerous.

▶ 21st-centuryは「21世紀の」という意味で、21stとcenturyがハイフン(-)で連結され、phenomenon「現象」を修飾している。

▶ nor「また～もない」は接続詞で、否定文に続けて用いる。〈nor＋(助)動詞＋主語〉の語順になることに注意。

✍ 英文を完成させなさい。

11歳の弟は体育の授業が好きではなく、私も好きではない。

My eleven-year-old little brother doesn't like P.E., (　　　) (　　　) I.

② **Sometimes fake news is the result of misunderstanding, like the toilet paper scare of 2020.**

▶ ～ is the result of ... は「～は…の結果だ」の意味で、因果関係を表す。

例 The doctor thinks my fatigue *is the result of* malnutrition.
「医師は私の疲労感は栄養不足の結果だと考えている」

▶ the toilet paper scare of 2020「2020年のトイレットペーパー恐怖」とは、Section 1にあるトイレットペーパー不足を招いたパニックを表す。

③ **Other times, it is a simple mistake, like the day in 1874 when a newspaper reported that America's beloved author, Mark Twain, had died.**

▶ Other timesは、②の文にあるSometimesと呼応し、「～な場合もあれば…な場合もある」という意味。

▶ whenはthe day in 1874を先行詞とする関係副詞。when以下で、1874年のその日に起きた出来事を説明している。

▶ America's beloved authorとMark Twainは同格の関係。マーク・トウェインは『トム・ソーヤーの冒険』などで知られるアメリカの小説家。

④ **Everyone was saddened, except Mark Twain, who was perfectly fine and traveling in Europe.**

▶ saddenは「～を悲しませる」の意味で、人が主語のときは受け身になる。

▶ 〈, who〉は非制限用法の関係代名詞。Mark Twainについて補足説明している。固有名詞のあとでは、ふつう関係代名詞は非制限用法になる。

⑤ **Twain sent a telegram: "The reports of my death have been greatly exaggerated."**

▶ コロン(:)以下にa telegram「電報」の内容が示されている。

▶ have been greatly exaggeratedは現在完了形の受け身で、「ひどく誇張された」の意味。

⑥ **Consider the Nazi propaganda (official government fake news) that controlled the thinking of millions of Germans in the 1930s and contributed to the massacre of millions of Jews.**

このセクションの内容 の答え→ A. 現象　B. プロパガンダ　C. 洞察力[識別力]

▶ Consider ～「～を考えてみなさい」で始まる命令文。

▶ (official government fake news) はthe Nazi propagandaの補足説明。

▶ thatはthe Nazi propagandaを先行詞とする主格の関係代名詞。controlled「～を支配した」とcontributed to ～「～の一因となった」(≒ became one of the causes of ～)が並列している。

✍ ほぼ同じ意味を表すように、英文を完成させなさい。

Lack of sleep became one of the causes of his illness.

Lack of sleep (　　　) (　　　) his illness.

▶ millions of ～は「何百万もの～」、massacreは「大虐殺」。

⑦ Up until the 21st century, fake news spread from person to person or over radio and TV.

▶ up until ～は「～に至るまで」の意味で、until「～まで」の強意表現。

▶ spreadは「広がる」。ここでは過去形で用いられている。

⑧ But in the current century, it spreads faster and farther and much more dangerously on social media.

▶ itは⑦の文にあるfake newsを指す。

▶ *A* and *B* and *C*と、3つの副詞の比較級が2つのandで並列されている。

▶ muchは副詞の比較級more dangerouslyを修飾し、「はるかに」の意味。

⑨ In fact, millions of people are exposed to extremely destructive false information on the Internet.

▶ in factは「実際」、be exposed to ～は「(危険など)にさらされる」(≒ be endangered by ～)、destructiveは「破壊的な」の意味。

例 The whole area *was exposed to* yellow sand.
「地域全域が黄砂にさらされた」

⑩ It is a matter of the greatest importance to have a discerning mind in order to identify and reject fake news.

▶ It is a matter of the greatest importance to *do*は「～することが最も重要な問題だ」。Itはto以下を指す形式主語。of the greatest importanceは〈of＋抽象名詞〉の形で、a matterを修飾している。

✍ 次の英文を日本語に直しなさい。

Global warming is a matter of importance to everyone.

地球温暖化は、＿＿＿＿＿＿＿＿＿＿＿＿＿＿＿＿＿＿＿＿＿＿＿＿＿＿。

▶ discerning mindは「洞察力」。discerningは、discern「～を識別する、～を見分ける」の形容詞形。mindは、ここでは「知力、思考力」を表す。

教科書pp.40～41　Section 3

3

①One way to control fake news is for social media sites to police themselves. ②Government regulation may also be necessary. ③But in the end, it is up to each one of us, as individuals, to recognize fake news and to stop passing it along. ④Here are some strategies you can use to evaluate what you see and read.

⑤First, admit that you don't understand everything. ⑥The world is complex, and issues like politics, economics, and medicine are complicated. ⑦Don't be ashamed if you don't know everything, and don't expect simple answers. ⑧The recognition of ignorance is the beginning of wisdom. ⑨The Greek philosopher Socrates said, "The only thing I know for sure is that I know nothing for sure." ⑩Don't accept the first, simple explanation you hear. ⑪Find out what experts are saying.

⑫Second, admit that you probably have some biases and prejudices. ⑬Challenge what you read and hear by asking yourself if you agree or disagree on a "gut level." ⑭If you immediately accept or reject an idea, without really thinking, think again. ⑮We tend to accept without question whatever conforms to the ideas and attitudes we began to develop when we were children. ⑯Psychologists call this "confirmation bias": the tendency to believe things that support what we have always believed and to reject, without much thought, anything that is different. ⑰Be critical of your ideas and attitudes. Learn to recognize your own biases. ⑱When you read or hear something that your "gut" immediately accepts or rejects, check it out with a reliable source.

このセクションの内容

（A.　　　　　　）の規制は、私たち一人ひとりがそれに気付いて広めるのをやめることにかかっている。見たり読んだりするものの評価に使える（B.　　　　　　）がある。第一に、何もかもを理解できるわけではないことを認め、単純な説明を受け入れないこと。第二に、自分が（C.　　　　　　）を持っている可能性があると認め、自分の考えや態度を批判的に見て、自分の偏見に気付くことだ。

① One way to control fake news is for social media sites to police themselves.

▶ for social media sitesはto police themselvesの意味上の主語を表す。

▶ policeは「～を監視する」(≒ monitor)。ここでは監視の対象がソーシャルメディア自身なので、再帰代名詞themselvesが使われている。

② Government regulation may also be necessary.

▶ Government regulationは「政府による規制」。①の文に加えて必要かもしれないことを述べている。

③ But in the end, it is up to each one of us, as individuals, to recognize fake news and to stop passing it along.

▶ be up to ～ (to *do*)は「(…することは) ～次第である、～にかかっている」(≒ depend on ～)。このitは、andで並列された2つの不定詞句を指す形式主語。不定詞のほかに、wh節が使われることもある。

✍ 次の英文を日本語に直しなさい。

It's up to you whether you can enjoy your life.

____

▶ each one of usは「私たちそれぞれ」、as individualsは「個人として」。

▶ pass ～ alongは「～を人に伝える、～を広める」(≒ spread ～)。目的語のitはfake newsを指す。

④ Here are some strategies you can use to evaluate what you see and read.

▶ Here is[are] ～は「(これから以下に述べることが) ～である」。

▶ strategies you can useは「あなたが使うことのできる戦略」。

▶ to evaluate ～は「～を評価するために」(副詞的用法の不定詞)。whatは先行詞を含む関係代名詞で、what以下がevaluateの目的語になる。

⑤ First, admit that you don't understand everything.

▶ admit that ～は「～ということを認めなさい」。

▶ not ～ everythingで「全部が～というわけではない」という部分否定を表す。文全体で「まず、自分が全部を理解しているわけではないと認めなさい」の意味。

⑥ The world is complex, and issues like politics, economics, and medicine are complicated.

▶ The world is complexまでが1つ目の文。issues以下が2つ目の文。

▶ issues like politics, economics, and medicineは「政治学、経済学、医学のような問題」。*A*, *B*, and *C*の形でissuesの具体例を挙げている。

⑦ Don't be ashamed if you don't know everything, and don't

このセクションの内容 の答え→ A. フェイクニュース B. 戦略 C. 偏見[先入観]

expect simple answers.

▶ be ashamedは「恥ずかしく思う」。

▶ ifは「たとえ～でも」(≒ even if) という譲歩を表す。

⑧ **The recognition of ignorance is the beginning of wisdom.**

▶ recognition of ～は「～についての認識」、ignoranceは「無知」。

⑨ **The Greek philosopher Socrates said, "The only thing I know for sure is that I know nothing for sure."**

▶ ソクラテスは古代ギリシャの哲学者で、自分が無知であることについての認識の重要性を表す「無知の知」という考え方で知られる。

▶ 引用符 (" ") 内は「私が確かにわかっている唯一のことは、私が何も確かには知らないということだ」の意味。thatは補語になる節を導く接続詞。

⑩ **Don't accept the first, simple explanation you hear.**

▶ ２つの形容詞firstとsimpleは共にexplanation「説明」を修飾している。

▶ explanation you hearは「あなたが耳にする説明」。

⑪ **Find out what experts are saying.**

▶ whatは先行詞を含む関係代名詞。what experts are sayingで「専門家が話していること」の意味。

⑫ **Second, admit that you probably have some biases and prejudices.**

▶ ２つ目の戦略についての文。

▶ biasとprejudiceは共に「偏見、先入観」の意味。biasは公平でない偏った見方、prejudiceは正確な情報を欠くことによる先入観を表す。

⑬ **Challenge what you read and hear by asking yourself if you agree or disagree on a "gut level."**

▶ Challenge ～は「～の妥当性を疑いなさい」。

▶ what you read and hearは「あなたが読んだり聞いたりすること」の意味で、whatは先行詞を含む関係代名詞。

▶ by asking *oneself*は「自問することによって」の意味で手段を表す。if *A* or *B*は「AかBか」の意味で、if節がaskingの２つ目の目的語になっている。

▶ on a gut levelは「直感的に」(≒ instinctively) の意味で、ここでは強調のためにgut levelに引用符 (" ") がついている。

⑭ **If you immediately accept or reject an idea, without really thinking, think again.**

▶ immediatelyは「すぐに」、without really thinkingは「じっくり考えることなく」。

⑮ **We tend to accept without question whatever conforms to**

the ideas and attitudes we began to develop when we were children.

▶ We tend to accept without question ～は「私たちは～を、疑問を持たずに受け入れる傾向にある[疑うことなく受け入れがちだ]」の意味。

▶ whatever ～は「～するものは何でも」の意味で、ここでは動詞acceptの目的語になっている。conform to ～は「～に従う、～に合う」。

▶ we began ～以下は、the ideas and attitudesを後ろから修飾する節。

▶ whatever以下は「私たちが子どもだったときに持ち始めた考えや意見に合うものなら何でも」という意味になる。

✍ 次の英文を日本語に直しなさい。

He tends to accept without question whatever the newspaper reports.

____

⑯ **Psychologists call this "confirmation bias": the tendency to believe things that support what we have always believed and to reject, without much thought, anything that is different.**

▶〈call + O + C〉「OをCと呼ぶ」の文。Oに当たるthisは⑮の文で述べられた傾向のこと。Cに当たるconfirmation biasは「確証バイアス」(心理学用語)。

▶ the tendency to *do*は「～する傾向」。2つの不定詞to believe ～とto reject ～が並列している。

▶ things that support what we have always believedは「私たちがいつも信じてきたことを支持すること」。thatは主格の関係代名詞。

▶ anything that is differentは「(信じてきたこととは)異なることは何でも」。

▶ 挿入句のwithout much thoughtは「十分に考えずに」。

⑰ **Be critical of your ideas and attitudes.**

▶ be critical of ～は「～を批判的に判断する」(≒ make careful judgments about ～)。

✍ ほぼ同じ意味を表すように、英文を完成させなさい。

I tried to make careful judgments about the online article.

I tried to be (　　　) (　　　) the online article.

⑱ **When you read or hear something that your "gut" immediately accepts or rejects, check it out with a reliable source.**

▶ thatは目的格の関係代名詞。something that your "gut" immediately accepts or rejectsで「あなたの『直感』がすぐに受け入れたり拒絶したりする何か」という意味。

▶ check it outは「それ(= something)を検討する[真偽を調べる]」、with a reliable sourceは「信頼できる情報源を使って」。

4

①Third, check the source. ②To know if a piece of information is true or not, we need to know where it comes from. ③The most reliable news will come from edited and fact-checked sources: newspapers, TV stations, and digital platforms that list their editors, publish signed articles, and name their sources.

④Be cautious about news articles that say: "Lots of people believe...," "Experts agree that...," "An anonymous insider said...." ⑤These are trick words to get you to bypass your critical thinking and go with your "gut." ⑥Don't be taken in.

⑦Finally, don't get caught up in feedback networks that reward you with "likes" and "shares." ⑧You are more likely to send on information that appeals to your biases than to send on the truth, especially if the fake information is more sensational than the plain truth. ⑨You get positive feedback and are encouraged to send on more fake news in the future. ⑩Social media often rewards you more for sending on fake news than for sending on the truth.

⑪The Internet brings us all sorts of information, ideas, and opinions. ⑫Media companies and the government have an obligation to protect us from fake news. ⑬In the end, however, everything depends upon each one of us becoming more discerning and critical in the way we manage information.

⑭Remember, you are surrounded by massive amounts of information, and more than a little of it is fake news. Protect yourself, your family, your community, and your country. Think twice before you click "Like." ⑮Think thrice before you click "Share."

このセクションの内容

第三に、記事の（A.　　　　　）を確認し、さらに批判的な思考を鈍らせて（B.　　　　　）に頼らせるだまし文句に注意すること。最後に、「いいね」などのフィードバックのネットワークに関わらないこと。すべては一人ひとりが情報管理の方法において、より鋭い洞察力を持ち、（C.　　　　　）になれるかどうかにかかっている。

① Third, check the source.

▶情報を評価するための3つ目の戦略についての文。sourceは「情報源」。

② To know if a piece of information is true or not, we need to know where it comes from.

▶To know ～は「～を知るために」、if ～ or notは「～かどうか」。

▶information「情報」は不可算名詞なので、a piece of ～を用いて数える。

▶where it comes fromは間接疑問で、「それ(＝a piece of information)がどこから来ているのか」の意味。

③ The most reliable news will come from edited and fact-checked sources: newspapers, TV stations, and digital platforms that list their editors, publish signed articles, and name their sources.

▶edited and fact-checked sourcesは「編集済みかつ事実確認のとれた[ファクトチェックがなされた]情報源」。コロン(：)以下にその具体例を挙げている。

▶thatはnewspapers, TV stations, and digital platformsを先行詞とする主格の関係代名詞。that節内で、list ～「～を一覧で載せる」、publish ～「～を掲載する」、name ～「～の名前を伝える」の3つの動詞が並列されている。signed articles「署名記事」は記者の名前が入った記事のこと。

④ Be cautious about news articles that say: "Lots of people believe...," "Experts agree that...," "An anonymous insider said...."

▶be cautious about ～は「～に気を付ける、注意する」。

▶thatはnews articlesを先行詞とする主格の関係代名詞。

▶コロン(：)以下で、注意すべきニュース記事の文言の具体例を3つ挙げている。

⑤ These are trick words to get you to bypass your critical thinking and go with your "gut."

▶These「これらのもの」とは、④の文で示された3つの文言を指す。

▶trick words to *do*は「～するためのだまし文句」。

▶get ～ to *do*は「～に…させる」という使役を表す。

例 Tina *got* her husband *to have* a medical checkup.
「ティナは夫に健康診断を受けさせた」

▶bypassは「～を迂回する、～を無視する」、go with ～は「～で進行する」(≒proceed with ～)。「批判的思考を迂回して『直感』で進行する」とはつまり、3つの文言によって、人は批判的に考えることをせずに、直観に頼って判断してしまうということ。

このセクションの内容 の答え→ A. 情報源 B. 直感 C. 批判的

✍ 英文を完成させなさい。

直感で突き進むことにはしばしばリスクを伴う。

(　　　) (　　　) your gut often involves risks.

⑥ Don't be taken in.

▶ be taken inは「だまされる」(≒ be deceived)。受け身の表現。

⑦ Finally, don't get caught up in feedback networks that reward you with "likes" and "shares."

▶ 情報を評価するための最後(4つ目)の戦略についての文。

▶ get caught up in ～は「～にとらわれる、～に巻き込まれる」(≒ get involved in ～)の意味で、〈get + 過去分詞〉「～される」を用いた表現。

✍ 次の英文を日本語に直しなさい。

The taxi driver cleverly avoided getting caught up in the traffic jam.

タクシー運転手は、＿＿＿＿＿＿＿＿＿＿＿＿＿＿＿＿＿＿＿＿。

▶ feedback networks「フィードバックのネットワーク」とは、SNS上の友人やフォロワーのコミュニティのこと。thatは主格の関係代名詞。

▶ reward ～ with ... は「～に…で報いる」。likeは名詞で、「(ソーシャルメディア上での)いいね」を表す。

⑧ You are more likely to send on information that appeals to your biases than to send on the truth, especially if the fake information is more sensational than the plain truth.

▶ be likely to *do*は「～する傾向がある、～しそうだ」。さらにこの文は、more likely to ～ than to ...「…するよりも～する傾向がある」と比較の文になっていることに注意。

✍ 次の英文を日本語に直しなさい。

People are more likely to live long if they do some regular exercise.

習慣的に運動をする人は、＿＿＿＿＿＿＿＿＿＿＿＿＿＿＿＿＿＿＿＿。

▶ send on ～は「(情報など)を回す、広める」(≒ spread ～)、appeal to ～は「～の心に訴えかける」。文の前半は「真実を広めるよりも自分の偏見に合う[自分好みの]情報を広める傾向がある」ということ。

▶ especially if ～は「特に～の場合には」。if節のmore sensational than ～は「～よりも扇情的な」の意味。

⑨ You get positive feedback and are encouraged to send on more fake news in the future.

▶ positive feedback「肯定的なフィードバック」とは、⑦の文の"likes" and "shares"の言いかえで、友人からの「いいね」などの反応のこと。

▶ be encouraged to *do*は「～するように促される」。

⑩ **Social media often rewards you more for sending on fake news than for sending on the truth.**

▶ reward ～ for ... は「～に…に対して報いる」。ここではmore *A* than *B*の形で、for sending on fake news「フェイクニュースを広めることに」とfor sending on the truth「真実を広めることに」を比較している。

⑪ **The Internet brings us all sorts of information, ideas, and opinions.**

▶〈bring＋O（人）＋O（物）〉「O（人）にO（物）をもたらす」の文。

⑫ **Media companies and the government have an obligation to protect us from fake news.**

▶ have an obligation to *do*は「～する義務がある」、protect ～ from ... は「…から～を守る」。

⑬ **In the end, however, everything depends upon each one of us becoming more discerning and critical in the way we manage information.**

▶ in the endは「結局は」。howeverは「しかしながら」と逆接を表す。

▶ depend upon ～は「～次第だ」。

▶ each one of us「私たち一人ひとり」は動名詞becomingの意味上の主語。become more discerning and criticalで「より洞察力を持ち、批判的になる」。

▶〈in the way＋主語＋動詞〉で「～が…する方法において」。

⑭ **Remember, you are surrounded by massive amounts of information, and more than a little of it is fake news.**

▶ Remember, ～は「～ということを覚えておいてください」（≒ Remember that ～）。

▶ be surrounded by ～は「～に囲まれている」、massive amounts of ～は「大量の～」。

▶ more than a little of ～は「少量以上の～」→「かなりの～」の意味で、量などが決して少なくはないことを表し、a lot of ～の遠回しの表現として使われている。大量の情報の中に含まれているフェイクニュースの量は少なくない（＝かなり多い）ということ。

⑮ **Think thrice before you click "Share."**

▶ thriceは「3回」（≒ three times）という意味の文語表現。ここでは、直前の文にあるthink twice「再考する」のtwice「2回」とかけて用いている。

確認問題

語彙

1 次の英文の（　）の中に与えられた文字で始まる適切な語を書きなさい。

(1) Journalists are trying to (o　　　) accurate information for news stories.

(2) The rock band denied the (r　　　) that they would break up soon.

(3) Meg said, "I (d　　　) with your plan because it doesn't sound good."

2 次の各組で下線部の発音がほかと異なるものを１つずつ選び、記号で答えなさい。

(1) ア stock　イ psychologist　ウ philosopher　エ expose

(2) ア epidemic　イ telegram　ウ extremely　エ tendency

(3) ア ashamed　イ sensational　ウ massive　エ regulation

(4) ア proceed　イ contribute　ウ protective　エ recognition

文法・表現

1 各組の文がほぼ同じ意味になるように、（　）内に適切な語を入れなさい。

(1) You passed the examination because of your hard work.
Your passing the examination is the (　　　) (　　　) your hard work.

(2) Critical thinking allows you to spot fake news.
Critical thinking (　　　) it possible (　　　) you to spot fake news.

(3) I didn't notice the article was full of errors. John didn't notice that, either.
I didn't notice the article was full of errors, (　　　) (　　　) John.

2 日本語に合うように、（　）内に適切な語を入れなさい。

(1) 私たちは、メディアが語ることを鵜呑(うの)みにする傾向がある。
We (　　　) to accept (　　　) question what the media says.

(2) 彼らは道すがら、不測のトラブルに巻き込まれた。
They got (　　　) (　　　) in some unexpected trouble on the way.

(3) 直感で正しいと思ったものがいつも正しいとは限らない。
What you thought was right on a (　　　) (　　　) is not always right.

(4) その記事は、私たちが手にする情報を批判的に見る方法についてのものだ。
The article is about how to be (　　　) (　　　) the information we get.

3 日本語に合うように、(　)内の語句を並べかえなさい。

(1) 選挙に勝つことが最も重要だ。
(a matter / the greatest / is / of / importance / it) to win the election.
______________________________ to win the election.

(2) ストレスでまいっているとき、人はより怒りっぽくなる。
You (get / are / to / angry / more / when / likely) you are stressed out.
You ______________________________ you are stressed out.

(3) その親は一人娘に、自分のしたいことを何でもやらせてあげた。
The parents (whatever / do / their / she / let / wanted / only daughter).
The parents ______________________________.

(4) 私はトムに、彼の自転車を貸してもらおうと考えている。
I'm (to / Tom / of / thinking / me / lend / getting) his bicycle.
I'm ______________________________ his bicycle.

総合

次の文を読んで、あとの問いに答えなさい。

①One way to control fake news is for social media sites to police themselves. Government regulation may also be necessary. But in the end, ②it is up to each one of us, as individuals, to recognize fake news and to stop passing it along. Here are some strategies you can use to evaluate what you see and read.

First, admit that you don't understand everything. The world is complex, and issues like politics, economics, and medicine are complicated. Don't (③) if you don't know everything, and don't expect simple answers. The recognition of ignorance is the beginning of wisdom. The Greek philosopher Socrates said, "④(I / for sure / know / the only / is / thing) that I know nothing for sure." Don't accept the first, simple explanation you hear. Find out what experts are saying.

問1　下線部①を日本語に直しなさい。
問2　下線部②の内容を具体的に日本語で説明しなさい。
問3　(　③　)に「恥ずかしがる」という意味の２語を書きなさい。
問4　下線部④が「私が確かにわかっている唯一のことは、私が何も確かには知らないということだ」という意味になるように、(　)内の語句を並べかえて、英文を完成させなさい。

Lesson 4 Beyond What Nature Intends

教科書p.54 *ll*.1～10 I

①When he was 17, Hugh Herr was one of America's most prominent rock climbers. ②But he had a severe accident while climbing. ③In this lesson, we will find out how he coped with hardship and developed his career.

④Hugh Herr was a born climber. ⑤By age 8, he had scaled the face of 11,627-foot Mt. Temple in southern Alberta, Canada. Later, he began climbing without a rope. ⑥He ascended tough climbing routes, some of which no adult had ever attempted before. ⑦By the time he was a teenager, Herr was one of the top rock climbers on the East Coast.

このセクションの内容

ヒュー・ハーは生まれながらのロッククライマーで、(A.　　　　　) 歳のときにはすでに、11,627フィートの標高を誇るカナダのテンプル山の急斜面を登っていた。のちに、彼は (B.　　　　　) なしで登り始め、それまでに一人の大人も挑戦したことがなかった困難なルートも登った。ティーンエイジャーになるまでには、ハーはアメリカの (C.　　　　　) でトップクラスのロッククライマーの一人となっていた。

① When he was 17, Hugh Herr was one of America's most prominent rock climbers.

▶ Whenのあとのheは、主節のHugh Herrを指す。

▶ prominentは「卓越した、重要な」。America's most prominent rock climbersで「アメリカで最も優れたロッククライマー」(≒ the most prominent rock climbers of America)。

▶ ロッククライミングは、岸壁や岩山を登る登山の一種。

② But he had a severe accident while climbing.

▶ whileの後ろは、主語のheとbe動詞wasが省略されている (= while he was climbing)。

③ In this lesson, we will find out how he coped with hardship and developed his career.

▶ find out ～は「(事実など) を知る、見つけ出す」の意味で、wh節やthat節などを目的語にとる。

✍ 次の英文を日本語に直しなさい。

We found out how the accident happened.

私たちは ＿＿＿＿＿＿＿＿＿＿＿＿＿＿＿＿＿＿＿＿＿＿＿＿。

▶ cope with ～は「～にうまく対処する」(≒ deal with ～)。

④ Hugh Herr was a born climber.

▶ born は形容詞で、「生まれながらの」の意味。

⑤ By age 8, he had scaled the face of 11,627-foot Mt. Temple in southern Alberta, Canada.

▶ By age 8 は「8歳のときにはすでに」。「8歳のとき」という過去の時点よりも以前の彼の行為を表すために、過去完了 had scaled が用いられている。scale は「～をよじ登る」。

▶ face は「(山などの) 急斜面」。

▶ 11,627-foot Mt. Temple は「11,627フィートのテンプル山」。foot「フィート」は長さの単位で、1フィートは約30.48センチメートル。複数形は feet だが、11,627-foot のように形容詞として用いる場合は単数形になる。*cf.* 12-year-old boy「12歳の少年」、three-hour walk「3時間の徒歩」

▶ Alberta「アルバータ州 (province)」はカナダ西部の州。

⑥ He ascended tough climbing routes, some of which no adult had ever attempted before.

▶ ascend は「～を登る」、tough climbing routes は「難しい登山ルート」。

▶〈, some of which ～〉は非制限用法の関係代名詞節。〈不定代名詞 (some や one など) + of + 関係代名詞〉の形で、「そのうちのいくつか[1つ]は～」と先行詞 (ここでは climbing routes) について補足説明をする。

例 I bought several books, *one of which* was about Japanese history.
「私は数冊の本を買ったが、そのうちの1冊は日本史に関するものだった」

▶ no adult had ever attempted before は「一人の大人もそれまでに挑戦したことがなかった」の意味で、経験を表す過去完了の文。

⑦ By the time he was a teenager, Herr was one of the top rock climbers on the East Coast.

▶ by the time ～は「～になるまでには」。後ろには主語と動詞を続ける。

✍ 英文を完成させなさい。

18歳になるまでには、その少年は事業を立ち上げていた。

(　　　) the (　　　) the boy turned 18, he had started a business.

▶ teenager は「10代の若者」の意味で、ふつう13歳から19歳までの若者を指す。

▶ the East Coast は「(アメリカの) 東海岸」の意味。

このセクションの内容 の答え→ A. 8　B. ロープ　C. 東海岸

教科書pp.54～55 *ll*.11～36 II

Climbing Accident

①In January 1982, 17-year-old Hugh Herr and his friend, Jeff Batzer, age 20, set out to climb Mt. Washington. ②Located in New Hampshire, Mt. Washington is the highest peak in the Northeastern United States, at 6,288 feet. ③Their climb began in reasonable weather, but winters in New Hampshire can be brutal, and very quickly, the two boys were fighting 100-mile-per-hour winds. ④The temperature dropped to a windchill factor of minus 110 degrees Fahrenheit.

⑤The boys became disoriented. ⑥Herr slipped and fell into a river, and they were stranded on the wilderness side of Mt. Washington. ⑦Cell phones did not yet exist, so the boys were on their own as the winds howled and the temperature dropped.

⑧"We survived by building snow caves and hugging each other to stay warm," Herr said later. ⑨They lost track of time. ⑩One day passed and then another.

⑪"When you're hypothermic, you can't think clearly," Herr said. ⑫"So even though we were approaching four days, we thought we were still in the same 24-hour day."

⑬Hypothermia gave way to surrender. ⑭"We were no longer able to walk," Herr said. ⑮"We just gave up all hope and we actually stopped hugging each other to stay warm. ⑯We just reasoned the sooner we died, the better."

⑰Almost by a miracle, the two boys were discovered by a snowshoer, and that evening they were airlifted to a hospital.

このセクションの内容

1982年1月に、当時17歳だったヒュー・ハーは、友人と共にワシントン山を登り始めたが、時速100マイルの風と（A.　　　　　）マイナス110度の体感温度の中、（B.　　　　　）がわからなくなった。ハーは川に転落し、2人は未開の山腹に取り残された。（C.　　　　　）によって、歩くこともできなくなった2人は希望を捨てたが、奇跡的に発見されて病院へと空輸された。

① In January 1982, 17-year-old Hugh Herr and his friend, Jeff Batzer, age 20, set out to climb Mt. Washington.

▶ Jeff Batzerとage 20は、his (= Herr's) friendの補足説明。

▶ set out to *do*は「〜し始める」(≒ start to *do*)の意味。

✍ ほぼ同じ意味を表すように、英文を完成させなさい。

Those teenagers started to travel around the world.

Those teenagers (　　　) (　　　) to travel around the world.

② Located in New Hampshire, Mt. Washington is the highest peak in the Northeastern United States, at 6,288 feet.

▶ Located in 〜は受け身の分詞構文で〈付帯状況〉を表す。be located in 〜で「(建物などが) 〜に位置している」。受け身の分詞構文ではbeingは省略されることが多い。

▶ peakは「頂上、山頂」のほかに「とがった山頂の山」を表す。the highest peak in 〜で「〜で最も高い山」。

▶ at 6,288 feetはMt. Washingtonの標高を表す。

③ Their climb began in reasonable weather, but winters in New Hampshire can be brutal, and very quickly, the two boys were fighting 100-mile-per-hour winds.

▶ Their climbは、Hugh HerrとJeff Batzerの登山のこと。

▶ reasonable weatherは「穏やかな天候」。

▶ canは「〜することがある」という可能性を表し、can be brutalで「ひどくなることがある」の意味。

▶ very quicklyは「(山に登り始めてから)すぐに、あっという間に」。

▶ the two boysはHugh HerrとJeff Batzerのこと。

▶ 100-mile-per-hour windsは「時速100マイルの風」。1マイルは約1,609メートル。

④ The temperature dropped to a windchill factor of minus 110 degrees Fahrenheit.

▶ drop to 〜は「〜にまで下がる」、windchill factorは「(風の影響による)体感温度」。

▶ minus 110 degrees Fahrenheitは「華氏マイナス110度」。Fahrenheit「華氏」は温度の単位のひとつ。アメリカでは気温を表すのに華氏が使われている。温度の単位には、ケルビンや、日本で使われている摂氏(Celsius)などがある。華氏マイナス110度は、およそ摂氏マイナス79度になる。

⑤ The boys became disoriented.

▶ The boysはHugh HerrとJeff Batzerのこと。

このセクションの内容 の答え→　A. 華氏　B. 方向　C. 低体温症

▶ become disorientedで「方向がわからなくなる」(≒ lose *one's* way)。

✍ 次の英文を日本語に直しなさい。

I became disoriented on the way to the festival venue.

私は祭りの会場に行く途中、＿＿＿＿＿＿＿＿＿＿＿＿＿＿＿＿＿＿。

⑥ Herr slipped and fell into a river, and they were stranded on the wilderness side of Mt. Washington.

▶ be stranded on ～は「～に取り残される」。

▶ wildernessは「荒野、未開地」、sideは「側、山腹」の意味で、ここでは登山ルートを外れたところのこと。

⑦ Cell phones did not yet exist, so the boys were on their own as the winds howled and the temperature dropped.

▶ Cell phonesは「携帯電話」。

▶ yetは、ここでは「1982年ではまだ」の意味。

▶ on *one's* ownは「ただ～だけで、一人で」の意味(≒ alone)。

▶ asは「～するとき、～する間」という意味で、同時性を表す接続詞。

▶ the winds howledは「風がビュービューと吹いている」様子を表す。

⑧ "We survived by building snow caves and hugging each other to stay warm," Herr said later.

▶ by V-ingは「～することによって」の意味で、２人が生き残るためにとった手段を説明している。

▶ building snow cavesは「(風よけのための)雪洞をつくること」、hugging each other to stay warmは「暖かくしているために[体温を保つために]お互いに抱き合うこと」。

⑨ They lost track of time.

▶ lose track of ～は「～がわからなくなる」(≒ no longer know ～)。

✍ 次の英文を日本語に直しなさい。

I lost track of where I was heading.

＿＿＿＿＿＿＿＿＿＿＿＿＿＿＿＿＿＿＿＿＿＿＿＿＿＿＿＿

⑩ One day passed and then another.

▶ anotherは、another day passed「もう１日が過ぎた」ということ。day passedは繰り返しの表現になるので省略されている。文全体で「１日が過ぎ、それからもう１日が過ぎた」となる。

⑪ "When you're hypothermic, you can't think clearly," Herr said.

▶ hypothermicは「低体温症の」、名詞はhypothermia「低体温症」。

▶ 代名詞のyouは読み手を含めた一般の人を指す。発言内容は「低体温症になると、人は[誰もが]はっきりと物を考えられなくなる」という意味。

⑫ "So even though we were approaching four days, we thought we were still in the same 24-hour day."

▶ even though ～は「～だけれども、～にもかかわらず」の意味で、though の強調表現。

例 He decided to climb the mountain *even though* the route was tough.
「彼はルートが困難だったにもかかわらず、その山を登ることにした」

▶ the same 24-hour day とは「(遭難した日と) 同じ24時間の１日」を表す。つまり、遭難してから４日を過ぎようとしていたにもかかわらず、２人はまだ遭難の初日だと思っていたということ。

⑬ Hypothermia gave way to surrender.

▶ give way to ～は「～に取って代わられる、～になる」(≒ be replaced with ～)。surrender は「(敵などに) 降伏すること」→「あきらめて状況に身をゆだねること」。ここでは、低体温症によって生き残ろうとする気力が失われたということ。

✍ 英文を完成させなさい。

嵐のような天気があけて、すがすがしい晴れた日になった。

The stormy weather (　　　) (　　　) to a beautiful sunny day.

⑭ "We were no longer able to walk," Herr said.

▶ no longer ～は「もはや～ない」、be able to *do* は「～することができる」。

✍ 英文を完成させなさい。

リリーはもはや、人形遊びをすることに興味がない。

Lily is (　　　) (　　　) interested in playing with her dolls.

⑮ "We just gave up all hope and we actually stopped hugging each other to stay warm.

▶ gave up all hope は「(生き残る) すべての希望をあきらめた」。

⑯ We just reasoned the sooner we died, the better."

▶ reason (that) ～は「～と判断する」。

▶ 〈the＋比較級～, the＋比較級 ...〉は「～すればするほどますます…」。文全体で、「私たちはただ、死ぬのが早ければ早いほどよいと思った」となる。

例 Sarah is sociable and believes *the more, the merrier.*
「サラは社交的で、人が多ければ多いほど楽しいと考えている」

⑰ Almost by a miracle, the two boys were discovered by a snowshoer, and that evening they were airlifted to a hospital.

▶ Almost by a miracle は「ほぼ奇跡的に、奇跡と言ってもいいほどに」。

▶ snowshoer は「かんじきを履いて歩く人」。

▶ airlift は「～を空輸する」で、ここでは受け身で使われている。

教科書pp.56～57 *ll*.37～65 III

"Walk, Not Climb"

①Herr woke up after surgery to find that he had lost both legs below the knee from frostbite. ②A nurse tried to offer encouragement by telling him that he would be able to walk with artificial legs. ③He was given crude plaster legs and, eventually, acrylic ones.

④When Herr asked the doctors if he would ever be able to climb again, they answered, "Walk, not climb." ⑤They told him that he would be able to drive a car, using hand controls, but not to ride a bike or return to mountain climbing.

⑥Herr told his friends that the artificial legs were far more rudimentary than he had hoped they would be. ⑦He said, "This is it? Are you kidding me?"

Back to the Mountains

The doctors were wrong. ⑧Herr started climbing again while he was still in the rehabilitation center.

⑨First, he noticed that because the amputations had left him 14 pounds lighter, he was able to move faster than before. ⑩He realized that there was no reason that his new feet needed to mimic his old ones. ⑪He started to make his own modifications to his artificial legs. ⑫He cut off a heel to reduce weight, increased his legs' stiffness where it was useful, added spikes for ice climbing, and made feet narrow enough to stick in small cracks.

⑬Soon, thanks to various types of prosthetic legs, Herr's climbing was better than ever. ⑭He began ascending rock faces that he actually could not have climbed before his accident.

Herr was again a major competitor in the climbing world. ⑮Just one year after the accident on Mt. Washington, he was featured on the cover of *Outside Magazine*.

このセクションの内容

凍傷によって（A.　　　　　）を失ったハーは、医師らにはもう二度と登山はできないと言われた。しかし、ハーはリハビリ施設にいる間に再び登山を始め、（B.　　　　　）に改良を加えて、再びクライミングの世界における主要な（C.　　　　　）となった。

① Herr woke up after surgery to find that he had lost both legs below the knee from frostbite.

▶ wake up to find that ～は「目覚めて～とわかる」の意味で、結果を表す副詞的用法の不定詞を用いた表現。ここではtoの前にafter surgery「手術後に」が挿入されている。

▶ that節内は「目覚めた」時点での完了を表すhad lostが使われている。

✍ 次の英文を日本語に直しなさい。

I woke up to find that she had left the house.

____

▶ fromは「～で、～のために」という原因を表す。frostbiteは「凍傷」。

② A nurse tried to offer encouragement by telling him that he would be able to walk with artificial legs.

▶ try to *do*は「～しようと試みる[努力する]」、offer encouragementは「励ます」（≒ encourage）。

▶ by V-ingは手段を表し、by telling him that ～で「彼（= Herr）に～だと話すことによって」の意味。ここでは、看護師がどのように励ましたのかを説明している。

▶ with artificial legsは「義足を使えば」。

③ He was given crude plaster legs and, eventually, acrylic ones.

▶「彼（= Herr）は～を与えられた」という受け身の文。*A* and, eventually, *B*の形なので、A→Bの順に与えられたということ。

▶ crude plaster legsは「未加工の石膏（せっこう）の脚」、acrylic onesは「アクリル製の脚」。onesはlegsのこと。

④ When Herr asked the doctors if he would ever be able to climb again, they answered, "Walk, not climb."

▶〈ask + O（人）+ O（= if節）〉の文。asked the doctors if ～で「～かどうか医師にたずねた」。

▶ if節のwouldは、時制の一致により過去形になっている。everは「いつか、今後」の意味で、たずねた時点における未来を表している。

▶"Walk, not climb."は、Herrの質問に対する医師の答えで、「今後、再び歩けるようにはなるが、登れるようにはならないだろう」ということ。

⑤ They told him that he would be able to drive a car, using hand controls, but not to ride a bike or return to mountain climbing.

▶〈tell + O (人) + O (= that節)〉の文。

▶using 〜は「〜しながら」という〈付帯状況〉を表す分詞構文で、「ハンドコントロールを使いながら」の意味。

▶but not to 〜は、*but* he would *not* be able *to* 〜ということ。

▶return to 〜は「〜を再開する」の意味で、returnはrideと並列している。つまり、自転車に乗ったり、再び登山をしたりはできないだろうということ。

⑥ Herr told his friends that the artificial legs were far more rudimentary than he had hoped they would be.

▶farは「はるかに」の意味で比較級を強める。rudimentaryは「原始的な」。

▶than he had hoped 〜は「彼が〜と予想したよりも」。「義足がはるかに原始的だった(とわかった)」時点よりも前のことを表す。

▶they would be の they は the artificial legs を指す。be のあとに rudimentaryが省略されている。Herrは義足が原始的なものだと予想していたが、その予想よりもはるかに原始的なものだったということ。

⑦ He said, "This is it? Are you kidding me?"

▶This is it?は「これだけ?」の意味で、ここでは「これが、自分が予想[期待]していたものなのか」(≒ Is this what I was expecting?)と義足に対する失望感を表している。

▶Are you kidding me?は「冗談でしょう」。

⑧ Herr started climbing again while he was still in the rehabilitation center.

▶rehabilitation centerは「リハビリ施設」。re-は「再び、元に」という意味の接頭辞。*cf.* rethink「〜を再考する」

⑨ First, he noticed that because the amputations had left him 14 pounds lighter, he was able to move faster than before.

▶amputationは「切断(手術)」、poundは「ポンド(重さの単位で、1ポンドは約454グラム)」。

▶had left him 14 pounds lighterは〈leave + O (人) + C (形容詞)〉「OをCのままにしておく」の形。had leftと過去完了が使われているのは、Herrが気付くよりも前のことだから。because節は「切断(手術)は彼を14ポンド軽くしたので」となる。

このセクションの内容 の答え→ A. 両脚 B. 義足 C. 競争参加者

⑩ **He realized that there was no reason that his new feet needed to mimic his old ones.**

▶ there is no reason that ～で「～という理由はない」。

✍ 英文を完成させなさい。

その女性は、「彼を憎む理由はない」と言った。

The woman said, "There is (　　　) (　　　) that I hate him."

▶ need to *do*は「～する必要がある」、mimicは「～をまねる、擬態する」。

▶ his old onesとはhis old legsのこと。

⑪ **He started to make his own modifications to his artificial legs.**

▶ make a modification to ～は「～に変更[改良]を加える」、*one's* ownは「自分なりの」。

⑫ **He cut off a heel to reduce weight, increased his legs' stiffness where it was useful, added spikes for ice climbing, and made feet narrow enough to stick in small cracks.**

▶ *A*, *B*, *C*, and *D*の形で、cut ～、increased ～、added ～、made ～の4つの動詞が並列している。Herrが義足をどのように改良したかを説明している。

▶ whereは「～する場合には」という意味の接続詞。itはstiffnessを指し、「それ（＝硬さ）が役立つ場合には、彼の脚の硬さを高めた」の意味。

▶ made feet narrow ～は〈make + O + C〉の形。feetは義足の「足」の部分のこと。to stick in small cracksは「小さな割れ目に突き刺さるように」。

⑬ **Soon, thanks to various types of prosthetic legs, Herr's climbing was better than ever.**

▶ thanks to ～は「～のおかげで」。

▶ prosthetic legsは「義足」の意味だが、artificial legsの中でも、工学技術を用いて複雑な動きを可能にした義足のこと。

▶ better than everは「かつてないほどよい」。

⑭ **He began ascending rock faces that he actually could not have climbed before his accident.**

▶ thatはrock faces「岩壁」を先行詞とする目的格の関係代名詞。

▶ could not have climbedは、過去の状況に基づいての推測・可能性で、文全体で「彼は、事故以前には実際に登ることができなかっただろう岩壁を登り始めた」となる。

⑮ **Just one year after the accident on Mt. Washington, he was featured on the cover of *Outside Magazine*.**

▶ just one year after ～で「～のちょうど1年後に」。

▶ *Outside Magazine*はアメリカのアウトドア専門誌。

教科書pp.57〜58 *ll*.66〜95 IV

Next Step

①Herr had never been much interested in school. ②His goal was to be the best mountain climber in the world. ③He had no interest in even going to college.

④Inspired by his accident, Herr decided to attend college, where he enrolled in math and science courses. ⑤He even earned a master's degree in mechanical engineering at MIT in 1993, followed by a Ph.D. at Harvard in biophysics. ⑥Since then, Herr has produced a string of breakthrough products, starting with a computer-controlled artificial knee in 2003. ⑦In 2004, he created the biomechatronics group at MIT, a now 40-person R&D lab drawing on the fields of biology, mechanics, and electronics to restore function to those who have lost it.

⑧In 2007, the team produced powered bionic limbs that allow an amputee to walk with speed and effort comparable to people with biological legs. ⑨The ankle system is manufactured by a private company Herr started.

⑩In 2016, Herr advanced another of his lab's goals: to improve human performance "beyond what nature intends" by creating an innovative device that saves energy when you are walking. ⑪The implications are vast for people who want to get to places faster, or people who want to conserve energy on a long walk.

⑫In the near future, Herr and his colleagues at the MIT center are committed to treating paralysis caused by damage to the spinal cord. ⑬Herr's goal is to develop a synthetic spinal cord that aids the original.

⑭Herr sees a future where technology not only helps eliminate disability but also increases human potential. ⑮He believes his research will extend far beyond limb replacement and will fundamentally redefine what it means to be human.

このセクションの内容

修士号と博士号を取得したハーは、人工膝や電動生体義肢といった（A.　　　　　）な製品をつくり出した。2016年には、彼の研究所は、「自然の意図を超えて」人間のパフォーマンスを向上させることを目標に掲げた。ハーは、科学技術が（B.　　　　　）を取り除くことのみならず、人間の潜在能力を高める未来を見ており、自分の研究が人間であるとはどういうことかを根本的に（C.　　　　　）するだろうと考えている。

① Herr had never been much interested in school.

▶ had never been ～は経験を表す過去完了。

② His goal was to be the best mountain climber in the world.

▶ to be ～は「～になること」で、名詞的用法の不定詞。

③ He had no interest in even going to college.

▶ have no interest in ～で「～に関心がない」、evenは「～でさえ、～すら」。文全体で「彼は大学に通うことにすら関心がなかった」となる。

④ Inspired by his accident, Herr decided to attend college, where he enrolled in math and science courses.

▶ Inspired by ～は過去分詞で始まる分詞構文で、「～に触発されて、～の影響を受けて」という意味。beingが省略されている。

▶〈, where〉は非制限用法の関係副詞で、先行詞はcollege「大学」。

▶ enroll in ～は「～に入学する」（≒ enter）。

⑤ He even earned a master's degree in mechanical engineering at MIT in 1993, followed by a Ph.D. at Harvard in biophysics.

▶ even earned ～は「～さえ取得した」、master's degreeは「修士号」。

▶ in mechanical engineeringは「機械工学で」。MITはMassachusetts Institute of Technologyの略で「マサチューセッツ工科大学」。

▶ (being) followed by ～は分詞構文で、その後に続いて起こったことを表す。

▶ Ph.D.（＝Doctor of Philosophy）は「博士号」で、ラテン語のPhilosophiae Doctorの略。

▶ Harvardは「ハーバード大学」、biophysicsは「生物物理学」。

⑥ Since then, Herr has produced a string of breakthrough products, starting with a computer-controlled artificial knee in 2003.

▶ thenは、⑤の文のHerrが博士号を取得したとき。

▶ a string of ～は「一連の～」（≒ a series of ～）、breakthrough productsは「画期的な製品」。

▶ starting with ～は〈付帯状況〉を表す分詞構文で、「(一連の製品を) ～で始めて」の意味。computer-controlled artificial kneeは「コンピューターで制御された人工の膝」。

⑦ In 2004, he created the biomechatronics group at MIT, a now 40-person R&D lab drawing on the fields of biology, mechanics, and electronics to restore function to those who have lost it.

▶ biomechatronics「バイオメカトロニクス」は、生物学、機械工学、電子工学を組み合わせた新しい科学分野。

▶ a now 40-person R&D (＝research and development) lab「現在40人から成る研究開発ラボ」以下は、the biomechatronics group at MITについて具体的に説明している。labはlaboratory「研究所」を短くしたもの。

▶ draw on ～は「(知識など) を活用する」(≒ use knowledge of ～)。

▶ to restore function to those who have lost itは「(身体の) 機能をなくした人々に、その機能を取り戻させる」という意味。itはfunctionを指す。

⑧ In 2007, the team produced powered bionic limbs that allow an amputee to walk with speed and effort comparable to people with biological legs.

▶ the teamはHerrがMITで設立したグループのこと。

▶ powered bionic limbsは「電動の生体義肢」。

▶ allow ～ to *do*は「～に…することを可能にする」。amputeeは「手術で手足などをなくした人」で、動詞形はamputate「(手足などを) 切断する」。

▶ comparable to ～は「～と同等の、～に匹敵する」(≒ similar to ～)。電動の生体義肢を使えば、生物学上の[本物の]脚をもつ人と同等の速さと労力で歩くことができるようになるということ。

✍ 次の英文を日本語に直しなさい。

He is a saxophone player comparable to John Coltrane.

彼はジョン・コルトレーンに ________________________________。

⑨ The ankle system is manufactured by a private company Herr started.

▶ The ankle system「足首の機構」は、⑧の文のpowered bionic limbsの足首の部分のこと。

▶ be manufactured by ～は受け身で、「～によって製造される」。

⑩ In 2016, Herr advanced another of his lab's goals: to improve human performance "beyond what nature intends" by creating an innovative device that saves energy when you are walking.

このセクションの内容 の答え→ A. 画期的 B. (身体的) 障害 C. 再定義

▶ advanceは「～を提唱する」、another of his lab's goalsは「彼（= Herr）のラボのもう1つの目標」。⑦の文にあるものとは別の目標のこと。

▶ beyond what nature intendsは「自然が意図していることを超えて」。

▶ by creating an innovative device that saves energy when you are walkingは「歩行中のエネルギーを節約する革新的な装置をつくることによって」。

⑪ The implications are vast for people who want to get to places faster, or people who want to conserve energy on a long walk.

▶ The implications「その意味」とは、⑩の文の目標が実現したときの意味のこと。vastは「非常に大きい」。

▶ conserve energy on a long walkは「長距離の徒歩でエネルギーを節約する」。

⑫ In the near future, Herr and his colleagues at the MIT center are committed to treating paralysis caused by damage to the spinal cord.

▶ be committed to ～は「～に力を尽くす」（≒ be dedicated to ～）

✍ 英文を完成させなさい。

そのエンジニアは、新しいハイテク装置の開発に力を尽くしている。

The engineer is (　　　) (　　　) developing new hi-tech devices.

▶ caused ～はparalysis「麻痺（まひ）」を後ろから修飾している。paralysis以下は、「脊髄への損傷によって引き起こされる麻痺」の意味。

⑬ Herr's goal is to develop a synthetic spinal cord that aids the original.

▶ a synthetic spinal cord that aids the originalは「元の脊髄の補助をする合成脊髄」。thatは主格の関係代名詞。

⑭ Herr sees a future where technology not only helps eliminate disability but also increases human potential.

▶ whereはa futureを先行詞とする関係副詞。

▶ not only ～ but also ... は「～だけでなく…も」、help *do*は「～するのに役立つ、～するのを促進する」。

⑮ He believes his research will extend far beyond limb replacement and will fundamentally redefine what it means to be human.

▶ far beyond limb replacementは「四肢の交換をはるかに超えて」。

▶ what it means to be humanは「人間であるとはどういうことか」。

確認問題

語彙

1 次の文の意味が通るように、右から単語を選んで（　）内に補いなさい。

artificial rudimentary prominent crude

(1) She is one of the most (　　　) actors in Japan and has starred in many famous films.
(2) Did you know that AI is short for (　　　) intelligence?
(3) This piano lesson is for beginners, and it teaches a very (　　　) knowledge of how to play the piano.

2 第2音節にアクセント（強勢）のある語を3つ選び、記号で答えなさい。

ア　mi-nus　　イ　bru-tal　　ウ　re-store
エ　in-tend　　オ　mim-ic　　カ　en-roll

文法・表現

1 日本語に合うように、（　）内に適切な語を入れなさい。ただし、最初の文字が指定されているときは、その文字で書き始めなさい。

(1) 19歳になるまでには、彼は一人暮らしを始めていた。
(　　　) the (　　　) he reached the age of 19, he had started living alone.
(2) その旅行者は、方向がわからなくならないよう市の地図を持って行った。
The traveler took a city map along so as not to (　　　) (　　　).
(3) 彼女は過去の経験を生かして、教師として働き始めた。
She started to work as a teacher, (d　　　) (　　　) her experience.
(4) マキはとうの昔に海外移住をして、もはやここに住んでいない。
Maki moved abroad a long time ago and (　　　) (　　　) lives here.
(5) 少年はオンラインゲームに夢中になり、時間が経つのを忘れた。
The boy was caught up in online games and (　　　) (　　　) of time.

2 日本語に合うように、（　）内の語句を並べかえなさい。

(1) 彼女が非難されるべき理由はない。
(she / is / no / that / there / should / reason) be blamed.
____ be blamed.
(2) 彼女は目を覚ますと、雨が降り始めていたことがわかった。
She (find / up / it / that / woke / had / to) started raining.
She ____ started raining.

(3) 収入は高ければ高いほどよいと考える人もいる。
Some people (higher / that / the income / the / think), the better.
Some people ________________________________, the better.

(4) 彼は10の山を登り、その中には10,000フィートを超えるものもあった。
He climbed ten mountains, (some / 10,000 feet / which / were / of / over).
He climbed ten mountains, ________________________________.

(5) 時が経過するにつれ、彼への怒りは彼への同情に取って代わられた。
As time went by, (sympathy / gave / at / him / anger / to / way) for him.
As time went by, ________________________________ for him.

総合

次の文を読んで、あとの問いに答えなさい。

In 2007, the team produced ①powered bionic limbs that allow an amputee to walk with speed and effort comparable to people with biological legs. The ankle system is manufactured by a private company Herr started.

In 2016, Herr advanced another of his lab's goals: to improve human performance "beyond what nature intends" by creating an innovative device that saves energy when you are walking. ②The implications are vast for people who want to get to places faster, or people who want to conserve energy on a long walk.

In the near future, Herr and his colleagues at the MIT center are (③) to treating paralysis caused by damage to the spinal cord. Herr's goal is to develop a synthetic spinal cord that aids ④the original.

⑤Herr sees a future (helps / disability / where / not / eliminate / technology / but / only) also increases human potential. He believes his research will extend far beyond limb replacement and will fundamentally redefine what it means to be human.

問1　下線部①は何を可能にするか、日本語で説明しなさい。
問2　下線部②はどのような人々への意味か、日本語で2つ答えなさい。
問3　(③)に適するものを下から選び、記号で答えなさい。
ア　coped with　　イ　committed　　ウ　set out　　エ　accustomed
問4　下線部④が表すものを具体的に日本語で説明しなさい。
問5　下線部⑤の( )内の語を並べかえて、英文を完成させなさい。

Lesson 5 How to Beat Procrastination

教科書p.68 *ll*.1〜11 I

①Tim Urban, one of the Internet's most popular writers, shares his thoughts on a variety of topics from everyday psychology to artificial intelligence on his blog, *Wait But Why*. ②Here he writes a post on his own bad habit—procrastination.

③I'm just a lifelong procrastinator who thinks about this topic all the time. ④I'm still in a total battle with my own habits, but I have made some progress in the last few years, and I'm drawing my thoughts from what's worked for me.

⑤To understand why procrastinators procrastinate so much, let's start by comparing the non-procrastinator's brain with the procrastinator's brain:

このセクションの内容

ライターのティム・アーバンは、（A.　　　　　）に自分の悪癖について以下のように書いている。「私は終生変わらぬ先延ばし屋だが、ここ数年で（B.　　　　　）した。先延ばし屋がなぜ先延ばしをしてしまうのかを理解するために、先延ばし屋ではない人の脳と先延ばし屋の脳とを（C.　　　　　）することから始めよう。」

① Tim Urban, one of the Internet's most popular writers, shares his thoughts on a variety of topics from everyday psychology to artificial intelligence on his blog, *Wait But Why*.

▶ one of the Internet's most popular writers「インターネット上の最も人気のあるライターの一人」は、Tim Urbanの補足説明（同格）。

▶ share *one's* thoughts on 〜は「〜についての考えを話す」、a variety of 〜は「さまざまな〜」。

✍ 英文を完成させなさい。

私は、さまざまなロボットが人類のために働く未来を見通している。

I see a future where a (　　　) (　　　) robots work for human beings.

▶ from *A* to *B*は「AからBまで」の意味で、ブログのトピックが日常的な心理学から人工知能に至るまでの幅広いものであることを示している。

② Here he writes a post on his own bad habit—procrastination.

▶ Hereは、①の文を受けて「彼のブログに」の意味。

▶ダッシュ (—) は「つまり」の意味で、直前のhis own bad habit「彼自身の悪癖」をprocrastination「先延ばし(をすること)」と言いかえている。procrastinationとは、やるべき仕事を始めずにぐずぐずと先延ばしにすることをいう。動詞形はprocrastinate「先延ばしする」、さらに、先延ばしをする癖のある人のことをprocrastinator「先延ばし屋」という。

③ I'm just a lifelong procrastinator who thinks about this topic all the time.

▶who はa lifelong procrastinatorを先行詞とする主格の関係代名詞。

▶this topicとは、②の文のprocrastinationのこと。

④ I'm still in a total battle with my own habits, but I have made some progress in the last few years, and I'm drawing my thoughts from what's worked for me.

▶be in a battle with 〜は「〜と格闘している」。形容詞totalは「完全な、徹底した」の意味で、battleの程度を強調している。

▶have madeは現在完了で、make progressは「進歩する」。

✍ 次の英文を日本語に直しなさい。

Her writing skills have made a lot of progress.

彼女のライティングスキルは ＿＿＿＿＿＿＿＿＿＿＿＿＿＿＿＿ 。

▶draw 〜 from ... は「…から(教訓など)を引き出す」。fromの後ろは関係代名詞whatで始まる名詞節で、「私にとって効果があったこと」の意味。なお、what'sはwhat hasの短縮形。workは「うまくいく、効果がある」。

⑤ To understand why procrastinators procrastinate so much, let's start by comparing the non-procrastinator's brain with the procrastinator's brain:

▶To understand 〜は「〜を理解するために」。

▶why以下は間接疑問で、「先延ばし屋はなぜそんなにも先延ばしをするのか」の意味。

▶start by V-ingで「〜することから始める」。comparing以下がbyの目的語になっている。compare *A* with *B*は「AをBと比較する」。

例 *Compare* Illustration C *with* D. 「図Cを図Dと比較しなさい」

▶non-procrastinatorは「先延ばししない人」。ここでは所有格で使われている。non-は「非、不、〜ではない」の意味を持つ接頭辞。*cf.* non-Japanese「日本人ではない人」、nonsmoker「非喫煙者」、nonfiction「ノンフィクション」

▶文末のコロン(:)に続けて、教科書p.68で、「先延ばし屋ではない人の脳」と「先延ばし屋の脳」のイラストが示されている。

このセクションの内容 の答え→ A. ブログ B. 進歩[改善] C. 比較

教科書pp.69〜70 *ll*.12〜35 II

①Do you notice anything different? ②It seems the Rational Decision-Maker in the procrastinator's brain is coexisting with a pet—the Instant Gratification Monkey. ③This would be fine if only the Rational Decision-Maker knew how to own a monkey. ④But unfortunately, it wasn't a part of his training and he's left completely helpless as the monkey makes it impossible for him to do his job.

⑤The fact is, the monkey is the last creature that should be in charge of decisions. ⑥He thinks only about the present, trying to maximize the pleasure of the current moment. ⑦The monkey doesn't understand the Rational Decision-Maker; the Rational Decision-Maker doesn't understand the monkey either. ⑧Why would we continue jogging, the monkey thinks, when we could stop, which would feel better? ⑨Why would we practice that instrument when it's not fun? He thinks humans are insane. ⑩In the monkey world, he eats when he is hungry, sleeps when he is tired, and doesn't do anything difficult.

⑪There's one thing that scares the monkey. ⑫It is called the Panic Monster. ⑬The monster is inactive most of the time, but he suddenly wakes up when a deadline gets too close, or when there's danger of public embarrassment or some other scary consequence. ⑭It freaks the monkey out of the wheel and the Rational Decision-Maker regains control to finish the task in the last minute. ⑮However, some procrastinators don't even respond to the monster. ⑯In the most desperate moments, they run up the tree with the monkey, entering a state of shutdown.

このセクションの内容

先延ばし屋の脳内では、「合理的な決断を下す者」が「即座の快感を求めるサル」と（A.　　　　　）しており、後者（サル）のせいで前者は仕事ができない。サルは現在の快楽を（B.　　　　　）するように努める。しかし、恐ろしい結果の危険性があると、「パニックの怪獣」が目を覚まし、「合理的な決断を下す者」は支配権を取り戻してどたん場で仕事を終える。しかし、深刻な状況でも仕事から逃げて、（C.　　　　　）の状態になる先延ばし屋もいる。

① Do you notice anything different?

▶教科書p.68にある２つのイラストの違いについて読み手にたずねている。

② It seems the Rational Decision-Maker in the procrastinator's brain is coexisting with a pet—the Instant Gratification Monkey.

▶It seems (that) ～「～のように思える、～であるようだ」の構文。

▶the Rational Decision-Maker「合理的な決断を下す者」とthe Instant Gratification Monkey「即座の快感を求めるサル」は、教科書p.68のイラストに登場するキャラクターのこと。

▶coexistは「共存する」。co-は「共に」という意味の接頭辞。*cf.* cooperate「協力する」、coworker「同僚」

③ This would be fine if only the Rational Decision-Maker knew how to own a monkey.

▶Thisは、②の文を受け「合理的な決断を下す者と即座の快感を求めるサルが共存している状態」を指す。

▶仮定法過去の文で、if only ～は「～でありさえすれば」。文全体で、「合理的な決断を下す者がサルを飼いならす方法を知ってさえいれば、これ(＝共存)は問題ないだろう(実際はそうではない)」という意味。

④ But unfortunately, it wasn't a part of his training and he's left completely helpless as the monkey makes it impossible for him to do his job.

▶③の文を受けて、実際のことについて述べている文。

▶１つ目のitは「サルを飼いならすこと」で、合理的な決断を下す者は、それを習得する訓練を受けていないということ。文中のhis、he、himはthe Rational Decision-Makerを指す。

▶he's left completely helplessは、〈leave + O + C〉「OをCのままにしておく」の受け身の文。「彼はまったく無力のままにさせられる」の意味。

▶asは「～なので」と〈理由〉を表す。

▶make it impossible for ～ to *do*は「～が…することを不可能にする」の意味で、itはto以下を指す形式目的語。

⑤ The fact is, the monkey is the last creature that should be in charge of decisions.

▶The fact is, ～は「事実は～」の意味(≒The fact is that ～)。

✍ 英文を完成させなさい。

事実、おじが先延ばしをすることは決してない。

The (　　　) (　　　), my uncle never procrastinates.

▶the last ～ that ...は「最も…するには望ましくない～」、in charge of ～は

このセクションの内容 の答え→ A. 共存　B. 最大化　C. 停止[シャットダウン]

「～を管理して、～を担当して」。

▶ thatはthe last creatureを先行詞とする主格の関係代名詞。文全体で「事実、サルは決断を担当すべき生き物としては最も望ましくない」となる。

⑥ He thinks only about the present, trying to maximize the pleasure of the current moment.

▶ only about the presentは「現在についてのみ」。

▶ trying ～は〈付帯状況〉の分詞構文で、動作の連続を表す。「そして、今現在の快楽を最大化しようとする」の意味。

⑦ The monkey doesn't understand the Rational Decision-Maker; the Rational Decision-Maker doesn't understand the monkey either.

▶ セミコロン（；）は接続詞と同じ働きをする。ここでは対照的な２文をつなげ、両者が理解し合っていないことを述べている。

▶ eitherは否定文で「～もまた（…ない）」の意味。

⑧ Why would we continue jogging, the monkey thinks, when we could stop, which would feel better?

▶ 挿入句the monkey thinks以外が、サルが考えている内容になる。

▶ １つ目のwouldは「～するとは」という、話し手の驚きや困惑などを表し、反語の意味で使われることが多い。ここでは、「なぜジョギングなんかし続けるのか（し続けなくてもよいではないか）」ということ。

▶ when we could stopは「（ジョギングを）やめられるのに」。このwhenは「～なのに」という〈譲歩〉を表し、whyやhowの疑問文で使われる。

▶〈, which〉は非制限用法の関係代名詞で、when we could stopが先行詞。

▶ 文全体は、「『やめられるのに、その方がより楽だろうに、どうしてジョギングなんかし続けるんだ』とサルは思う」という意味。

⑨ Why would we practice that instrument when it's not fun?

▶ サルの思考を別の例で示している。「楽しくないのに、なぜその楽器を練習するのか（しなくてもよいではないか）」という意味。

✍ 次の英文を日本語に直しなさい。

Why would she study hard when the exam is already over?

____________________ なぜ彼女は熱心に勉強するのか。

⑩ In the monkey world, he eats when he is hungry, sleeps when he is tired, and doesn't do anything difficult.

▶ In the monkey world「サルの世界」とはつまり、「サルの価値観」のこと。

▶ eats ～、sleeps ～、doesn't do ～の３つの動詞が並列している。

⑪ There's one thing that scares the monkey.

▶ thatはone thingを先行詞とする主格の関係代名詞。scareは「～をこわがらせる、びっくりさせる」。

⑫ **It is called the Panic Monster.**

▶ Itは⑪の文のone thing that scares the monkeyを指す。

⑬ **The monster is inactive most of the time, but he suddenly wakes up when a deadline gets too close, or when there's danger of public embarrassment or some other scary consequence.**

▶ inactiveは「不活発な」、most of the timeは「ほとんどいつも」。

▶ heはThe monster (= the Panic Monster) を指す。

▶ *A*, or *B*の形で、２つのwhenで始まる副詞節が並列し、怪獣が目覚めるのがどのようなときかを示している。

▶ ２つ目のorは、public embarrassmentとsome other scary consequenceを並列させている。

▶ but以下は、「締め切りが近づきすぎているときに、あるいは人前でばつの悪い思いをすることやその他の恐ろしい結果の危険性があるときに、彼 (=怪獣) は突然目を覚ます」となる。

⑭ **It freaks the monkey out of the wheel and the Rational Decision-Maker regains control to finish the task in the last minute.**

▶ Itはthe monsterのこと。

▶ freak ～ out of the wheelは「～を取り乱させて舵輪(だりん)から引き離す」(≒ make ～ very upset and get it away from the wheel)。the wheel「舵輪」は、行動を決めることの比喩表現。

▶ in the last minuteは「どたん場で」(≒ just before it is too late)。

⑮ **However, some procrastinators don't even respond to the monster.**

▶ don't even respond to ～は「～に反応することさえしない」。

⑯ **In the most desperate moments, they run up the tree with the monkey, entering a state of shutdown.**

▶ In the most desperate momentsは「最も絶望的な瞬間に」→「深刻な状況で」。

▶ theyは⑮の文のsome procrastinatorsを指す。

▶ entering ～は〈付帯状況〉の分詞構文。a state of shutdown「停止の状態」とは、仕事から目を背けたまま、あきらめてしまうこと。

教科書pp.70~72 *ll*.36~66 III

①Now, let's examine the diagram which represents the challenge at hand anytime you take on a task. ②The Critical Entrance is where you go when you start the task; the Dark Woods is where you're actually doing the work; and once you finish, you're rewarded by ending up in the Happy Playground—a place where you feel satisfaction because you got something done. ③You occasionally even enter a state of Flow, where you're so immersed in the task that you lose track of time. Sounds pretty simple, right?

④Unfortunately, procrastinators tend to miss out on both the Happy Playground and Flow. ⑤For example, consider a procrastinator who couldn't bring himself to get started. ⑥He spent hours in the Dark Playground, one of the monkey's favorite places, knowing the deadline was drawing near. ⑦He was only making his life harder by not starting. ⑧Eventually, the deadline got so close, the Panic Monster suddenly came roaring into the room, causing him to fly through the task to hit the deadline. ⑨After he finishes, he feels decent because he accomplished something, but he's not that pleased because he knows he rushed to do it. ⑩He also feels he wasted most of his day procrastinating. ⑪This lands him in Mixed Feelings Park.

⑫What should you do to keep this from happening? ⑬First, you must make it through the Critical Entrance. ⑭This means stopping whatever you're doing when it's time to begin the task. You put away all distractions and get started. ⑮This is the hardest part, because this is where the monkey puts up his fiercest resistance. He absolutely hates stopping something fun to start something hard. You need to be the strongest. ⑯If you can get started and force the monkey into the Dark Woods, you've broken a bit of his will.

The Dark Woods is where you're working. ⑰It's not a fun place to be, and the monkey wants nothing to do with it. ⑱To make things harder, the Dark Woods is surrounded by the Dark Playground. ⑲And the monkey will try as hard as he can to leave the Dark Woods.

このセクションの内容

先延ばし屋は、仕事を始めずに暗い（A.　　　　　）で何時間も過ごし、急いで締め切りまでに仕事を終えても、あまり満足感を得られない。これを防ぐには、「重要な（B.　　　　　）」をうまく通り抜けて仕事をし始める必要がある。サルが激しく（C.　　　　　）するため、ここが最難関の部分だ。

① Now, let's examine the diagram which represents the challenge at hand anytime you take on a task.

▶ the diagram「図」は、教科書p.71上部にあるイラストのこと。

▶ at handは「差し迫った、目の前の」（≒ immediately in front of you）。

▶〈anytime＋主語＋動詞〉は「～するときはいつでも」、take on ～は「（仕事など）を引き受ける」（≒ decide to do ～）。

② The Critical Entrance is where you go when you start the task; the Dark Woods is where you're actually doing the work; and once you finish, you're rewarded by ending up in the Happy Playground—a place where you feel satisfaction because you got something done.

▶ The Critical Entrance「重要な入口」、the Dark Woods「暗い森」、the Happy Playground「楽しい遊び場」という３つの場所について、それぞれセミコロン（；）で区切りながら説明している。

▶ １つ目と２つ目のwhereは、先行詞を含む関係副詞で、「～する場所」の意味。３つ目のwhereはa placeを先行詞とする関係副詞。

▶ onceは接続詞で、〈once＋主語＋動詞〉は「いったん～すると」。

▶ be rewardedは受け身で、「報われる」の意味。

▶ end up in ～は「ついに～にいる、～にたどり着く」。

▶ ダッシュ（—）以下で、the Happy Playgroundについて説明している。

▶ get something doneは〈get＋O＋C〉の形で、「何か（＝仕事）を終わらせる」。

③ You occasionally even enter a state of Flow, where you're so immersed in the task that you lose track of time.

▶〈, where〉は非制限用法の関係副詞で、a state of Flow「フローの状態」について説明している。

▶ so ～ that ...は「とても～なので…」、be immersed in ～は「～に没頭する」（≒ be absorbed in ～）。

▶ lose track of timeは「時間がわからなくなる、時がたつのを忘れる」。

④ Unfortunately, procrastinators tend to miss out on both the Happy Playground and Flow.

▶ miss out on 〜は「(機会など) を逃す」(≒ lose the chance to enjoy 〜)。

✍ 英文を完成させなさい。

皆さん、この絶好の機会をお見逃しなく！

Don't (　　　) (　　　) on this golden chance, everyone!

⑤ **For example, consider a procrastinator who couldn't bring himself to get started.**

▶ couldn't bring himself to get started は「彼自身に始めさせることができなかった」→「どうしても彼は始める気にならなかった」。

⑥ **He spent hours in the Dark Playground, one of the monkey's favorite places, knowing the deadline was drawing near.**

▶ knowing 〜は〈付帯状況〉の分詞構文で、「〜と知りながら」。

▶ draw near は「(時期などが) 近づく」。

⑦ **He was only making his life harder by not starting.**

▶〈make + O + C〉は「O を C (の状態) にする」。

▶ by not starting は「始めないことによって」。否定語は動名詞の前に置く。

⑧ **Eventually, the deadline got so close, the Panic Monster suddenly came roaring into the room, causing him to fly through the task to hit the deadline.**

▶ so 〜 that ...「とても〜なので…」の that を省略し、代わりにコンマを置いた口語的な文。come V-ing は「〜しながら来る」。

▶ causing 〜は〈付帯状況〉の分詞構文で、動作の連続を表す。cause 〜 to *do* は「〜に…させる」。

▶ fly through 〜は「〜にすばやく取り組む」(≒ work on 〜 quickly)、hit the deadline は「締め切りに間に合って終える」(≒ finish in time for the deadline)。

⑨ **After he finishes, he feels decent because he accomplished something, but he's not that pleased because he knows he rushed to do it.**

▶ feel decent は「(ある程度) 満足感を得る」。

▶ he's not that pleased で「彼はあまり[それほど]満足していない」。

⑩ **He also feels he wasted most of his day procrastinating.**

▶ waste 〜 V-ing は「〜を…して無駄にする」。

✍ 次の英文を日本語に直しなさい。

I was told not to waste my time playing video games.

---

⑪ **This lands him in Mixed Feelings Park.**

このセクションの内容 の答え→ A. 遊び場　B. 入口　C. 抵抗

▶ Thisは、⑩の文を受けて「先延ばしをして1日の大半を無駄にしたと感じること」を指す。land ~ in ... は「~を…の状態に陥らせる」。

▶ Mixed Feelings Parkは「複雑な心境の公園」。

⑫ What should you do to keep this from happening?

▶ keep ~ from V-ingは「~が…するのを防ぐ」(≒ prevent ~ from V-ing)。

▶ thisは、⑪の文の「複雑な心境の公園に行き着くこと」を指す。

⑬ First, you must make it through the Critical Entrance.

▶ make it through ~は「~をうまく通り抜ける」(≒ successfully go through ~)。このitは、取り巻く(漠然とした)状況を表す。

⑭ This means stopping whatever you're doing when it's time to begin the task.

▶ whatever you're doingは「していることは何でも」。

▶ 文全体で、「このことはつまり、仕事を始めるべきときに、何をしていてもそれをやめる[やめて仕事を始める]」という意味になる。

⑮ This is the hardest part, because this is where the monkey puts up his fiercest resistance.

▶ whereは先行詞を含む関係副詞で「~する場所」。

▶ put up ~は「(抵抗など)を示す」(≒ show ~)。

⑯ If you can get started and force the monkey into the Dark Woods, you've broken a bit of his will.

▶ force ~ into ... は「~を…へ押し込む、追いやる」。

▶ a bit of ~「わずかな~」は不可算名詞に用いられることが多い。

▶ his will「彼(=サル)の意志」とは、楽しいことをすること。

⑰ It's not a fun place to be, and the monkey wants nothing to do with it.

▶ Itとitはどちらも⑯の文のthe Dark Woodsを指す。

▶ want nothing to do with ~は「~に関わりたくない」。

⑱ To make things harder, the Dark Woods is surrounded by the Dark Playground.

▶ To make things harder「事態がより厳しいものとなることには」は独立不定詞で、文全体を修飾する働きがある。

⑲ And the monkey will try as hard as he can to leave the Dark Woods.

▶ try to *do*「~しようとする」のtoの前に、as hard as he can「できるだけ熱心に[しつこく]」が挿入されている。

教科書pp.73~74 *ll*.67~96 IV

①If you can power through a bit of the Dark Woods, something funny happens. ②Making progress on a task produces positive feelings of accomplishment and raises your self-esteem. ③When you feel a jolt of self-satisfaction, the monkey finds a High Self-Esteem Banana in his path. ④It doesn't suppress his resistance entirely, but it goes a long way toward distracting him for a while; you'll find that the urge to procrastinate has diminished. ⑤If you continue along, something magical happens. ⑥Once you get two-thirds of the way through a task, you start to feel great about things and suddenly, the end is in sight. ⑦This is the Tipping Point.

⑧The Tipping Point is important because it's not just you who can smell the Happy Playground up ahead—the monkey can smell it too. ⑨Once you hit the Tipping Point, the monkey becomes more interested in getting to the Happy Playground than the Dark Playground. ⑩When this happens, you lose all impulse to procrastinate, and now both you and the monkey are speeding toward the finish. ⑪Before you know it, you're done, and you're in the Happy Playground.

⑫One last word of caution: what makes procrastination so hard to beat is that the Instant Gratification Monkey has a terribly short-term memory. ⑬Even if you succeed on Monday, when you begin a task on Tuesday, he has forgotten everything and will again resist entering the Dark Woods. ⑭And that's why persistence is such a critical component of success. ⑮Laying each brick yields an inner struggle. ⑯But in the end, your ability to lay brick after brick, day after day, is what lies at the core of a procrastinator's struggle to gain control over his world.

⑰So much of what makes people happy or unhappy—their level of satisfaction, their self-esteem, the regrets they carry with them—is severely affected by procrastination. So the time to start improving is now.

このセクションの内容

「（A.　　　　　）」に達すると、サルも「楽しい遊び場」に行くことに興味を持ち、先延ばしの衝動は失われ、あっという間に仕事を終えられる。しかし、サルが記憶している時間は非常に（B.　　　　　）ので、先延ばしをやめるのは簡単ではない。そのため、（C.　　　　　）が成功の決定的な要素になる。人々の幸不幸は、先延ばしによって深刻な影響を受ける。今こそ改善に取り組むべき時なのだ。

① If you can power through a bit of the Dark Woods, something funny happens.

▶ power through ～は「～を勢いよく進む」（≒ move quickly through ～）。

② Making progress on a task produces positive feelings of accomplishment and raises your self-esteem.

▶ 主語は動名詞句のMaking progress on a task「仕事がはかどること」。

▶ positive feelings of accomplishmentは「前向きな達成感」、self-esteemは「自己肯定感、自尊心」。

③ When you feel a jolt of self-satisfaction, the monkey finds a High Self-Esteem Banana in his path.

▶ a jolt of ～は「～という突然の感情」（≒ a sudden feeling of ～）。

▶ High Self-Esteem Banana「高い自己肯定感のバナナ」とは、抵抗するサルの気を紛らわせるものを表す。

④ It doesn't suppress his resistance entirely, but it goes a long way toward distracting him for a while; you'll find that the urge to procrastinate has diminished.

▶ 2つのItとitは、③の文のa High Self-Esteem Bananaを指す。

▶ not ～ entirelyは「完全には～ない」（部分否定）。

▶ go a long way toward V-ingは「～するのに大いに役立つ」（≒ be very useful in V-ing）。

✍ 英文を完成させなさい。

この文章は、フェイクニュースを見つけるのに大いに役立つだろう。

This passage will go a (　　　) (　　　) toward spotting fake news.

▶ セミコロン（；）は、ここでは「そして」の意味。

▶ the urge to procrastinateは「先延ばしをしようとする衝動」。

▶ has diminished「減少した」は完了を表す現在完了。

⑤ If you continue along, something magical happens.

▶ continue alongは「先へ進む、続ける」。alongは「先へ」の意味。

⑥ Once you get two-thirds of the way through a task, you start to feel great about things and suddenly, the end is in sight.

▶ Onceは接続詞で、〈once＋主語＋動詞〉で「いったん～すると」。

▶ two-thirds of the way through a taskは「仕事の３分の２」。

▶ thingsは「状況」、be in sightは「見える」（≒ be visible）。

⑦ This is the Tipping Point.

▶ Thisは、⑥の文で述べられている状況を指す。tipping pointは「転換点」（≒ where a significant change takes place）。

⑧ The Tipping Point is important because it's not just you who can smell the Happy Playground up ahead—the monkey can smell it too.

▶ it's ～ who ...は強調構文で、youを強調する。

✍ 次の英文を日本語に直しなさい。

It was Saki who won first prize in the contest.

____咲だった。

▶ smellは「～のにおいを感じる」の意味だが、ここでは仕事の終わり（＝the Happy Playground）が見えてきたことを表している。

▶ up aheadは「この先すぐに」（≒ nearby）。

▶ ダッシュ（—）は、not justと対応して、but (also)の意味。

⑨ Once you hit the Tipping Point, the monkey becomes more interested in getting to the Happy Playground than the Dark Playground.

▶ Once you hit the Tipping Pointは「いったん転換点に達すると」。

▶ thanの後ろにgetting toが省略されている。

⑩ When this happens, you lose all impulse to procrastinate, and now both you and the monkey are speeding toward the finish.

▶ thisは、⑨の文の「サルが暗い遊び場よりも楽しい遊び場に行くことに、より興味を持つこと」を指す。

▶ impulse to procrastinateは「先延ばしをしようとする衝動」。impulseはurgeの類義語。

⑪ Before you know it, you're done, and you're in the Happy Playground.

▶ before you know itは「気が付くと、あっという間に」（≒ in a moment）。

▶ be doneは「（仕事などを）終えている」（≒ finish the task）。

⑫ One last word of caution: what makes procrastination so

このセクションの内容 の答え→ A. 転換点　B. 短い　C. 粘り強さ

hard to beat is that the Instant Gratification Monkey has a terribly short-term memory.

▶ One last word of caution は「最後の注意の一言」。

▶ コロン（：）以下は注意の内容で、what ～ beatが文の主語。〈make + O + C〉は「OをC（の状態）にする」、hard to *do*は「～しづらい」。

▶ that以下は、文の補語。have a terribly short-term memoryは「ひどく期間の短い記憶を持つ」→「ひどく忘れやすい」。

⑬ **Even if you succeed on Monday, when you begin a task on Tuesday, he has forgotten everything and will again resist entering the Dark Woods.**

▶ Even if ～ Tuesdayが従属節で、「たとえ月曜日に成功したとしても、火曜日に仕事をし始めたとき」の意味。

▶ 主節のheは、the Instant Gratification Monkeyを指す。

⑭ **And that's why persistence is such a critical component of success.**

▶ that's why ～は「そういうわけで～、だから～」。

▶〈such (a) + 形容詞 + 名詞〉は「とても～な…」の意味で、程度を強調する。

⑮ **Laying each brick yields an inner struggle.**

▶ 主語のLaying each brick「れんがを一つひとつ積むこと」とは、粘り強く地道に作業することを比喩的に表現している。

▶ yields an inner struggleは「内面の闘争を生む」。

⑯ **But in the end, your ability to lay brick after brick, day after day, is what lies at the core of a procrastinator's struggle to gain control over his world.**

▶ in the endは「結局のところ」。

▶ your ～ dayまでが文の主語で、what以下が補語になる。

▶ 文全体は、「しかし結局は、来る日も来る日もれんがを次から次へと積むことのできる能力が、自分の世界を支配するための、先延ばし屋の闘争の核心部分にあるものだ」となる。

⑰ **So much of what makes people happy or unhappy—their level of satisfaction, their self-esteem, the regrets they carry with them—is severely affected by procrastination.**

▶ So much of ～は「～の大部分」。ダッシュ（—）の終わりまでが主語。what makes people happy or unhappyは「人を幸せに、あるいは不幸にするもの」で、ダッシュ（—）ではさまれた語句はその言いかえになる。

▶ is severely affected by ～は受け身で、「～にひどく影響を受ける」。

確認問題

語彙

1 次の語を( )内の指示にしたがって書きかえなさい。

(1) embarrassed (名詞形に)　(2) accomplish (名詞形に)

(3) resistance (動詞形に)　(4) terrible (副詞形に)

2 次の各組で下線部の発音がほかと異なるものを1つずつ選び、記号で答えなさい。

(1)	ア insane	イ inactive	ウ gratification	エ occasionally
(2)	ア impulse	イ diminish	ウ diagram	エ coexist
(3)	ア topic	イ jolt	ウ psychology	エ monster

文法・表現

1 日本語に合うように、( )内に適切な語を入れなさい。

(1) 君はあっという間に新しい学校に慣れるよ。

You'll get used to your new school (　　) (　　) know it.

(2) 夏休みの終わりが見えてきている。

The end of the summer vacation (　　) in (　　).

(3) 事実、私は子どものころスリランカに住んでいた。

The (　　) (　　), I lived in Sri Lanka as a child.

(4) マイルズは目の前の作業に取り組み出した。

Miles set out to work on the task (　　) (　　).

(5) その映画監督はどたん場で計画を変更した。

The movie director changed his plan in the (　　) (　　).

(6) 来る日も来る日も、少年はトランペットを練習した。

The boy practiced the trumpet (　　) after (　　).

2 日本語に合うように、( )内の語を並べかえなさい。

(1) 外はとても暑いのに、どうして外出なんてするだろうか。

(when / out / would / I / why / it / go) is really hot outside?

______________________________ is really hot outside?

(2) ほほえむことは、よい印象を与えるのにとても役立つだろう。

Smiling will (way / go / long / a / making / toward) a good impression.

Smiling will ______________________________ a good impression.

(3) 悩みについて話したければ、いつでも私に電話をかけて。
Call me up (want / talk / about / to / you / anytime) your worries.
Call me up ________________________________ your worries.

(4) 正直、あのうそつきとは関わりたくない。
Honestly, (do / nothing / with / want / I / to) that liar.
Honestly, ________________________________ that liar.

総合

次の文を読んで、あとの問いに答えなさい。

Unfortunately, procrastinators tend to (①) out on both the Happy Playground and Flow. For example, consider a procrastinator who couldn't bring himself to get started. He spent hours in the Dark Playground, one of the monkey's favorite places, ②(the deadline / was / knowing / near / drawing). He was only making his life harder by not starting. Eventually, the deadline got so close, the Panic Monster suddenly came roaring into the room, causing him to fly through the task to (③) the deadline. After he finishes, he feels decent because he accomplished something, but he's not that pleased because he knows he rushed to do it. He also feels he wasted most of his day procrastinating. ④This lands him in Mixed Feelings Park.

What should you do to (⑤) this from happening? First, you must make it through the Critical Entrance. ⑥This means stopping whatever you're doing when it's time to begin the task. You put away all distractions and get started. This is the hardest part, because this is where ⑦the monkey puts up his fiercest resistance. He absolutely hates stopping something fun to start something hard.

問1 (①)(③)(⑤)に適する語を下から選んで入れなさい。
〔power hit keep miss freak finish〕

問2 下線部②が「締め切りが近づいているということを知りながら」という意味になるように、( )内の語句を並べかえなさい。

問3 下線部④の内容を具体的に日本語で説明しなさい。

問4 下線部⑥を日本語に直しなさい。ただし、Thisの内容を明らかにすること。

問5 下線部⑦についての次の説明を完成させなさい。
サルは、(　　　)を始めるために(　　　)をやめるのをひどく嫌う。

Lesson 6 Today's Treasure, Tomorrow's Trash

教科書p.86 *ll.*1～18 I

①All sorts of electrical and electronic products are being sold today. ②We keep buying them, while dumping old ones. ③The consequence of this trend is ever-increasing e-waste, which is damaging the environment. ④How do we deal with this problem?

⑤In this consumer society we live in, new products are introduced into the market every day. ⑥A certain high-tech company in the US shipped so many new tablet computers in 2020 that if they were all laid flat and stacked, they would be as tall as 862 Empire State Buildings.

⑦This is a magnificent accomplishment on the part of the manufacturer. ⑧But if you look at the other side of the coin, you may have a different idea. ⑨A UN study reports that about 53.6 million tons of e-waste was generated worldwide in 2019. ⑩The amount of global e-waste is expected to increase to 74 million tons by 2030. ⑪The negative impact of e-waste on the environment is quite serious. ⑫E-waste is often highly toxic, leaking heavy metals and dangerous chemicals into the soil around landfills, and emitting greenhouse gases and mercury when burned.

このセクションの内容

(A.　　　　　　) の調査によると、2019年に世界で約5,360万トンの電気・電子機器が廃棄され、その量は2030年までには7,400万トンに増えると予想されている。電気・電子機器廃棄物はしばしば非常に (B.　　　　　　) で、埋め立て地の土壌に重金属や化学物質が流出したり、燃やすと (C.　　　　　　) や水銀が出たりする。

① All sorts of electrical and electronic products are being sold today.

▶ all sorts of ～は「あらゆる種類の～」。

▶ are being sold「売られている」は受け身の進行形〈be being＋過去分詞〉。

② We keep buying them, while dumping old ones.

▶ keep V-ingは「～し続ける」。themは、①の文のAll sorts of electrical and electronic products「あらゆる種類の電気・電子製品」を指す。

▶ whileは「だが一方では～、それと同時に～」。while dumpingはwhile we keep dumpingを短くしたもの。

▶ old onesは、「古い[使わなくなった]電気・電子製品」のこと。

③ The consequence of this trend is ever-increasing e-waste, which is damaging the environment.

▶ this trendとは、②の文で述べられている「私たちが電気・電子製品を買い続ける一方で、その古いものを捨てている」傾向のこと。

▶ ever-increasingは「絶えず増加する」。ever-は接頭辞で、「常に、絶えず」の意味。*cf.* evergreen「常緑樹」、everlasting「永遠の」

▶ e-wasteのe-も接頭辞で、「電子の、オンラインの」。

▶〈, which〉は非制限用法の関係代名詞で、直前のever-increasing e-wasteを補足説明している。

④ How do we deal with this problem?

▶ deal with ～は「(問題の解決など)に取り組む、対処する」。

✍ 次の英文を日本語に直しなさい。

They are dealing with issues of poverty.

____

▶ this problemとは、③の文の「増え続ける電気・電子機器廃棄物(e-waste)が環境を破壊している」という問題。

⑤ In this consumer society we live in, new products are introduced into the market every day.

▶ we live inはthis consumer societyを修飾している。consumer society「消費社会」とは、企業が消費者の購買意欲を促すことで、商品やサービスが大量に消費される社会のこと。

▶ are introduced into the marketは受け身で「市場に売り出されている」。

⑥ A certain high-tech company in the US shipped so many new tablet computers in 2020 that if they were all laid flat and stacked, they would be as tall as 862 Empire State Buildings.

▶ A certain high-tech companyは「ある特定のハイテク企業」の意味で、筆者は意図して企業名を伏せている。shipは「(商品など)を出荷する」。

▶ so ～ that ...「とても～なので…、…なほど～」の文。that節内は仮定法過去の文になっている。

▶ if節と帰結節のtheyはnew tablet computersを指す。

▶ be laid flat and stackedは「平積みにされる」。

▶ Empire State Building「エンパイアステートビルディング」は、ニューヨークにある高層ビルの1つで、約443メートルの高さがある。as tall as

このセクションの内容 の答え→ A. 国際連合 B. 有毒 C. 温室効果ガス

862 Empire State Buildingsとは、(仮に2020年に出荷された新しいタブレットコンピューターを平積みにすると)エンパイアステートビルディング862棟分の高さになるということ。

⑦ This is a magnificent accomplishment on the part of the manufacturer.

▶ Thisは、⑥の文の「2020年に非常に多くのタブレットコンピューターが出荷されたこと」を指す。

▶ on the part of ～は「～の側としては」。

⑧ But if you look at the other side of the coin, you may have a different idea.

▶ if you look at the other side of the coinは「別の見方をすると」(≒ if you see it from a different perspective)。視点を硬貨の裏表に例えた表現。

✍ 次の英文を日本語に直しなさい。

On the other side of the coin, agriculture damages the environment.

____

⑨ A UN study reports that about 53.6 million tons of e-waste was generated worldwide in 2019.

▶ UNはUnited Nations「国際連合」の省略表記。

▶ was generatedは「生み出された」という受け身。

⑩ The amount of global e-waste is expected to increase to 74 million tons by 2030.

▶ be expected to *do*は「～すると予想[期待]されている」。

✍ 英文を完成させなさい。

その新薬は世界中の人々を救うと期待されている。

The new medicine is (　　　) (　　　) save people around the world.

⑪ The negative impact of e-waste on the environment is quite serious.

▶ impact of ～ on ...は「…に対する～の影響」。

⑫ E-waste is often highly toxic, leaking heavy metals and dangerous chemicals into the soil around landfills, and emitting greenhouse gases and mercury when burned.

▶ highly toxicは「非常に有毒な」。

▶ leaking ～, and emitting ～は、〈原因・理由〉を表す2つの分詞構文を並列している。

▶ when burnedはwhen e-waste is burnedということ。

教科書p.87 *ll*.19～39 II

Factors behind E-waste

①A recent study by the Federal Environment Agency in Germany tried to uncover the factors which brought about the present situation. ②The findings suggest that the lifespan of household appliances is getting shorter. ③This is partly because consumers are demanding better products. ④A third of all replacement purchases for household appliances were motivated simply by desire for a better unit while the old one still worked fine. ⑤That proportion rose to 60 percent when it came to televisions. ⑥Old ones are replaced as outdated even if they are still perfectly usable.

⑦More importantly, the study reveals another concerning problem. ⑧The results show that the proportion of large household appliances that needed to be replaced within five years of purchase due to a defect grew from 3.5 percent in 2004 to 8.3 percent in 2012. ⑨The agency described that rise as "remarkable." ⑩Although the study has not provided any conclusive proof, it speculates that manufacturers intentionally shorten the lives of products to boost sales—a strategy often referred to as "planned obsolescence." ⑪This simply means to design a product with an intentionally limited lifespan.

このセクションの内容

ドイツの連邦環境庁の調査によると、家電製品の（A.　　　　　）が短くなっている。これは、（B.　　　　　）がよりよい製品を望んで、製品が壊れる前に買い替えることが原因の一部にある。さらに調査結果は、故障で5年以内に交換された家電製品の割合が増えていることを示した。連邦環境庁は、製造業者が製品の寿命を（C.　　　　　）に短くしていると推測している。

① A recent study by the Federal Environment Agency in Germany tried to uncover the factors which brought about the present situation.

▶ Federal Environment Agencyは「連邦環境庁」。

▶ uncoverは「～を明らかにする」の意味で、cover「～をおおう」に接頭辞のun-がついた動詞。*cf.* unpack「荷ほどきをする」⇔pack「荷造りをする」

▶ whichはthe factorsを先行詞とする主格の関係代名詞。

▶ bring about ～は「～をもたらす」(≒ cause ～)。

▶ the present situationとは、大量のe-wasteが出ている現状のこと。

② **The findings suggest that the lifespan of household appliances is getting shorter.**

▶ The findings suggest that ～は「調査結果は～ということを示唆している」の意味。連邦環境庁の調査結果のこと。

▶ get shorterは〈get＋形容詞〉「～の状態になる」の形で、「より短くなる」。

③ **This is partly because consumers are demanding better products.**

▶ Thisは、②の文の「家電製品の寿命が短くなっていること」を指す。

▶ This is partly because ～は「これは部分的には～のためだ[～が原因だ]」の意味で、理由の一端を表す表現。家電製品の寿命が短くなっている理由はほかにもあることを含意している。

✍ 英文を完成させなさい。

彼はよく朝食を抜く。これは部分的には、彼がダイエット中だからだ。

He often skips breakfast. This is (　　　) (　　　) he is on a diet.

④ **A third of all replacement purchases for household appliances were motivated simply by desire for a better unit while the old one still worked fine.**

▶ A third of ～「～の３分の１」からappliancesまでが主節の主語で、「家電製品のすべての買い替えのうちの３分の１」という意味。

▶ be motivated by ～は「～に動機付けられる」という受け身を表す。

▶ whileは「～なのに、一方で～」。the old oneはthe old unitのこと。unitとは、ここでは組み立てられた１個の製品のこと。

⑤ **That proportion rose to 60 percent when it came to televisions.**

▶ That proportion「その割合」とは、④の文の「まだ使用できる古い家電製品の買い替えの割合」のこと。

▶ when it comes to ～は「～に関しては」(≒ regarding ～)。

✍ 次の英文を日本語に直しなさい。

When it comes to cooking, Nancy is the best in the class.

＿＿＿＿＿＿＿＿＿＿＿＿＿＿＿＿ ナンシーがクラスで一番だ。

⑥ **Old ones are replaced as outdated even if they are still perfectly usable.**

▶ theyはold ones (= old televisions) を指す。

このセクションの内容 の答え→ A. 寿命　B. 消費者　C. 意図的[故意]

⑦ **More importantly, the study reveals another concerning problem.**

▶ More importantlyは「さらに重要なことには」。

▶ another concerning problemは、②～⑥の文で説明されているものとは別の問題のこと。⑧の文以降で説明している。

⑧ **The results show that the proportion of large household appliances that needed to be replaced within five years of purchase due to a defect grew from 3.5 percent in 2004 to 8.3 percent in 2012.**

▶ The resultsは、連邦環境庁による調査結果のこと。

▶ that節内では、the proportion ～ a defectが主語で、large household appliancesを先行詞とする関係代名詞thatの節が含まれている。

▶ due to ～は「～のせいで、～が原因で」(≒ because of ～、owing to ～)。

▶ that節は、「故障で購入から5年以内に交換の必要があった大型の家電製品の割合は、2004年の3.5パーセントから2012年には8.3パーセントに増加した」となる。

⑨ **The agency described that rise as "remarkable."**

▶ that riseとは、⑧の文の増加のこと。

▶ describe ～ as ...は「～を…だと言う」。remarkableに引用符(" ")がついているのは、連邦環境庁がそのように表現しているため。

⑩ **Although the study has not provided any conclusive proof, it speculates that manufacturers intentionally shorten the lives of products to boost sales—a strategy often referred to as "planned obsolescence."**

▶ itは連邦環境庁を指す。speculate that ～は「～だと推測する」。

▶ shorten the lives of productsは「製品の寿命を短くする」。

▶ ダッシュ(—)以下で「売り上げを伸ばすために、製造業者が製品の寿命を意図的に短くすること」を言いかえている。

▶ (be) referred to as ～は「～と呼ばれる」(≒ (be) called～)、planned obsolescenceは「計画的陳腐化」。*cf.* obsolete「旧型の、役に立たない」

✍ 英文を完成させなさい。

あの時計は、一般的に「ビッグベン」と呼ばれている。

That clock is commonly (　　　) (　　　) (　　　) "Big Ben."

⑪ **This simply means to design a product with an intentionally limited lifespan.**

▶ Thisは、⑩の文のplanned obsolescenceを指す。

pp.88~89 *ll*.40~66 III

Coping with "Planned Obsolescence"

①Is there anything we can do to cope with planned obsolescence? ②One thing we can do is to repair and keep using our electrical and electronic devices for as long as possible. ③When products break, we can either repair them by ourselves, or have them repaired by the shop where we bought them. ④The longer we can use them, the less impact they will have on the environment. ⑤We can extend the life of our devices, save money, and reduce the burden of the many gadgets that have turned into the world's junk. ⑥Furthermore, we can reduce the amount of waste and greenhouse gas emissions associated with the production of new products.

⑦In recent years, however, a new way to make products obsolete is on the rise: "repair prevention." ⑧Now it is getting more and more difficult for individuals and repair shops to troubleshoot electrical and electronic devices. ⑨This is partly because devices have become more complex, but it is partly by design. ⑩Manufacturers are limiting access to repair information to authorized service centers, leaving private repairers unable to deal with even simple problems. ⑪Some companies also refuse to provide repair manuals. ⑫Thus, it's just easier and sometimes cheaper to buy something new.

⑬Obviously, companies have an incentive to make it difficult to repair their products. If they can control the repairs, they can make money. ⑭The profit is increased because companies with a monopoly on repair can set prices higher than the market would otherwise bear. ⑮The result: more and more e-waste is being dumped into landfills.

このセクションの内容

私たちは、電気・電子機器を（A.　　　　　）して使い続けることで、環境への影響を減らすことができる。しかし近年は、個人や民間の修理業者が製品を修理することが（B.　　　　　）なってきている。製造業者は、修理に関する情報提供を制限して高額な修理代で（C.　　　　　）を得ようとする。その結果、ますます多くの電気・電子機器の廃棄物が埋め立て地に捨てられている。

① Is there anything we can do to cope with planned obsolescence?

▶ Is there anything we can do to ～?は「～するために私たちにできることはあるだろうか」。we can doはanythingを修飾する。

▶ cope with ～は「～に対処する」(≒ deal with ～)。

② One thing we can do is to repair and keep using our electrical and electronic devices for as long as possible.

▶ to repair ～(名詞的用法の不定詞)が主格補語の文。

▶ our electrical and electronic devices「私たちの電気・電子製品」は、repairとkeep usingの両方の目的語になる。

▶ for as long as possibleは「できるだけ長い間」。

③ When products break, we can either repair them by ourselves, or have them repaired by the shop where we bought them.

▶ either *A* or *B*「AまたはB」を用いた文。ここでは、Aがrepair them by ourselvesで、Bがhave ～ bought themになる。

▶ have ～ *done*は「～を…してもらう」という使役を表す。have them repairedで「それら(＝電気・電子製品)を修理してもらう」の意味。

▶ whereはthe shopを先行詞とする関係副詞。

▶ 文全体で「製品が故障したとき、私たちは自分でそれを修理することができるし、あるいはその購入店に修理してもらうことができる」となる。

④ The longer we can use them, the less impact they will have on the environment.

▶ 〈The＋比較級 ～, the＋比較級 ...〉「～すればするほどますます…」の文。ここでは、後半がthe less ～(劣勢比較)なので、「(製品を長く使うほど)環境への影響がより少ない」ということ。

✍ 次の英文を日本語に直しなさい。

The more you practice, the less nervous you'll feel.

____

⑤ We can extend the life of our devices, save money, and reduce the burden of the many gadgets that have turned into the world's junk.

▶ *A*, *B*, and *C*の形で、extend、save、reduceが並列している。

▶ thatはthe many gadgets「多くの装置」を先行詞とする関係代名詞。

▶ have turned into ～は現在完了で、turn into ～は「～に変わる、～になる」(≒ become ～)の意味。

このセクションの内容 の答え→ A. 修理 B. 難しく C. 利益

✍ 英文を完成させなさい。

大型冷凍庫内で、水はすぐに氷に変わった。

In the deep freezer, water has quickly (　　　) (　　　) ice.

⑥ Furthermore, we can reduce the amount of waste and greenhouse gas emissions associated with the production of new products.

▶ associated with the production of new products「新製品の生産と関連した」は直前の waste and greenhouse gas emissions「廃棄物や温室効果ガスの排出」を修飾する。(be) associated with ～は「～と関連した」(≒ (be) involved in ～)。

⑦ In recent years, however, a new way to make products obsolete is on the rise: "repair prevention."

▶ to make は形容詞的用法の不定詞。〈make + O + C〉は「O を C（の状態）にする」、on the rise は「増加して」(≒ increasing)。

✍ ほぼ同じ意味を表すように、英文を完成させなさい。

The prices of eggs and milk are increasing.

The prices of eggs and milk are (　　　) the (　　　).

▶ コロン（：）以下で、増加している、製品を使えなくする新しい方法について言いかえている。repair prevention は「修理妨害」。

⑧ Now it is getting more and more difficult for individuals and repair shops to troubleshoot electrical and electronic devices.

▶〈it is (getting) + 形容詞 + for ― to ...〉「―にとって…することは～だ[になってきている]」の文。get more and more difficult は「ますます難しくなる」、to troubleshoot ～は「～を修理すること」。

▶ 文全体で、「現在、個人や修理店が電気・電子機器を修理するのはますます難しくなってきている」となる。

⑨ This is partly because devices have become more complex, but it is partly by design.

▶ This は⑧の文全体を指す。but 以下の it も同じ。

▶ partly because ～は「部分的には～だから」、have become more complex は「(機器の構造が) より複雑になった」。

▶ by design は「故意に、計画的に」の意味で、電気・電子機器の修理が難しくなっているのは、一部は故意によるものだということ。

⑩ Manufacturers are limiting access to repair information to authorized service centers, leaving private repairers unable

to deal with even simple problems.

▶ limit *A* to *B*は「AをBに制限する」。ここでは、Aがaccess to repair information「修理に関する情報へのアクセス」、Bがauthorized service centers「認可されたサービスセンター」になる。

▶ leaving ～は〈付帯状況〉の分詞構文。〈leave + O + C〉は「OをCのままにしておく」の形で、leaving以下は「(認可を受けていない)民間の修理業者が、単純な問題[故障]にすら対処できなくなっている」ということ。

⑪ **Some companies also refuse to provide repair manuals.**

▶ refuse to *do*は「～することを拒否する」。

⑫ **Thus, it's just easier and sometimes cheaper to buy something new.**

▶ Thusは「したがって、その結果」。

▶〈it is + 形容詞 + to ...〉「…することは～だ」の文。

⑬ **Obviously, companies have an incentive to make it difficult to repair their products.**

▶ incentiveは「動機、インセンティブ」。

▶ make it difficult to *do*は「～することを難しくする」の意味で、itはto以下を指す形式目的語。

▶ 文全体で、「明らかに企業には、製品の修理を難しくするための動機がある」となる。

⑭ **The profit is increased because companies with a monopoly on repair can set prices higher than the market would otherwise bear.**

▶ monopoly on ～は「～の独占」。companies with a monopoly on repairで「修理を独占している企業」。

▶〈set + O + C〉は「OをC(の状態)にする」。

▶ than the market would otherwise bearは仮定法過去で、「そうでなければ(＝独占がなければ)市場[自由市場]が決めるであろう(価格)よりも」という意味になる。the marketの前にpricesが省略されている。

▶ 動詞bearは「～を持ちこたえる、～に耐える、～を生む」などの意味がある。ここでは、市場の自由競争によって決まる価格、または市場が維持するのに耐えられる価格ということ。

⑮ **The result: more and more e-waste is being dumped into landfills.**

▶ The resultは、企業による「修理妨害」の結果のこと。

▶ is being dumpedは「捨てられている」という現在進行形の受け身。

pp.89~90 *ll*.67~109 IV

"Right to Repair"

So, what should we do? ①A new and powerful approach to this problem is a movement to protect the "right to repair," which is gaining momentum in the US and Europe. ②This movement aims to force manufacturers of electrical and electronic products to recognize the right of consumers and technicians to obtain information necessary for repairs and perform repairs on their own.

③The right-to-repair campaign is gaining ground in the UK and EU. ④In the UK, a new law will require manufacturers to provide spare parts for their products to consumers for the first time. ⑤The goal is to protect consumers and reduce environmental impact at the same time. ⑥The UK government claims that this will reduce e-waste by 1.5 million tons each year, as well as carbon dioxide emissions.

⑦In the EU, the first eco-design regulations that set standards for repair have come into effect. ⑧This means that manufacturers of washing machines, dishwashers, refrigerators, etc. have to ensure that customers can replace components using easily obtainable tools. ⑨The French government has set the goal of making 60 percent of electrical and electronic devices in France repairable by 2026.

⑩Furthermore, in the US, about 20 states have already filed right-to-repair bills. ⑪It is expected that other states will follow suit. ⑫However, some of the big companies are lobbying against the legislation, making it difficult for the government to push the new laws through.

"Owner Society"

⑬In a "consumer society" where people continue to consume disposable products, ecological destruction is inevitable. ⑭On the other hand, in an "owner society" where products are cherished and repaired, companies and consumers can move toward reducing the burden on the environment by sharing responsibility.

Which society do you want to live in: a "consumer society" or an "owner society"? ⑮ Your choice may determine the long-term fate of this planet.

このセクションの内容

アメリカやヨーロッパでは、「修理する権利」を守ろうとする運動が勢いづいている。(A.　　　　　　)の法律は、予備の部品を消費者に提供するよう製造業者に求めている。EUでは、手に入れやすい(B.　　　　　　)で部品交換ができるようにする規制が導入された。アメリカでは、約20州で「修理する権利」の法案が提出されたが、大企業が反発している。私たちは、地球の運命を決める「消費社会」と「所有社会」の(C.　　　　　　)を迫られている。

① A new and powerful approach to this problem is a movement to protect the "right to repair," which is gaining momentum in the US and Europe.

▶ this problemは、「修理の難しさや市場の独占による高い修理代が電気・電子機器の廃棄物の増加につながっている」という問題のこと。

▶〈, which〉は非制限用法の関係代名詞で、「修理する権利を守る運動」を補足説明している。gain momentumは「勢いづく」(≒ keep developing)。

✍ 次の英文を日本語に直しなさい。

This trend is beginning to gain momentum among teenagers.

この流行は、＿＿＿＿＿＿＿＿＿＿＿＿＿＿＿＿＿＿＿＿。

② This movement aims to force manufacturers of electrical and electronic products to recognize the right of consumers and technicians to obtain information necessary for repairs and perform repairs on their own.

▶ This movementは、①の文の修理する権利を守る運動のこと。

▶ aim to *do*は「～することを目指す」、force ～ to *do*で「～に…することを強制する」。ここでは、manufacturers of electrical and electronic productsがforceの目的語。

▶ to obtain ～ and (to) perform ...は形容詞的用法の不定詞で、the right of consumers and technicians「消費者と技術者の権利」を修飾している。

▶ 文全体で、「この運動は、電気・電子製品の製造業者に、修理に必要な情報を得たり、自身で修理したりする消費者と技術者の権利を認めさせることを目指している」となる。

③ The right-to-repair campaign is gaining ground in the UK

and EU.

▶ right-to-repair「修理する権利の」はcampaignを修飾する。

▶ gain groundは「受け入れられる、支持を得る」(≒ become more popular)。

④ **In the UK, a new law will require manufacturers to provide spare parts for their products to consumers for the first time.**

▶ require ～ to *do*は「～に…することを求める」、provide ～ to ... は「…に～を提供する」。

⑤ **The goal is to protect consumers and reduce environmental impact at the same time.**

▶ to protect ～ and (to) reduce ... は名詞的用法の不定詞。

⑥ **The UK government claims that this will reduce e-waste by 1.5 million tons each year, as well as carbon dioxide emissions.**

▶ that節のthisは、新しい法律によって製造業者に課された内容のこと。

▶ byは「～だけ」という程度や差を表す。reduce e-waste by 1.5 million tonsで「電気・電子機器廃棄物を150万トン減らす」となる。

▶ as well as ～は「～も」の意味で、e-wasteに加えてさらにcarbon dioxide emissions「二酸化炭素の排出」も減らすだろうということ。

⑦ **In the EU, the first eco-design regulations that set standards for repair have come into effect.**

▶ the first ～ repairが文の主語。that set standards for repair「修理の基準を設けた」は関係代名詞節で、the first eco-design regulations「最初のエコデザインの規制」を修飾している。

▶ come into effectは「有効になる、実施される」(≒ officially begin to apply)。

✍ 次の英文を日本語に直しなさい。

The ban on plastic bags will come into effect from next week.

ビニール袋の禁止が ＿＿＿＿＿＿＿＿＿＿＿＿＿＿＿＿＿＿＿＿ 。

⑧ **This means that manufacturers of washing machines, dishwashers, refrigerators, etc. have to ensure that customers can replace components using easily obtainable tools.**

▶ that節の中に、さらにhave to ensure that ～「～を確実にしなければならない」と、that節が使われている。

▶ using ～は〈付帯状況〉の分詞構文で、「～を使いながら」の意味。

⑨ **The French government has set the goal of making 60 percent of electrical and electronic devices in France repairable by 2026.**

▶ has set the goal of ～は「～という目標を設定した」。goalのあとのofは「～という」の意味で、前後は〈同格〉の関係になる。

このセクションの内容 の答え→ A. 英国[イギリス] B. 道具 C. 選択

✍ 英文を完成させなさい。

私は１年で映画を100本見るという目標を設定した。

I have (　　　) the goal (　　　) watching 100 movies a year.

▶ making以下は、〈make + O + C〉「OをC（の状態）にする」の形で、Oは60 percent of electrical and electronic devices in France「フランスの60パーセントの電気・電子機器」、Cはrepairable「修理できる」。

⑩ Furthermore, in the US, about 20 states have already filed right-to-repair bills.

▶ have already filed right-to-repair billsは「修理する権利に関する法案をすでに提出した」。fileは「（法案など）を提出する」。

⑪ It is expected that other states will follow suit.

▶ It is expected that ～は「～と予想［期待］されている」。Itはthat節の内容を指す形式主語。follow suitは「先例にならう」（≒ do the same）。

⑫ However, some of the big companies are lobbying against the legislation, making it difficult for the government to push the new laws through.

▶ lobby against ～は「～に反対するように議員などに圧力をかける」。*cf.* oppose ～「～に反対する」。

▶ making ～は〈付帯状況〉の分詞構文。make it difficult for ～ to *do*は「～が…するのを困難にする」（itは形式目的語）。

▶ push ～ throughは「（法案など）を強引に通過させる」（≒ force ～ to pass）。

⑬ In a "consumer society" where people continue to consume disposable products, ecological destruction is inevitable.

▶ "consumer society"「消費社会」の引用符（" "）は、⑭の文の"owner society"「所有社会」と対比するため。

▶ ecological destructionは「環境破壊」、inevitableは「避けられない」。

⑭ On the other hand, in an "owner society" where products are cherished and repaired, companies and consumers can move toward reducing the burden on the environment by sharing responsibility.

▶ On the other handは「他方では、これに対し」。

▶ move toward reducing the burden on the environmentは「環境への負荷を減らす方向へ向かう」。

⑮ Your choice may determine the long-term fate of this planet.

▶ Your choiceとは、「消費社会」と「所有社会」の選択。

▶ the long-term fate of this planetは「この惑星（＝地球）の遠い未来の運命」。

確認問題

語彙

1 次の文の意味が通るように、右から単語を選んで（　）内に補いなさい。

disposable unable inevitable repairable

(1) The writer was (　　　) to update his blog because of an internet connection problem.
(2) These are (　　　) items, which means they are single-use and destined to be thrown away after use.
(3) Since the members cannot reach an agreement, further discussion is (　　　).

2 次の各組でアクセントの位置が同じなら○、異なるなら×を書きなさい。

(1) (stan-dard　gadg-et)　(2) (tox-ic　cam-paign)
(3) (tech-ni-cian　mo-men-tum)　(4) (in-cen-tive　mer-cu-ry)

文法・表現

1 日本語に合うように、（　）内に適切な語を入れなさい。

(1) 父は毎朝腕立て伏せをするという目標を設定した。
My father has set the (　　　) (　　　) doing push-ups every morning.
(2) その宇宙船は、火星で貴重なデータを収集することが期待されている。
The spaceship is (　　　) (　　　) collect valuable data on Mars.
(3) 別の見方をすれば、解決策が見つかるかもしれない。
You may find a solution if you look at the other (　　　) of the (　　　).
(4) 1匹のペンギンが駆け出し、間もなくその他のペンギンもそれにならった。
One penguin started to run, and soon the others (　　　) (　　　).
(5) その都市の人口は当時、増え続けていた。
The population of the city was (　　　) (　　　) rise at that time.

2 日本語に合うように、（　）内の語句を並べかえなさい。

(1) 宿題は終わらせるのが早ければ早いほどよいものですよ。
(homework / your / you / get / the sooner / done), the better.
______________________________________, the better.
(2) サイバー犯罪に対する新しい法律が間もなく実施される予定だ。
The new law (come / will / into / cybercrimes / effect / against) soon.
The new law ________________________________ soon.

(3) その運動は世界的に支持を得ると予想されていた。
(was / would / the movement / it / expected / gain / ground / that) internationally.

____ internationally.

(4) 森林破壊に関する問題について話し合われているところだ。
Problems (being / deforestation / are / associated / discussed / with).
Problems __________________________________.

総合

次の文を読んで、あとの問いに答えなさい。

A recent study by the Federal Environment Agency in Germany tried to uncover the factors which (①) the present situation. The findings suggest that the lifespan of household appliances is getting shorter. ②This is partly because consumers are demanding better products. A third of all replacement purchases for household appliances were motivated simply by desire for a better unit while the old one still worked fine. That proportion rose to 60 percent when it came to televisions. ③Old ones are replaced as outdated even if they are still perfectly usable.

More importantly, the study reveals ④another concerning problem. The results show that the proportion of large household appliances that needed to be replaced within five years of purchase due to a defect grew from 3.5 percent in 2004 to 8.3 percent in 2012. The agency described that rise as "remarkable." Although the study has not provided any conclusive proof, it speculates that manufacturers intentionally shorten the lives of products to boost sales—a strategy often referred to as ⑤"planned obsolescence."

問1 (①)に適するものを下から選び、記号で答えなさい。
ア aimed at　イ brought about　ウ lobbied against

問2 下線部②が指すものを具体的に日本語で説明しなさい。

問3 下線部③を、onesが指すものを明らかにして日本語に直しなさい。

問4 下線部④の「別の懸念すべき問題」とはどのような問題か。具体的に日本語で説明しなさい。

問5 下線部⑤はどのような戦略か。具体的に日本語で説明しなさい。

Lesson 7 Only a Camera Lens between Us

教科書p.100 *ll*.1～25 I

①When conflicts end, they leave behind hundreds of thousands of soldiers to be reintegrated into society and millions of small arms to be destroyed. ②This work is done by experts in Disarmament, Demobilization and Reintegration (DDR). Seya Rumiko is one of these experts. This is her story.

③As a child, Seya was always drawn to the "unknown." ④In her mind, foreign countries seemed so far away, and, of course, "unknown" to her. ⑤She got all excited when she opened her atlas and found Africa.

⑥When Seya was a high school student, she was shocked to see a photo of a dying mother and her small child in a refugee camp for Rwandans. ⑦She asked herself: "What am I doing here in Japan, looking at this photo while eating snacks?" ⑧She thought, "There is only a camera lens between us, but there is a crucial difference between *my* life in Japan and *their* lives." ⑨She was living in a country where she could make a difference if she wanted; those refugees had no choice but to accept their plight.

このセクションの内容

幼いころから（A.　　　　　）にひかれていた瀬谷さんは、高校生のとき、ルワンダの（B.　　　　　）で死にかけている母親と幼い子どもの写真を見て衝撃を受けた。彼女は、自分の生活と彼らの生活には決定的な（C.　　　　　）があると感じた。

① When conflicts end, they leave behind hundreds of thousands of soldiers to be reintegrated into society and millions of small arms to be destroyed.

▶ conflictは「紛争、戦争」。theyはconflictsを指す。

▶ leave ～ behindは「～をあとに残す[置き去りにする]」。ここでは、leaveの目的語に当たる語句がbehindの後ろに置かれている。

▶ leaveの目的語は、hundreds ～ societyとmillions ～ destroyed。

▶ to be reintegrated into societyは「社会に再統合されるべき」→「社会復帰しなければならない」の意味で、直前のhundreds of thousands of soldiers「数十万の兵士」を修飾する。

▶ millions of small arms to be destroyedは「破棄されるべき数百万の小型武器」。

② This work is done by experts in Disarmament, Demobilization and Reintegration (DDR).

▶ This workとは、①の文の数十万の兵士を社会復帰させ、数百万の小型の武器を廃棄することを指す。

▶ is done by ～は「～によってなされる」、expertは「専門家」。

▶ Disarmament, Demobilization and Reintegration (DDR)は「武装解除、動員解除、社会復帰」の意味で、紛争地域における紛争後の復興活動のこと。

③ As a child, Seya was always drawn to the "unknown."

▶ As a childは「子どものときに」(≒ When she was a child)。

▶ be drawn to ～は「～に魅力を感じる、ひきつけられる」。drawnはdraw「～を引く」の過去分詞。

✍ 次の英文を日本語に直しなさい。

When he was young, he used to be drawn to insect collecting.

____

▶ the "unknown"は「『未知の』もの」(≒ the unknown things)。〈the＋形容詞[分詞]〉で「～なもの[こと、人]」の意味を表す。

④ In her mind, foreign countries seemed so far away, and, of course, "unknown" to her.

▶ seemed (to be) ～は「～に思えた」、so far awayは「非常に遠くに」。

⑤ She got all excited when she opened her atlas and found Africa.

▶ get all excitedは「とても[すっかり]わくわくする」。allはexcitedを修飾して、〈強調〉を表す。

▶ atlasは「地図帳」。なお、mapは「一枚の地図」のこと。

⑥ When Seya was a high school student, she was shocked to see a photo of a dying mother and her small child in a refugee camp for Rwandans.

▶ be shockedは「ショックを受けた」。

▶ to *do*は感情の原因・理由を表す副詞的用法の不定詞。ここでは、瀬谷さんがショックを受けた理由を表す。

✍ 次の英文を日本語に直しなさい。

She was shocked to hear the news of the accident.

____

▶ dyingは「死にかけている、瀕死の」の意味で、dieのing形。

このセクションの内容の答え→ A. 未知(のもの) B. 難民キャンプ C. 違い

▶ a refugee camp for Rwandansは「ルワンダ人のための難民キャンプ」。

⑦ **She asked herself: "What am I doing here in Japan, looking at this photo while eating snacks?"**

▶ ask *oneself*は「自分自身に問いかける、自問する」。

▶ コロン（：）以下が問いかけた内容になる。

▶ looking at ～は〈付帯状況〉を表す分詞構文で、「～を見ながら、～を見て」の意味。

▶ while V-ingは「～している間」。whileのあとにI amが省略されている。

⑧ **She thought, "There is only a camera lens between us, but there is a crucial difference between *my* life in Japan and *their* lives."**

▶ There is only a camera lensは「カメラのレンズがあるだけ」。

▶ between us「私たちの間に」とは、（高校生の）瀬谷さんとルワンダで瀕死の状態にある母子との間のこと。

▶ crucial differenceは「決定的な［重大な］違い」。

▶ between *my* life in Japan and *their* livesはbetween usの言いかえ。レンズのこちら側（日本）と向こう側（ルワンダ）を対比するために、myとtheirがイタリック体になっている。theirは⑥の文のa dying mother and her small childを指している。

▶ livesはlife「生活」の複数形。

⑨ **She was living in a country where she could make a difference if she wanted; those refugees had no choice but to accept their plight.**

▶ was livingは「（一時的に）生活をしていた」の意味。動詞liveは、進行形で一時的な状況を表す。

▶ whereは関係副詞で、先行詞のa countryを修飾している。

▶ make a differenceは「違いをもたらす、（状況を）変える」。wantedのあとにto make a differenceが省略されている。

▶ セミコロン（；）は、ここでは「しかし、一方で」の意味で対比を表す。

▶ have no choice but to *do*は「～すること以外に選択肢はない、～せざるを得ない」。butは「～を除いて、～以外に」の意味。

✍ 英文を完成させなさい。

大雨のために、私たちはイベントを中止にせざるを得なかった。

Because of the heavy rain, we had (　　　) (　　　) (　　　) to cancel the event.

▶ plightは「（悪い）状態、苦境」。

教科書pp.100～101 *ll*.26～54 Ⅱ

Visits to Rwanda

①As a university student, Seya began to read about conflicts in the world, talked with specialists, and saved money from part-time jobs to visit Rwanda. ②In 1997, when she was a junior, her dream came true. ③She visited Rwanda, hoping that she might be of some help to the people there who had been devastated by severe conflicts between the majority Hutu and the minority Tutsi peoples. ④During the conflicts, somewhere between 800,000 and one million people were killed in about three months, and two million people fled to refugee camps.

⑤While staying with a family which had survived the genocide, Seya tried to learn about what had happened. ⑥Most people, however, simply remained silent; their trauma had not been healed yet, and they couldn't bring themselves to reveal their true feelings to an outsider. ⑦Seya felt that she was of no use to them. ⑧She realized she lacked skills, knowledge, and experience, all of which are absolutely necessary to help solve the problems of people like those she met in Rwanda.

このセクションの内容

大学３年生のときに瀬谷さんは、（A.　　　　　）を訪れ、部族間の紛争で打ちのめされた現地の人々を助けようとした。しかし、彼らの（B.　　　　　）は癒されておらず、体験を瀬谷さんに話そうとはしなかった。瀬谷さんは、自分には技術、知識、（C.　　　　　）のすべてがないことを痛感した。

① As a university student, Seya began to read about conflicts in the world, talked with specialists, and saved money from part-time jobs to visit Rwanda.

- ▶ As a university student は「大学生のときに」（≒ When she was a university student）。
- ▶ began ～, talked ～, and saved ～と、３つの動詞が並列する文。
- ▶ save money from ～は「～でお金を貯める」。from はお金の出所を表す。
- ▶ part-time job は「アルバイト」。

② In 1997, when she was a junior, her dream came true.

▶ juniorは「（4年制大学の）3年生」の意味。*cf.* freshman「大学1年生」、sophomore「大学2年生」、senior「大学4年生」

例 I'm a *junior* at the university. / I'm in my *junior* year.
「私は大学3年生です」

▶ her dreamとは、ルワンダを訪れること。come trueは「実現する」。

③ She visited Rwanda, hoping that she might be of some help to the people there who had been devastated by severe conflicts between the majority Hutu and the minority Tutsi peoples.

▶ hoping ～は〈付帯状況〉の分詞構文で、「～と願いながら」の意味。

▶ mightは〈可能性・推量〉を表す。

▶ be of helpは「役に立つ、助けになる」（≒ be helpful）。〈of＋抽象名詞〉で形容詞と同様の意味になる。*cf.* of value「価値のある」

✍ 次の英文を日本語に直しなさい。

His research will be of great importance to our society.
彼の研究は、私たちの社会に ＿＿＿＿＿＿＿＿＿＿＿＿＿＿＿＿。

▶ the people there「そこの人々」とは、ルワンダの人々のこと。

▶ whoは主格の関係代名詞で、先行詞the people thereを修飾する。

▶ be devastated by ～は「～によって打ちのめされる」。had been devastatedと過去完了形が使われているのは、瀬谷さんがルワンダを訪れた時（visited）よりも前のことを表すため。

▶ severe conflicts between *A* and *B*は「AとBの間の激しい紛争」。

▶ the majority Hutu and the minority Tutsi peoplesは「多数派のフツ族と少数派のツチ族」。peoplesはpeople「民族、部族」の複数形。

④ During the conflicts, somewhere between 800,000 and one million people were killed in about three months, and two million people fled to refugee camps.

▶ somewhere between 800,000 and one million peopleは、「80万人から100万人の間のどこか」→「だいたい80万人から100万人」。

▶ fledはflee「逃げる、避難する」の過去形（過去分詞も同形）。

⑤ While staying with a family which had survived the genocide, Seya tried to learn about what had happened.

▶ While V-ingは「～している間」。she wasが省略されている。

▶ whichは先行詞a familyを修飾する主格の関係代名詞。

▶ surviveは「生き延びる」、genocideは「大虐殺」。

▶ what had happenedは、瀬谷さんが知ろうとした時（tried to learn about）よりも過去のことを表す。whatを疑問代名詞と考える場合は「何が起こっ

このセクションの内容 の答え→ A. ルワンダ B. 心の傷［トラウマ］ C. 経験

たか」、関係代名詞と考える場合は「起こったこと」の意味になる。

⑥ Most people, however, simply remained silent; their trauma had not been healed yet, and they couldn't bring themselves to reveal their true feelings to an outsider.

▶ simplyは「単に、ただ」、remain silentは「だまっている」。

▶セミコロン(;)以下で、直前の内容を補足説明している。

▶ traumaは「心の傷、心的外傷、トラウマ」、healは「～を治す、癒す」。

▶ cannot bring *oneself* to *do*は「～するのを躊躇する、～する気が起きない」。
cf. bring *oneself* to *do*「自身に～させる」(≒ force *oneself* to *do*)

✍ 英文を完成させなさい。

トラブルにもかかわらず、彼は助けを求めるのを躊躇した。

Despite his troubles, he couldn't (　　　) (　　　) to ask for help.

▶ revealは「～を明らかにする[示す]」、outsiderは「部外者」。

⑦ Seya felt that she was of no use to them.

▶ be of no useは「(まったく)役に立たない」(≒ be useless)。

✍ 英文を完成させなさい。

お役に立てなくてごめんなさい。

I'm sorry that I could be (　　　) (　　　) use to you.

▶ themは、ルワンダの大虐殺を生き延びた人々のこと。

⑧ She realized she lacked skills, knowledge, and experience, all of which are absolutely necessary to help solve the problems of people like those she met in Rwanda.

▶ realize (that) ～は「～だと理解する」。

▶ lackは「～を持っていない、～が足りない」。skills「技術、技量」、knowledge「知識」、experience「経験」が目的語になる。

▶〈, all of which〉のwhichは非制限用法の関係代名詞で、先行詞のskills, knowledge, and experienceについて補足説明する。「そしてそれらすべては～」という意味になる。

▶ absolutely necessaryは「絶対に必要な」。

▶ to help solve ～は「～の解決を手助けするために」。help *do*は「～することを助ける」の意味。

▶ people like those she met in Rwandaは「彼女(=瀬谷さん)がルワンダで会ったような人々」。those she metはthose who[whom] she metと同じ。

✍ 次の英文を日本語に直しなさい。

I admire people like those I interviewed for the article.

私は、＿＿＿＿＿＿＿＿＿＿＿＿＿＿＿＿＿＿を尊敬している。

教科書p.101 ll.55~85 Ⅲ

①In her fourth year, Seya made plans to go to the UK for her graduate work. ②She knew that she had to narrow down her area of specialty in the field of conflict resolution. ③She spent hours in the library reading books, as well as collecting information from the websites of international organizations and NGOs. ④In three months, she had absorbed so much information that she could not decide what to specialize in. ⑤Then all of a sudden, the following sentence jumped out at her: "Conflict areas are now faced with the problem of how to reintegrate ex-soldiers and child soldiers into society." ⑥*This is it*, Seya thought.

In 1999, Seya started her graduate work in the UK. ⑦While she was a graduate student, she was asked by a Japanese NGO to work in Rwanda. ⑧Part of her mission was to open their office in Kigali, the capital of Rwanda, and to initiate a project to provide job training for women who had lost their husbands in conflicts. ⑨She selected 10 trainees, most of whom were single mothers in their 20s and 30s, and taught them sewing and dressmaking skills so that they could support themselves.

このセクションの内容

瀬谷さんは兵士の（A.　　　　　）を専門分野に決めて、英国の大学院で研究を始めた。大学院生のとき、日本のNGOから、ルワンダの紛争で夫を失った女性たちに（B.　　　　　）を提供するプロジェクトを依頼され、彼女たちが（C.　　　　　）できるように裁縫や仕立ての技術を教えた。

① In her fourth year, Seya made plans to go to the UK for her graduate work.

▶ In her fourth yearは「彼女（＝瀬谷さん）が大学4年生のとき」（≒ When she was in her fourth year）。

▶ make a plan to *do*は「～する計画を立てる」、graduate workは「大学院での研究」。

② She knew that she had to narrow down her area of specialty in the field of conflict resolution.

▶ had to ～はhave to ～「～しなければならない」の過去形。主節の動詞

knewが過去形なので、that以下の時制も過去になる(時制の一致)。

▶ narrow down ～は「～を絞り込む」。

✍ 次の英文を日本語に直しなさい。

The police narrowed down the suspects to three individuals.

警察は、容疑者を ＿＿＿＿＿＿＿＿＿＿＿＿＿＿＿＿＿＿＿＿。

▶ her area of specialtyは「彼女の専門領域」、in the field of conflict resolutionは「紛争解決の分野に」。

③ She spent hours in the library reading books, as well as collecting information from the websites of international organizations and NGOs.

▶ spend hoursは「何時間も過ごす[費やす]」。

▶ spend ～ V-ingは「…することに～を費やす」。

✍ 英文を完成させなさい。

彼女は小論文の執筆に多くの時間を費やした。

She spent a lot of (　　　) (　　　) the essay.

▶ as well as ～は「さらに～」の意味(≒ and ～)。*A* as well as *B*は、本来「BだけでなくAも」の意味でAに焦点が置かれるが、ここではas well as以下の内容を加える意図で使われている。

④ In three months, she had absorbed so much information that she could not decide what to specialize in.

▶ had absorbedは「～を吸収した、取り入れた」の意味で、過去の時点における完了を表す。

▶ so ～ that ...は「とても～なので…」。ここでは「とても多くの情報[知識]を吸収したので…」となる。

▶ what to *do*は「何を～すべきか」、specialize in ～は「～を専攻する[専門に研究する]」。

⑤ Then all of a sudden, the following sentence jumped out at her: "Conflict areas are now faced with the problem of how to reintegrate ex-soldiers and child soldiers into society."

▶ all of a suddenは「突然、急に、不意に」(≒ suddenly)。

▶ jump out at ～は「～の目に飛び込んでくる、～の目につく」。

▶ コロン(：)以下の引用符(" ")の文がthe following sentenceの内容。

▶ be faced with ～は「(困難・危険など)に直面している」(≒ encounter ～)。

✍ 英文を完成させなさい。

その企業は現在、財政難に直面している。

The company is currently (　　　) (　　　) financial challenges.

このセクションの内容 の答え→ A. 社会復帰　B. 職業訓練　C. 自活[自立]

▶ the problem of how to *do*「どのように～するかという問題」。ofの前後は〈同格〉になる。

▶ reintegrate ex-soldiers and child soldiers into societyは「元兵士と少年兵を社会に復帰させる」。ex-は「前の」という意味の接頭辞で、地位や身分などを表す名詞の前に付く。*cf.* ex-colleague「元同僚」

⑥ ***This is it*, Seya thought.**

▶ *This is it*は「まさにこれだ」。*it*は、瀬谷さんが探し求めていた自分の専門分野のこと。強調を表すためにイタリック体で書かれている。

⑦ **While she was a graduate student, she was asked by a Japanese NGO to work in Rwanda.**

▶ graduate studentは「大学院生」。

▶ be asked (by ～) to *do*は「(～に) …するように頼まれる」の意味で、〈ask＋人＋to *do*〉の受け身の形。

▶ NGOはnon-governmental organization「非政府組織」の略。

⑧ **Part of her mission was to open their office in Kigali, the capital of Rwanda, and to initiate a project to provide job training for women who had lost their husbands in conflicts.**

▶ Part of her missionは「彼女の任務の一部」。

▶ to open ～「～を開設すること」とto initiate ～「～を始めること」の2つの不定詞が文の補語になっている。

▶ to provide job training for ～は「～に職業訓練を提供するための(という)」。

⑨ **She selected 10 trainees, most of whom were single mothers in their 20s and 30s, and taught them sewing and dressmaking skills so that they could support themselves.**

▶ 動詞のselectedとtaughtが並列する文。selectは「～を選び出す」。

▶ traineeは「研修生、訓練生」。*cf.* trainer「訓練をする人」

▶ 挿入句のmost of whom ～ 30sは非制限用法の関係代名詞節で、10 traineesについて補足説明をする。前置詞ofのあとなので、関係代名詞は目的格のwhomになる。「(そして)その研修生のほとんどは～」の意味。

✍ 次の英文を日本語に直しなさい。

There were many kids, most of whom enjoyed board games.

多くの子どもがいて、＿＿＿＿＿＿＿＿＿＿＿＿＿＿＿＿＿＿。

▶ in their 20s and 30sは「20代と30代の」。

▶ sewing and dressmaking skillsは「裁縫や服の仕立ての技術」。

▶ so that ～は、「～するために、～するように」(≒ in order that ～)。

▶ support *oneself*は「自活する」。

教科書pp.102〜103 *ll*.86〜128 Ⅳ

Project in Sierra Leone

①When the Kigali project was almost finished, Seya heard about a DDR project which was in progress in Sierra Leone. ②She decided to go there in order to observe the actual DDR process with her own eyes, but she faced challenges. ③Could she find people who understood the local situation and knew in detail what the problems were? ④If not, how could she ever dream of working as a specialist in conflict resolution? ⑤Seya was undaunted. ⑥She made contacts and was able to visit camps for war victims as well as a care center for former child soldiers. ⑦She even had an interview with one of the top leaders of the DDR projects.

⑧Having finished her graduate work in 2001, she was back again in Sierra Leone in January 2002. ⑨This time she was not a visitor but a UN volunteer; her mission was to facilitate the reintegration of ex-soldiers into society by providing them with job training. ⑩Working together with a team of 15 staff members from various countries, Seya gradually developed her expertise in DDR.

⑪After a ceasefire, there is still much work to be done. ⑫Soldiers may be thrown into the streets with no jobs, no houses to live in, and no money to support their families. ⑬There is always a risk that ex-soldiers will return to armed conflict. ⑭They must be able to return to society and lead productive lives. ⑮This is reintegration.

⑯From 2003 to 2005, Seya was in Afghanistan with the DDR team, which disarmed 63,380 soldiers and collected more than 12,000 heavy weapons and almost 58,000 small arms.

このセクションの内容

瀬谷さんは、シエラレオネでのDDRプロジェクトを視察するために、自ら（A.　　　　）をつくり、現地のキャンプや元少年兵の施設を訪れた。2002年には、国連の（B.　　　　）として、シエラレオネで元兵士の社会復帰を促す任務についた。彼女は徐々に専門知識を深め、2003年から2005年にはアフガニスタンで、多くの（C.　　　　）を回収した。

① When the Kigali project was almost finished, Seya heard about a DDR project which was in progress in Sierra Leone.

▶ finishedは「終えた、完成した」という意味の形容詞。

例 When will you be *finished*?「いつ終わりますか」

▶ hear about ～は「～について（詳しく）聞く」。

▶ whichは主格の関係代名詞で、先行詞a DDR projectを修飾する。

▶ be in progressは「進行中の」（≒ be going on）。

✍ 次の英文を日本語に直しなさい。

The construction of the new library is currently in progress.

新しい図書館の建設が、＿＿＿＿＿＿＿＿＿＿＿＿＿＿＿＿＿＿。

▶ Sierra Leone「シエラレオネ」はアフリカ西部の大西洋岸にある共和国。

② She decided to go there in order to observe the actual DDR process with her own eyes, but she faced challenges.

▶ thereはSierra Leoneを指す。

▶ with *one's* own eyesは「自分の目で」。

▶ challengeは「課題、難問」。

③ Could she find people who understood the local situation and knew in detail what the problems were?

▶ ②の文のchallengesの内容を述べる文。

▶ who以下はpeopleを修飾する関係代名詞節。people who understood ～ and knew ... で「～を理解し、…を知っている人々」となる。

▶ in detailは「詳しく、詳細に」。*cf.* thoroughly「完全に、徹底的に」

▶ what the problems wereは「問題は何か」の意味で、knewの目的語（間接疑問）。

④ If not, how could she ever dream of working as a specialist in conflict resolution?

▶ ②の文のchallengesの内容の続き。

▶ If not「もしそうでなければ」とは、③の文を受けて、現地の状況を理解し、問題は何かを詳細に知っている人を見つけられなければということ。

▶ everは疑問文を強調する役割があり、how ～ everで「いったい[そもそも]どうやって～」の意味になる。

例 *How* will he *ever* find his way without a map?

「地図もなしに彼はいったいどうやって道がわかるのだろうか」

▶ dream of V-ingは「～することを夢見る」。

⑤ Seya was undaunted.

▶ undauntedは「くじけない、ひるまない」。③と④の文の課題に対する瀬

 このセクションの内容 の答え→ A. 人脈 B. ボランティア C. 武器

谷さんの態度を述べた文。

⑥ **She made contacts and was able to visit camps for war victims as well as a care center for former child soldiers.**

▶ contactsは「人脈、仲介者、橋渡しとなる人」で、make contactsで「人脈をつくる」の意味(≒ meet people who are useful)。

✍ 次の英文を日本語に直しなさい。

He made contacts that helped him get a new business opportunity.

___

▶ camps for war victimsは「戦争の被害者のためのキャンプ地」。

▶ as well as ～は「さらに～」(≒ and ～)。

▶ a care center for former child soldiersは「元少年兵のための養護施設」。

⑦ **She even had an interview with one of the top leaders of the DDR projects.**

▶ evenは「～さえ(した)」と強調を表す。

▶ have an interview with ～は「～にインタビューをする」。

⑧ **Having finished her graduate work in 2001, she was back again in Sierra Leone in January 2002.**

▶ Having finished ～は完了の分詞構文で、「～を終えたので」(理由)の意味。主節より前の時を表す。

⑨ **This time she was not a visitor but a UN volunteer; her mission was to facilitate the reintegration of ex-soldiers into society by providing them with job training.**

▶ not *A* but *B*は「AではなくB」。

▶ セミコロン(;)以下で、a UN volunteer「国連のボランティア」の内容を説明している。

▶ her mission was to ～は「彼女の任務は～することだった」。

▶ facilitateは「～を促進する」、the reintegration of ex-soldiers into societyは「元兵士の社会復帰」。

▶ by V-ingは「～することによって」という手段を表す。

▶ provide ～ with ... は「～に…を提供する」(≒ give ... to ～)。

✍ ほぼ同じ意味を表すように、英文を完成させなさい。

The school gives pencils and notebooks to kids.

The school (　　　) kids (　　　) pencils and notebooks.

⑩ **Working together with a team of 15 staff members from various countries, Seya gradually developed her expertise in DDR.**

▶ Working ～は〈付帯状況〉の分詞構文で、「～しながら、～して」の意味。

▶ a team of 15 staff membersは「15人のスタッフのチーム」。ofの前後は〈同格〉の関係。

▶ expertiseは「専門知識、専門技術」。

⑪ After a ceasefire, there is still much work to be done.

▶ ceasefire「停戦」は、cease「終わる」とfire「砲撃」が合わさった語。

▶ much work to be doneは「されるべき多くの仕事」。

⑫ Soldiers may be thrown into the streets with no jobs, no houses to live in, and no money to support their families.

▶ be thrown into ～は「～に投げ込まれる[放り出される]」の意味で、throw ... into ～「…を～に投げ込む[放り出す]」の受け身の形。

英文を完成させなさい。

そのニュースが広まったとき、彼らはパニックにおちいった。

They were (　　　) (　　　) a panic when the news spread.

▶ with以下で、兵士が路上に放り出されるときの状態を表している。with no jobsは「仕事[職]もなく」、(with) no houses to live inは「住む家もなく」、(with) no money to support their familiesは「家族を養うお金もなく」。

⑬ There is always a risk that ex-soldiers will return to armed conflict.

▶ a risk that ～は「～というリスク[危険(性)]」。

▶ armed conflictは「武力紛争」。

⑭ They must be able to return to society and lead productive lives.

▶ Theyは、⑬の文のex-soldiersを指す。

▶ must be able to *do*は「～できなければならない」。

▶ lead a ～ lifeは「～な生活を送る」(≒ live a ～ life)、productiveは「生産的な」。

⑮ This is reintegration.

▶ Thisは、⑭の文の「社会に戻り、生産的な生活を送ること」を指す。

⑯ From 2003 to 2005, Seya was in Afghanistan with the DDR team, which disarmed 63,380 soldiers and collected more than 12,000 heavy weapons and almost 58,000 small arms.

▶〈, which〉は非制限用法の関係代名詞で、直前のthe DDR teamについて補足説明する。

▶ 関係代名詞節内では、2つの動詞disarmed「～を武装解除した」とcollected「～を回収した」が並列している。more ～ armsはcollectedの目的語。

▶ heavy weaponsは「重火器」、small armsは「小型武器」。

教科書p.103 *ll*.129〜162 V

A Child Soldier in Sudan

①In 2009, Seya found herself in Sudan with a mission to launch a new project to support vulnerable youths, including child soldiers. ②She knew that she must earn the trust of these children and of the communities to which they would return. ③Trust plays an important part in DDR.

④Seya met a boy named Michael, who had been a soldier in the civil war for five years. ⑤When the war ended, he had been transferred to the police force. Now he wanted to go back to school. ⑥But he couldn't figure out how to proceed. ⑦Seya offered to help him, but he didn't trust her. ⑧Too many people had made promises that they did not keep. First, Seya had to gain Michael's trust. ⑨Then she had to persuade Michael's senior officers to allow him to return to school. ⑩She succeeded in both tasks.

⑪Michael's future would be difficult and uncertain. ⑫He would have to learn to trust other people. He would have to learn to trust himself.

⑬Seya told him that he was now on his own. "This is your life, not mine," she said. ⑭"You must think for yourself from now on." ⑮Michael answered, "Now I know what I'm going to do. This is my life." ⑯One small success for Seya Rumiko.

このセクションの内容

(A.　　　　　) で新しいプロジェクトを立ち上げた瀬谷さんは、元少年兵のマイケルを手助けするため、まず彼の (B.　　　　　) を得て、それから彼の上官も説得した。瀬谷さんはマイケルに、自分の (C.　　　　　) を歩んでゆくために、自分で考えるように励ました。

① In 2009, Seya found herself in Sudan with a mission to launch a new project to support vulnerable youths, including child soldiers.

▶ find *oneself* in 〜は「〜にいる自分を発見する」→「〜にいる」。ここでは、瀬谷さんの意図とは別に、求められてスーダンにいたことを表す。

▶ with a mission to *do* は「〜するという任務と共に」。

▶ launch a new project は「新しいプロジェクトを始める」。to support 以下

はprojectの内容。

▶ vulnerableは「傷つきやすい、もろい」、includingは「～を含めて」という意味の前置詞。

② She knew that she must earn the trust of these children and of the communities to which they would return.

▶ mustには過去形がないため、that節内ではmustのままになる（≒ that she had to earn ～）。

▶ earn the trust of ～は「～の信頼を得る」。

▶ to whichは〈前置詞＋関係代名詞〉の形で、the communitiesを修飾する。

③ Trust plays an important part in DDR.

▶ play a ～ part in ... は「…で～な役割を果たす」（≒ play a ～ role in ...）。

✍ 次の英文を日本語に直しなさい。

Teamwork plays a significant part in achieving goals.

____

④ Seya met a boy named Michael, who had been a soldier in the civil war for five years.

▶ a boy named ～は「～と名づけられた[～という名の]少年」。

▶ who以下は、先行詞Michaelについて補足説明する非制限用法の関係代名詞節。先行詞が固有名詞の場合は、非制限用法になる。

▶ had beenは、瀬谷さんが少年に会った時よりも前のことを表す。

⑤ When the war ended, he had been transferred to the police force.

▶ had been transferred to ～は受動態の過去完了形で、「(すでに) ～に転任させられていた、異動になっていた」の意味。

▶ the police forceは「警察(隊)」。

⑥ But he couldn't figure out how to proceed.

▶ figure out ～は「～がわかる、～を理解する」。

✍ 次の英文を日本語に直しなさい。

I couldn't figure out how to solve the problem.

私にはその問題の______________________________。

▶ how to proceed「進む方法」とは、直前のhe wanted to go back to schoolを受けて、学校へ戻る方法のことを表している。

⑦ Seya offered to help him, but he didn't trust her.

▶ offer to *do*は「～することを申し出る」。

⑧ Too many people had made promises that they did not keep.

▶ ⑦の文の時より前のことなので、過去完了形が使われている。

 このセクションの内容 の答え→ A. スーダン B. 信頼[信用] C. 人生

▶ make a promiseは「約束する」、keep a promiseは「約束を守る」。

▶ 文全体で、「あまりに多くの人が、守らない約束をしてきた[約束を守らなかった]」ということ。

⑨ Then she had to persuade Michael's senior officers to allow him to return to school.

▶ Then「次に」は直前の文のFirstに対応している。

▶〈persuade＋人＋to *do*〉は「(人)を説得して〜させる」、senior officersは「(警察の)上官」。

▶〈allow＋人＋to *do*〉は「(人)に〜することを許す」。

⑩ She succeeded in both tasks.

▶ succeed in 〜は「〜に成功する」。

▶ both tasks「2つの作業」とは、「マイケルの信頼を得ること」と「彼(＝マイケル)が復学するのを許可するように、彼の上官を説得すること」。

⑪ Michael's future would be difficult and uncertain.

▶ 過去における未来のことなので、willの過去形wouldが使われている。

▶ uncertainは「不確かな、不安定な」。

⑫ He would have to learn to trust other people.

▶ ⑪の文と同様に、過去における未来を表す文。

▶ learn to *do*は「〜することを学ぶ」。

⑬ Seya told him that he was now on his own.

▶ on *one's* ownは「一人で、自力で」。ここでは、Michaelが瀬谷さんの手助けなしに、自力で(したいことを)するということ。

⑭ "You must think for yourself from now on."

▶ think for *oneself*は「自分で考える」(≒ form *one's* own opinions)。

✍ 英文を完成させなさい。

生徒が自分で考えるように促すことが重要だ。

It is important to encourage students to (　　　) (　　　) themselves.

▶ from now onは「これからは、今後は(ずっと)」。

⑮ Michael answered, "Now I know what I'm going to do. This is my life."

▶ what I'm going to doは「私がすること」(関係代名詞節)、または「私が何をするのか」(間接疑問)の意味。

▶ This is my life.は「自分の人生なのだから」の意味。

⑯ One small success for Seya Rumiko.

▶ small success「小さな成功」とは、Michaelの自立を助けたことを指す。

教科書pp.103〜104 *ll*.163〜212 Ⅵ

As an Expert

①Now, with her experience and expertise, Seya is convinced that just having knowledge and skills is not enough to find a solution. ②You don't go to areas devastated by war and conflicts with a ready-made solution. Seya believes that in order to find a solution, you need to meet people and listen to them.

③Seya is also convinced that giving too much assistance can deprive people of the willpower to stand on their own two feet. ④She says, "All I can do is to create an option and assist them a little bit. ⑤It is up to the people on the ground to manage their own lives and society."

⑥There is much to be done. There are not enough people. There is not enough money. ⑦There are successes, but success is limited.

⑧Seya says, "I feel that even if we manage to create something positive, there are some situations where we cannot solve everything." ⑨Asked when her work will be over, Seya says, "Our work will be over when people tell us they don't need us anymore."

⑩In dealing with the plight of people with different cultural backgrounds, Seya often finds herself in difficulty. ⑪But she has no regrets about choosing a career as a DDR specialist. ⑫When things get difficult, she tells herself, "Never try to find excuses for not doing something. ⑬Perhaps you may not be able to find a perfect solution to the problem, but you can start thinking what you can do to solve 10 percent of the problem. ⑭At least that's a step in the right direction."

Seya remains undaunted. ⑮Her colleagues say that she does not allow herself to be overwhelmed by emotion even in the face of terrible situations. ⑯She believes that it is not enough for us to sympathize with people in trouble. ⑰Her current ambition is to work closely with people on the ground to prevent the tragic consequences of conflict.

このセクションの内容

解決策を見つけるには、（A.　　　　　）に会って話を聞く必要があると瀬谷さんは信じている。さらに、自分たちは彼らの自立を少し助けるだけで、彼らの生活と社会は彼ら次第だと言う。自分たちの活動は、彼らが自分たちを（B.　　　　　）としなくなったときに終わる。紛争の（C.　　　　　）を防ぐために、瀬谷さんは現地の人々と協力していくことを願っている。

① Now, with her experience and expertise, Seya is convinced that just having knowledge and skills is not enough to find a solution.

▶ withは「～を備えて、～を身につけて」、expertiseは「専門知識」。

▶ be convinced that ～は「～だと確信している」（≒ believe that ～）。

✍ 次の英文を日本語に直しなさい。

Scientists are convinced that climate change is caused by human activity.

科学者たちは、＿＿＿＿＿＿＿＿＿＿＿＿＿＿＿＿＿＿＿＿＿。

▶ that節は動名詞が主語の文。just having ～ is not enoughは「ただ～を持っているだけでは十分ではない」。

▶ to find a solutionは「解決策を見つけるために」（不定詞の副詞的用法）。

② You don't go to areas devastated by war and conflicts with a ready-made solution.

▶ Youは一般の人々を指す。

▶ devastated by ～は「～で荒らされた」の意味で、areasを修飾する。

▶ with a ready-made solutionは「既成の解決策で」。

③ Seya is also convinced that giving too much assistance can deprive people of the willpower to stand on their own two feet.

▶ giving too much assistanceは「支援をしすぎること、過度の援助」。

▶ deprive ～ of ...は「～から…を奪う」（≒ take away ... from ～）。

✍ ほぼ同じ意味を表すように、英文を完成させなさい。

The storm took electricity away from us.

The storm (　　　) (　　　) (　　　) electricity.

▶ the willpower to *do*は「～する（という）意志の力」。

▶ stand on *one's* own two feetは「自分自身の２本の足で立つ」→「自立する」（≒ be independent）。

④ She says, "All I can do is to create an option and assist them a little bit.

▶引用符（“ ”）内は、All I can doが主語、to *do*が文の補語。all ～ can do is to *do*で、「～ができることは…することだけだ」（≒ the only thing ～ can do is to *do*）の意味。

✍ 英文を完成させなさい。

私たちにできたことは、彼女に同情することだけだった。

(　　　) we (　　　) (　　　) was to sympathize with her.

▶create an optionは「（１つの）選択肢をつくる［与えてやる］」。

⑤ It is up to the people on the ground to manage their own lives and society.”

▶It is up to ～は「～次第」（≒ It is *one's* responsibility）。Itはto manage以下を指す形式主語。

✍ 次の英文を日本語に直しなさい。

It is up to you to invite someone to the party.

____

▶on the groundは「現場の」（≒ actually present in that place）、manageは「～を管理する、～をやりくりする」。

⑥ There is much to be done.

▶much to be doneは「されるべき多くのこと」。

⑦ There are successes, but success is limited.

▶successesは「成功したこと［成功事例］」の意味で可算名詞、後ろのsuccessは「成功」という意味の抽象名詞（不可算）。

▶be limitedは「限定されている、限り［限界］がある」。

⑧ Seya says, “I feel that even if we manage to create something positive, there are some situations where we cannot solve everything.”

▶even if ～は「たとえ～でも」、manage to *do*は「なんとかして～する」、something positiveは「何か建設的［肯定的］なこと」。

▶whereはsome situationsを先行詞とする関係副詞。

▶not ～ everythingは「すべて～とは限らない」（部分否定）。

⑨ Asked when her work will be over, Seya says, “Our work will be over when people tell us they don't need us anymore.”

▶Asked ～は受け身の分詞構文で、「～とたずねられて」の意味。前にBeingが省略されている。

▶her workと引用符（“ ”）内のOur workは、これまで述べてきた元兵士の社会復帰を支援するDDRの活動のこと。

▶not ～ anymoreは「もう［もはや］～ない」。

 このセクションの内容 の答え→ A. 現地の人々 B. 必要 C. 悲劇的な結果

⑩ **In dealing with the plight of people with different cultural backgrounds, Seya often finds herself in difficulty.**

▶ in V-ingは「〜するときに(は)」、deal with 〜は「〜に対処する」、the plight of people with 〜は「〜を持つ人々の苦境」。

▶ find *oneself* in difficultyは「自分が困難な状況にあることに気付く」。

⑪ **But she has no regrets about choosing a career as a DDR specialist.**

▶ have no regrets about 〜は「〜について(まったく)後悔していない」。

⑫ **When things get difficult, she tells herself, "Never try to find excuses for not doing something.**

▶ tell *oneself* 〜は「〜と自分に言い聞かせる」(≒ remind *oneself* 〜)。

▶ Never try to *do*は「決して〜しようとしてはいけない」、find excuses for 〜は「〜に対する言い訳を見つける」。

⑬ **Perhaps you may not be able to find a perfect solution to the problem, but you can start thinking what you can do to solve 10 percent of the problem.**

▶ may not be able to *do*は「〜できないかもしれない」。

▶ start thinking what you can doは「何ができるか[できること]を考え始める」。

⑭ **At least that's a step in the right direction."**

▶ at leastは「少なくとも」。

▶ thatは、⑬の文のstart thinking 〜 the problemを指している。

▶ a step in the right directionは「正しい方向への1歩」。

⑮ **Her colleagues say that she does not allow herself to be overwhelmed by emotion even in the face of terrible situations.**

▶ allow *oneself* to *do*は「自分自身が〜することを許す」。

▶ be overwhelmed by 〜は「〜に(よって)圧倒される」。

▶ even in the face of 〜は「たとえ〜に直面しても」。

⑯ **She believes that it is not enough for us to sympathize with people in trouble.**

▶ that節は〈it is 〜 for — to ...〉の文で、itはto以下を指す形式主語。

▶ sympathize with 〜は「〜に同情する(だけでは)」、people in troubleは「困っている人々」。

⑰ **Her current ambition is to work closely with people on the ground to prevent the tragic consequences of conflict.**

▶ to work closely with 〜は「〜と親密に働く[協力する]こと」、to prevent the tragic consequences of conflictは「紛争の悲劇的な結果を防ぐために」。

確認問題

語彙

1 次の文の意味が通るように、( )内の語を適する形にしなさい。

(1) The (major) of the audience were young girls.
(2) They (initial) the project to collect small weapons ten years ago.
(3) We could not find a (resolve) to the problem.
(4) When we heard about the accident, we deeply (sympathy) with the victims.

2 第2音節にアクセント(強勢)のある語を2つ選び、記号で答えなさい。

ア op-tion　　イ web-site　　ウ cru-cial
エ per-suade　　オ train-ee　　カ back-ground

文法・表現

1 日本語に合うように、( )内に適切な語を入れなさい。

(1) 私はその情報はまったく役に立たないだろうと思った。
I thought the information would (　　) (　　) no use at all.
(2) その貧しい少年は学校をやめるしかなかった。
The poor boy had (　　) choice (　　) (　　) give up school.
(3) そのコミュニティは水不足に直面していた。
The community was (　　) (　　) a shortage of water.
(4) 突然、アリスは自分が穴の中にいることに気付いた。
(　　) of a (　　), Alice (　　) (　　) in a hole.
(5) 自由時間をどのように過ごすかはあなた次第だ。
It is (　　) (　　)(　　) to decide how you spend your free time.

2 各組の文がほぼ同じ意味になるように、( )内に適切な語を入れなさい。

(1) They believed that they were doing the right thing.
They were (　　) (　　) they were doing the right thing.
(2) The school gave laptop computers to students.
The school (　　) students (　　) laptop computers.
(3) She didn't feel like sharing her feelings with others.
She could not (　　) (　　) to reveal her feelings to others.

3 日本語に合うように、(　) 内の語句を並べかえなさい。

(1) 私たちは彼らが自立するのを手伝うことしかできない。

(can / stand / to help / we / do / all / is / them) on their own two feet.

____________________________________ on their own two feet.

(2) 彼らはたとえ住む家を奪われても、決して母国を離れないだろう。

Even if they (of / a house / live / were / in / deprived / to), they would never leave their home country.

Even if they __________________________________, they would never leave their home country.

総合

次の文を読んで、あとの問いに答えなさい。

Seya met a boy named Michael, who had been a soldier in the civil war for five years. ①When the war ended, (to / he / transferred / had / the police force / been). Now he wanted to go back to school. But he couldn't figure out how to proceed. Seya offered to help him, but ②he didn't trust her. Too many people had made promises that they did not keep. First, Seya had to gain Michael's trust. Then she had to persuade Michael's senior officers to allow him to return to school. She succeeded in ③both tasks.

Michael's future would be difficult and uncertain. He would have to learn to trust other people. He would have to learn to trust himself.

Seya told him that he was now on his own. "This is your life, not mine," she said. "You must think for yourself from now on." Michael answered, "④Now (going / do / I / I'm / know / to / what). This is my life." One small success for Seya Rumiko.

問1　下線部①、④の (　) 内の語句を並べかえて、英文を完成させなさい。

問2　下線部②の理由を具体的に日本語で説明しなさい。

問3　下線部③の内容を２つ、日本語で説明しなさい。

問4　次の英文が本文の内容に合っていれば○、合っていなければ×を書きなさい。

(1) Michael fought in the civil war for five years.

(2) Michael asked his senior officers to let him go back to school.

(3) Seya told Michael that she would help him forever.

Lesson 8 Super Clone Cultural Properties

教科書pp.116～117 *ll*.1～36 I

①Important cultural artifacts have been reproduced and put on display in a series of exhibits called "Super Clone Cultural Properties." ②The exhibits feature clones of important cultural artifacts, created by Professor Miyasako Masaaki in a project he directs at Tokyo University of the Arts. ③What does it mean to "clone" a work of art? What is the purpose?

④Professor Miyasako talks with Rie Davidson, host of the popular podcast, "Rie's Gallery."

Rie (R) : Welcome to "Rie's Gallery," Professor Miyasako.

Miyasako (M) : ⑤I'm delighted to be here, Ms. Davidson. May I call you "Rie-san"?

R : Please do! Most of my guests just call me Rie.

M : I know. ⑥I'm a regular listener.

R : ⑦Your "Super Clone Cultural Properties" exhibits have been a great success. Congratulations! ⑧Now, my first question for you is: What made you decide to create cloned cultural assets?

M : ⑨The short answer is: To keep great art safe and, at the same time, to make it accessible to as many people as possible.

R : And the long answer?

M : ⑩Museums face a dilemma. We need to preserve cultural properties. ⑪At the same time, we want to make them available to the public. ⑫Unfortunately, for reasons of security and preservation, people have only limited access to them.

R : An impossible dilemma! ⑬But you have a solution?

M : ⑭We are challenging the impossible. ⑮With our clone technology, we can exhibit the clone and keep the original safe, all at the same time.

R : That's ingenious. But I have a question. ⑯Why do you call these reproductions "clones"? ⑰Are they any different from ordinary replicas?

M : Good question! ⑱The term "clone" is usually used to refer to living things, as in the case of Dolly the sheep. ⑲So we are not using "clone" in the original sense. ⑳ But I couldn't think of anything more accurate to describe our creations. They really are "clones."

このセクションの内容

美術館は文化財を（A.　　　　　）する必要があると同時に、それらを一般に公開もしたい。このジレンマを解消するために、宮廻教授たちは文化財を複製して展示するプロジェクトを始め、その展示会は大成功を収めている。宮廻教授は、(B.　　　　　）した文化財のことを「（C.　　　　　）」と呼んでいる。

① Important cultural artifacts have been reproduced and put on display in a series of exhibits called "Super Clone Cultural Properties."

▶ cultural artifactは「文化遺産、文化財」（≒ cultural property）。

▶ have been reproducedは「複製されてきた」、(have been) put on displayは「陳列[展示]されてきた」。put ～ on displayは「～を展示する」（≒ exhibit ～）。

▶ "Super Clone Cultural Properties"は、「スーパークローン文化財」。clone「クローン」とは、ある個体から無性生殖した遺伝的に同一の個体のこと。サクラのソメイヨシノは同じ遺伝子を持つクローンだと言われている。

② The exhibits feature clones of important cultural artifacts, created by Professor Miyasako Masaaki in a project he directs at Tokyo University of the Arts.

▶ exhibitsは「展覧会」、featureは「～を特集する、～の特徴を持つ」。

▶ created by ～「～によってつくられた」は過去分詞で始まる句で、clones of important cultural artifactsを修飾する。

▶ he directs以下は直前のa projectを修飾する節。

▶ 宮廻正明教授は、2018年まで東京藝術大学で教授を務めた日本画家で、デジタル技術を用いて文化財を複製する「クローン文化財」の技術を開発した。

③ What does it mean to "clone" a work of art?

▶ itはto以下を指す形式主語。cloneは動詞で「～のクローンをつくる」。

④ Professor Miyasako talks with Rie Davidson, host of the popular podcast, "Rie's Gallery."

▶ hostは「主催者、管理人」。host以下がRie Davidsonについての説明。

▶ podcastはインターネットで音声データを配信するサービス、またはその番組を指す語。"Rie's Gallery"はそのタイトル。

⑤ **I'm delighted to be here, Ms. Davidson.**

▶ be delighted to *do* は「～してうれしい」(≒ be glad to *do*)。

⑥ **I'm a regular listener.**

▶ regular listener は「定期的な聴取者」→「いつも(番組を)聞いています」。

⑦ **Your "Super Clone Cultural Properties" exhibits have been a great success.**

▶ have been a great success は「大成功[大盛況]だった」(完了・結果)。

⑧ **Now, my first question for you is: What made you decide to create cloned cultural assets?**

▶ コロン(:)以下が my first question の内容。

▶ What made you *do* ～? は、「何があなたを～させたのか」→「なぜあなたは～したのか」と理由をたずねる表現(≒ Why did you *do* ～?)。

✍ 次の英文を日本語に直しなさい。

What made you say such words to your friend?

____

▶ cloned cultural assets は「複製された文化財[文化財の複製(品)]」。

⑨ **The short answer is: To keep great art safe and, at the same time, to make it accessible to as many people as possible.**

▶〈S + V + C(= 名詞的用法の不定詞)〉の文ではないので注意。コロン(:)以下が The short answer の内容で、理由や目的を表す副詞的用法の不定詞になる。

▶〈keep + O + C〉は「OをC(の状態)に保つ」。

▶〈make + O + C〉は「OをC(の状態)にする」。it は great art を指す。

▶ as ～ as possible は「できるだけ～」。accessible to as many people as possible で「できるだけ多くの人が(芸術に)触れられる」。

⑩ **Museums face a dilemma.**

▶ dilemma「ジレンマ」とは相反する事がらで板挟みになる状態のこと。ここでは、文化財の保存と公開の板挟みのこと。

⑪ **At the same time, we want to make them available to the public.**

▶〈make + O + C〉の文。them は、直前の文の cultural properties を指す。

▶ make ～ available to the public は「一般の人々が～を利用できる[鑑賞できる]ようにする」(≒ allow anyone access to ～)。

⑫ **Unfortunately, for reasons of security and preservation, people have only limited access to them.**

▶ for reasons of ～は「～という理由で」。of の前後は〈同格〉。

 このセクションの内容 の答え→ A. 保存 B. 複製 C. クローン

▶ security and preservationは「(文化財の) 安全[保全]と保存」。

▶ have only limited access to ～は「(文化財) に対して限られたアクセスしかない」→「(文化財) に触れる[鑑賞する]機会は限られている」。

⑬ But you have a solution?

▶肯定文にクエスチョン・マーク (?) がついた形。「～ですよね？」と確認している。≒ But you have a solution, don't you?

⑭ We are challenging the impossible.

▶ the impossibleは「不可能なこと」。〈the + 形容詞〉で「～なこと」を表す。

⑮ With our clone technology, we can exhibit the clone and keep the original safe, all at the same time.

▶ withは「～を使って」という手段を表す。

▶ keep the original safeは「原物[オリジナル]を安全に保つ」。

▶ all at the same timeは「すべて[まったく]同時に」の意味で、allは強調を表す。

⑯ Why do you call these reproductions "clones"?

▶ reproductionは「複製 (品)」の意味で、ここでは宮廻教授のクローン技術でつくった文化財の複製こと。

⑰ Are they any different from ordinary replicas?

▶ replicaは「(絵画などの) (精密な) 複製[レプリカ]」を表す語。

⑱ The term "clone" is usually used to refer to living things, as in the case of Dolly the sheep.

▶ refer to ～は「～に言及する」、living thingは「生き物」。

▶ as in the case of ～は「～の事例のように」(≒ as illustrated by ～)。

✍ 英文を完成させなさい。

ジグソーパズルのように、小さな断片が大きな絵をつくります。

Small pieces make a big picture, (　　　) in the (　　　) (　　　) a jigsaw puzzle.

▶ Dolly the sheep「羊のドリー」は、世界初の哺乳類のクローン動物のこと。

⑲ So we are not using "clone" in the original sense.

▶ in the original senseは「本来の意味で」。

⑳ But I couldn't think of anything more accurate to describe our creations.

▶ think of ～は「～を思いつく」。

▶ anything more accurateは「もっと正確な何か (＝言葉)」。

▶ our creations「私たちの創造物」とは、宮廻教授の文化財の複製のこと。

教科書pp.117～118 *ll*.37～62 Ⅱ

Shaka Triad Statue

R : ①Could you say a little more about that?

M : Sure. Let's talk about the Shaka Triad statue in Horyuji. It's very old. ②The metal is deteriorating and some parts are missing. ③We could make a reproduction of it as it looks today. ④However, we wanted to restore the statue to exactly the same condition it was in when it was created in 623. ⑤You might say we wanted to retain the original "genes."

R : ⑥So if we compare the actual statue in Horyuji with its clone, we'll notice some differences, right?

M : That's right. ⑦For one thing, look at the central figure. It has curls of hair on its head. ⑧Some of these were missing in the original, but they have been restored in the clone. ⑨We also restored the flying heavenly maidens around the halo behind the figures.

R : Very impressive! ⑩But how could you reproduce something you've never seen?

M : ⑪That's the tricky part. ⑫First of all, we learned everything we could about Buddhist statues. ⑬Then we supplemented that knowledge with 3-D measurements of the statues. ⑭We also consulted academic references and records in order to reproduce colors faithfully. ⑮The bronze we used was as close to the original as possible.

R : ⑯That must have taken a lot of time. And people.

M : Lots and lots of people. ⑰Art history professors, material analysis experts, painters, sculptors, and traditional craftsmen. ⑱Specialists in Takaoka copperware and Inami wood carving helped us make the castings. ⑲Without the partnership of cutting-edge technology and traditional craftsmanship, we couldn't have completed our project.

このセクションの内容

宮廻教授は、法隆寺の釈迦三尊像を複製する際に、（A.　　　　）の姿ではなく、最先端の技術を駆使して、それが（B.　　　　）ときと同じ状態に復元することをめざした。そのためには、多くの研究時間と各分野の（C.　　　　）の協力が必要だった。

① Could you say a little more about that?

▶ Could you ～?は「～していただけますか」。thatは宮廻教授が「クローン」と呼ぶ文化財の複製のこと。

② The metal is deteriorating and some parts are missing.

▶ The metal「金属」は、釈迦三尊像の素材。deterioratingは「劣化している」、missingは「失われている」。

③ We could make a reproduction of it as it looks today.

▶ couldは能力を表し、「(しようと思えば) ～できた」という意味。

▶ 2つのitはthe Shaka Triad statue in Horyujiを指す。

▶ as it looks todayは「それが現在見えるように」→「現在と同じ姿に」。

✍ 英文を完成させなさい。

その料理は見た目ほどおいしくなかった。

The food didn't taste as good (　　　) (　　　) (　　　).

④ However, we wanted to restore the statue to exactly the same condition it was in when it was created in 623.

▶ restore ～ to ... は「～を…に修復する、～を…に戻す」。

✍ 英文を完成させなさい。

彼らは、壊れた家を元のデザインに修復した。

They (　　　) the damaged house (　　　) its original design.

▶ 2つのitはthe statueを指す。conditionの後ろの関係代名詞が省略されているため、前置詞のinがwasの後ろに置かれている。≒ the same condition in which it was when it was created in 623

⑤ You might say we wanted to retain the original "genes."

▶ mightは「～かもしれない」〈推量〉、retainは「～を保持する」。

▶ the original "genes"は「元の［オリジナルの］『遺伝子』」。ここでは、現存する劣化したものではなく、制作当時の最初の素材や形状のこと。

⑥ So if we compare the actual statue in Horyuji with its clone, we'll notice some differences, right?

▶ compare ～ with ... は「～を…と比較する」。

▶ the actual statue「実際の像」は現存する像のこと。

⑦ For one thing, look at the central figure.

▶ For one thingは「1つには、まず」。

▶ the central figure「中央の像」とは、釈迦三尊像の中央の像のこと。

⑧ Some of these were missing in the original, but they have been restored in the clone.

▶ theseは、直前の文のcurls of hair on its head「頭の巻き髪」を指す。

▶ the originalは、複製[クローン]に対する「原物」の意味。ここでは、現存する法隆寺の釈迦三尊像を指す。

▶ 原物では(劣化して)失われていた頭の巻き髪が、クローンでは復元されたということ。

⑨ We also restored the flying heavenly maidens around the halo behind the figures.

▶ the flying heavenly maidensは「飛翔する天女」、the halo behind the figuresは「像の後ろの光輪」。

⑩ But how could you reproduce something you've never seen?

▶ how could you ～は「あなた方はどうやって～することができたのか」。

▶ something you've never seenは「一度も見たことがないもの」。you've以下の節がsomethingを修飾する。

⑪ That's the tricky part.

▶ Thatは、⑩の文の「見たこともないものを複製する」ことを表す。

▶ tricky partは「扱いにくい[困難な]部分」。

⑫ First of all, we learned everything we could about Buddhist statues.

▶ First of allは「第一に、まず」。

▶ everything we couldは「私たちが(学ぶことの)できるすべてのこと」。

⑬ Then we supplemented that knowledge with 3-D measurements of the statues.

▶ supplement ～ with ...は「～を…で補う、～に…を加える」(≒ add ... to ～)。

✍ 次の英文を日本語に直しなさい。

He supplemented his presentation with pictures and graphs.

____

▶ that knowledge「その知識」とは、⑫の文の仏像についての知識のこと。

▶ with 3-D measurementsは「3次元測定で」。3-Dは「3次元の」の意味で、Dはdimension「次元、寸法」の頭文字。

⑭ We also consulted academic references and records in order

このセクションの内容 の答え→ A. 現在[今日] B. つくられた C. 専門家

to reproduce colors faithfully.

▶ consultは「～を調べる、参照する」、academic references and recordsは「学術文献や記録」。

▶ reproduce colors faithfullyは「色を忠実に再現する」。

⑮ **The bronze we used was as close to the original as possible.**

▶ The bronze we usedは「私たちが使ったブロンズ[青銅]」。

▶ close to ～は「～に近い」、as ～ as possibleは「できる限り～」。

⑯ **That must have taken a lot of time.**

▶ Thatは、宮廻教授たちが行ったこと(⑫～⑮の文の内容)を指す。

▶ must have *done*は「～したに違いない」の意味で、過去の行為に対する(現在の)推量を表す。*cf.* should have *done*「～すべきだったのに」(後悔)

✍ 英文を完成させなさい。

鍵を家に忘れたに違いありません。かばんの中にないのですから。

I (　　　) (　　　) left my keys at home. They're not in my bag.

⑰ **Art history professors, material analysis experts, painters, sculptors, and traditional craftsmen.**

▶ 直前のLots and lots of people「非常に多くの人々」がどんな人々か説明する文。

▶ art history professorは「美術史の教授」、material analysis expertは「材料分析の専門家」、traditional craftsmanは「伝統工芸家」。

⑱ **Specialists in Takaoka copperware and Inami wood carving helped us make the castings.**

▶ Specialists ～ carvingが文の主語。Takaoka copperware「高岡銅器」とInami wood carving「井波彫刻」は伝統工芸品の名前。

▶〈help + 人 + *do*〉は「(人)が～するのを助ける」。

▶ castingは「鋳物」。溶かした金属を型に流し込んで固めた金属製品のこと。

⑲ **Without the partnership of cutting-edge technology and traditional craftsmanship, we couldn't have completed our project.**

▶ 仮定法過去完了の文。Without ～, we couldn't have ... で「もし～がなければ、私たちは…することができなかっただろう」。

✍ 次の英文を日本語に直しなさい。

Without your advice, I could not have avoided the accident.

____

▶ cutting-edgeは「最先端の」、craftsmanshipは「職人技」。

教科書p.119 *ll*.63～84 Ⅲ

Transcend the Original

R : ①The Shaka statue was only one of many clones. You also cloned modern art. ②My favorite was Manet's *The Fifer*. ③You not only cloned the painting, you also brought the boy—and his flute!—right off the canvas and into the audience in full 3-D. I could touch him!

M : ④One of the features of clones is that we don't have to worry so much about security or deterioration. You can touch them with your own hands. ⑤Currently, we're developing a clone boy who will actually play the flute live for you.

R : I can't wait!

M : We are also making *ukiyo-e* clones. ⑥Of course, you know Utagawa Hiroshige's blooming plum tree. ⑦What's amazing about our clone is that you can smell the blossoms. ⑧We soaked the clone in fragrance. ⑨You can touch it and feel the subtle irregularities of the surface. ⑩In fact, this kind of clone transcends the original and even expands the possibilities of art. ⑪That's why we call them "super" clones.

このセクションの内容

宮廻教授のプロジェクトでは、マネの作品の立体像や、（A.　　　　　）の出る浮世絵などを製作した。クローンには保全や劣化の心配はなく、それらに（B.　　　　　）こともできる。クローンはオリジナルを越えて、芸術の（C.　　　　　）さえも広げている。

① The Shaka statue was only one of many clones.

▶ onlyは副詞で、「ただ～だけ」。

▶ one of many clonesは「数多くのクローン[複製]の１つ」。

② My favorite was Manet's *The Fifer*.

▶ Manet（エドゥアール・マネ）は19世紀フランスの画家。*The Fifer*はマネの絵画のタイトルで、日本語で『笛を吹く少年』として知られている。

③ You not only cloned the painting, you also brought the boy—and his flute!—right off the canvas and into the audience in full 3-D.

▶ not only ～, but also ... の接続詞butが省略された文。なお、正式ではコンマ(,)のみで2文をつなげることはできない(コンマの誤用)。

▶ right off ～は「～をすっかり離れて」(≒ completely separately from ～)。

例 The strong winds tore the roof right off the house.
「強風は家から屋根をすっかり引き剝がした」

④ One of the features of clones is that we don't have to worry so much about security or deterioration.

▶〈S + V + C (= that節)〉の文。

▶ features of clonesは「クローンの特徴」。

▶ securityは「安全[保全]」、deteriorationは「劣化」。

⑤ Currently, we're developing a clone boy who will actually play the flute live for you.

▶ whoは主格の関係代名詞で、先行詞はa clone boy。

▶ play the flute liveは「フルートを生演奏する」。liveは副詞。

⑥ Of course, you know Utagawa Hiroshige's blooming plum tree.

▶ blooming plum tree「咲いている梅の木」とは、歌川広重が浮世絵に描いた梅のこと。連作「名所江戸百景」に『蒲田の梅園』と『亀戸梅屋舗』がある。

⑦ What's amazing about our clone is that you can smell the blossoms.

▶〈S (= what節) + V + C (= that節)〉の文。whatは関係代名詞。

▶ What's amazing about our cloneは「私たちのクローンの驚くべきこと」。

✍ 次の英文を日本語に直しなさい。

What's amazing about music is that it can bring back memories.

______________________________ 記憶を思い出させることだ。

⑧ We soaked the clone in fragrance.

▶ soak ～ in ... は「～を…に浸す」、fragranceは「香水」。

⑨ You can touch it and feel the subtle irregularities of the surface.

▶ the subtle irregularities of the surfaceは「表面のかすかなでこぼこ」。

⑩ In fact, this kind of clone transcends the original and even expands the possibilities of art.

▶ this kind of clone「この種のクローン」とは、⑤～⑧の文で述べたようなクローンのこと。

▶ transcendは「～を越える」、expandは「～を広げる」。

⑪ That's why we call them "super" clones.

▶ That's why ～は「そういうわけで～、だから～」。

このセクションの内容 の答え→ A. (梅の) 匂い B. 触れる C. 可能性

教科書pp.119〜120 *ll*.85〜109 Ⅳ

Build Peace through Art

R : ①Super clones! Transcending the original! ②Is there any limit to what you can do with technology? ③But now I have to ask you: What is your goal? ④It's fun, but do you have a higher purpose?

M : ⑤Well, I'd say my main goal is to protect our cultural heritage and pass it on to the next generation. ⑥Much of the world's great art is endangered. ⑦It is being lost to natural disasters, destroyed by conflict, damaged during restoration, displaced by history, or discolored by age. ⑧May I read you a few sentences from the exhibit catalog?

R : Of course. ⑨Please do.

M (*reading*) : "⑩With our clone project, we hope to restore damaged cultural properties and allow people all over the world, especially young people, to appreciate great human accomplishments. ⑪Cultural properties lead people to appreciate not just the individual artwork's ingenuity but also the diversity of cultures which is instrumental in creating great art. ⑫The greater your access to artworks, the greater your respect for different cultures. ⑬We hope that will contribute to making a peaceful world." ⑭In short, our mission is to build peace through art.

R : Build peace through art. ⑮That's a very appropriate closing thought. Professor Miyasako, thank you very much. ⑯I'm looking forward to the next exhibit of "Super Clone Cultural Properties." ⑰And I hope you'll join me again on Rie's Gallery.

M : ⑱It's been a pleasure, Rie-san.

R : Just call me Rie.

このセクションの内容

今日、さまざまな理由で、世界の偉大な芸術作品が（A.　　　　　）に瀕している。宮廻教授たちは、文化遺産に触れた人々が、芸術作品の技巧だけでなく、文化の（B.　　　　　）を理解することを願っている。つまり、芸術を通して（C.　　　　　）を築くことがプロジェクトの使命なのだ。

① Super clones! Transcending the original!

▶宮廻教授が述べたフレーズを、聞き手のリエさんが繰り返している。superには「優れた、すばらしい」のほかに「(程度などが)超越した」という意味がある。transcendingとほぼ同じ意味になる。*cf.* superhuman「超人的な」、supernatural「超自然的な」

② Is there any limit to what you can do with technology?

▶limit to ～は「～(へ)の限界」。

▶what you can do with ～は「～を使ってできること」。whatは関係代名詞。

▶この文は単なる疑問文ではなく、「(スーパークローンには)限界などなさそうに思える」という気持ちを含んでいる。

③ But now I have to ask you: What is your goal?

▶But nowは「しかしそれでは」の意味。

▶What is your goal?「あなたの(最終的な)目標は何ですか」は、スーパークローンの技術についてのこれまでの説明を受けての質問。

④ It's fun, but do you have a higher purpose?

▶higher purpose「より高い目的」とは、③の文のyour goalを言いかえたもの。

⑤ Well, I'd say my main goal is to protect our cultural heritage and pass it on to the next generation.

▶I'd (= I would) say (that) ～は「私の考えでは～といったところです、～だと私は思います」と自分の考えを控えめに伝える表現。

例 *I'd say that* every artwork has its own meaning.
「どんな芸術作品にも意味があると私は思います」

▶cultural heritageは「文化遺産」。

▶pass ～ on to ...[pass on ～ to ...]は「～を…に伝える[渡す]」(≒ hand down ～ to ...)。itはour cultural heritageを指す。

✍ 次の英文を日本語に直しなさい。

Please pass on your contact information to the organizer.

____

⑥ Much of the world's great art is endangered.

▶Much of ～は「大量の[多くの] ～」。

▶endangeredは「絶滅の危機にさらされた、危機に瀕している」。

⑦ It is being lost to natural disasters, destroyed by conflict, damaged during restoration, displaced by history, or discolored by age.

▶〈be動詞 + being + 過去分詞〉は受け身の現在進行形。Itは⑥の文のthe world's great artを指す。

このセクションの内容 の答え→ A. 危機 B. 多様性 C. 平和

✍ 英文を完成させなさい。

動物はそのシェルターで保護されている。

Some animals (　　　) (　　　) kept in the shelter.

▶過去分詞が5つ並列している。lostは「失われた」、destroyedは「破壊された」、damagedは「損傷を受けた」、displacedは「(元の場所から)移された」、discoloredは「変色した」。

⑧ May I read you a few sentences from the exhibit catalog?

▶May I ～?は「～してもよろしいですか」。

▶the exhibit catalogは、スーパークローン文化財の展覧会のカタログのこと。

⑨ Please do.

▶⑧の文を受けて、「どうぞ(そうしてください)」と勧めている。doはreadの代わりに使われている。

⑩ With our clone project, we hope to restore damaged cultural properties and allow people all over the world, especially young people, to appreciate great human accomplishments.

▶⑩～⑬の文は、展示会のカタログからの引用。

▶With our clone projectは「私たちのクローンプロジェクトで」(手段)。

▶hope to *do*は「～することを望む、～したいと思う」。

▶〈allow + 人 + to *do*〉は「(人)が～することを可能にする、(人)が～できるようにする」。people all over the world, especially young peopleが「人」に当たる。

✍ 次の英文を日本語に直しなさい。

The new policy allows employees to choose their own working hours.

新しい方針では、従業員は ＿＿＿＿＿＿＿＿＿＿＿＿＿＿＿＿。

▶appreciate great human accomplishmentsは「偉大な人類の功績をよく理解する」。great human accomplishmentsはcultural propertiesを言いかえたもの。

⑪ Cultural properties lead people to appreciate not just the individual artwork's ingenuity but also the diversity of cultures which is instrumental in creating great art.

▶〈lead + 人 + to *do*〉は「(人)に～させる」。

▶appreciateの目的語は、not just *A* but also *B*「AだけでなくBもまた」の形になっている。

▶the individual artwork's ingenuityは「個々の芸術作品の技巧」、the diversity of culturesは「文化の多様性」。

▶which以下は、the diversity of culturesを修飾する関係代名詞節。

▶ instrumentalは形容詞で「重要な、役立つ」という意味。instrumental in creating great artで「偉大な芸術を生み出すのに重要な」となる。

✍ 次の英文を日本語に直しなさい。

Her skills were instrumental in developing the new system.
新しいシステムを開発するのに、＿＿＿＿＿＿＿＿＿＿＿＿＿＿＿＿。

⑫ The greater your access to artworks, the greater your respect for different cultures.

▶〈The＋比較級～, the＋比較級 ...〉「～すればするほど（ますます）…」の文。artworksとculturesのあとに、動詞のgetsまたはbecomesが省略されている。

▶ access to ～は「～へのアクセス」、respect for ～は「～に対する敬意」。

⑬ We hope that will contribute to making a peaceful world.

▶ thatは、⑫の文の内容を指す。

▶ contribute to ～は「～に貢献する」、making a peaceful worldは「平和な世界を実現すること」。

⑭ In short, our mission is to build peace through art.

▶ in shortは「要約すると、つまり」。

▶ build ～ through ...は「…を通して[…によって]～を築く」。

⑮ That's a very appropriate closing thought.

▶ Thatは、「芸術を通して平和を築くこと」を指す。

▶ appropriate closing thoughtは「適切な締めくくりの考え」→「適切なまとめ（の考え）」。

⑯ I'm looking forward to the next exhibit of "Super Clone Cultural Properties."

▶ look forward to ～は「～を楽しみに待つ」。

⑰ And I hope you'll join me again on Rie's Gallery.

▶ joinは「（人）と落ち合う[合流する]」。ここでは、Rie's Gallery（ポッドキャストの番組）に出演すること。

⑱ It's been a pleasure, Rie-san.

▶ It's (＝It has) been a pleasureは「楽しかったです」。

▶ Rie-sanは「リエさん」で、日本語の「さん」がそのまま使われている。英語でMr.やMs.を付けるように、日本の方式にならって日本人名のあとに"-san"を付けることがある。

確認問題

語彙

1 次の語を（　）内の指示にしたがって書きかえなさい。

(1) impress（形容詞形に）　(2) restore（名詞形に）
(3) analyze（名詞形に）　(4) danger（動詞形に）
(5) deteriorate（名詞形に）　(6) possible（名詞形に）

2 次の各組でアクセントの位置が同じなら○、異なるなら×を書きなさい。

(1) (se-ries　as-set)　(2) (re-tain　pre-serve)
(3) (re-pro-duce　ref-er-ence)　(4) (ac-a-dem-ic　ap-pro-pri-ate)

文法・表現

1 日本語に合うように、（　）内に適切な語を入れなさい。ただし、最初の文字が指定されているときは、その文字で書き始めなさい。

(1) 彼は美術館を訪れることができてとてもうれしかった。
He (　　　) (d　　　) to visit the museum.
(2) 強風で帽子が彼女の頭から飛ばされてしまった。
The strong wind blew the hat (r　　　) (　　　) her head.
(3) 景気後退の事例と同じように、歴史は繰り返す。
History repeats itself, as (　　　) the (　　　) of economic recessions.
(4) その著者は、古い著作を一般の人々が無料で読めるようにした。
The author made her old titles (　　　) (　　　) the (　　　) for free.
(5) 美術館は来週新しい絵画を展示するでしょう。
The museum will put some new paintings (　　　) (d　　　) next week.
(6) 彼女は、健康のために食事を副菜のサラダで補っている。
She (　　　) her meals (　　　) a side salad for her health.

2 各組の文がほぼ同じ意味になるように、（　）内に適切な語を入れなさい。

(1) Why did she decide to cancel the trip?
(　　　) (　　　) her decide to cancel the trip?
(2) But for your support, the event wouldn't have been successful.
(　　　) your support, the event wouldn't have been successful.
(3) I'm sure he lost his way in the forest.
He (　　　) (　　　) (　　　) his way in the forest.

3 日本語に合うように、( )内の語句を並べかえなさい。

(1) この車の驚くべきことは、自動運転をすることだ。

(is / about / that / what's / this car / amazing) it drives itself.

________________________________ it drives itself.

(2)「タブレット」という言葉は、文字が彫られた平らな石のことを言う。

(is / to / the term / refer to / "tablet" / used) a piece of flat stone with words.

________________________________ a piece of flat stone with words.

総合

次の文を読んで、あとの問いに答えなさい。

R : Super clones! Transcending the original! ①<u>Is there (do / can / what / to / you / limit / any) with technology?</u> But now I have to ask you: What is your goal? It's fun, but do you have a higher purpose?

M : Well, I'd say my main goal is to protect our cultural heritage and (②) it on to the next generation. Much of the world's great art is endangered. ③<u>It</u> is being lost to natural disasters, destroyed by conflict, damaged during restoration, displaced by history, or discolored by age. May I read you a few sentences from the exhibit catalog?

R : Of course. Please do.

M (*reading*) : "With our clone project, we hope to (④) damaged cultural properties and allow people all over the world, especially young people, to appreciate great human accomplishments. Cultural properties lead people to appreciate not just the individual artwork's ingenuity but also the diversity of cultures which is ⑤(instrument) in creating great art. ⑥<u>The greater your access to artworks, the greater your respect for different cultures.</u> We hope that will contribute to making a peaceful world."

問1 下線部①の( )内の語を並べかえて、英文を完成させなさい。

問2 (②)(④)に適する語を下から選んで入れなさい。

〔bloom pass restore record soak〕

問3 下線部③が指すものを英文中から6語で抜き出して答えなさい。

問4 ⑤の( )内の語を適する形にしなさい。

問5 下線部⑥を日本語に直しなさい。

Lesson 9 Culture in the Animal Kingdom

教科書p.132 *ll*.1～15 I

①People have long thought that culture is what makes humans different from other animals. ②But recent studies have shown that this may not be the case. Let's examine various examples of "animal culture."

③Julie started a fashion fad. ④The 18-year-old chimpanzee stuck blades of grass into her ears and went around a wildlife sanctuary in Zambia showing off her new accessories. ⑤The other chimpanzees couldn't take their eyes off her. Pretty soon, they were also sticking grass in their ears. ⑥Eight out of the 10 in the group took up the fad.

⑦Julie died soon after, but her grass-in-the-ear fashion trend still lives on among her followers. ⑧The tradition arose spontaneously and spread through social networks, very much like a human fad.

⑨This is just one of many surprising examples of animal behavior that lead animal researchers to talk about animal "culture."

このセクションの内容

ジュリーという名の18歳の（A.　　　　　）が、草の葉を（B.　　　　　）に突き刺して仲間に見せびらかすと、彼らもそうし始めた。この流行はジュリーの死後も続いている。このような動物の行動から、研究者たちは動物の「（C.　　　　　）」について議論を始めている。

① People have long thought that culture is what makes humans different from other animals.

▶ that以下は〈S + V + C (= what節)〉の形。whatは関係代名詞。

▶〈make + O + 形容詞〉で「Oを～にする」。make ～ different from ... で、「～を…と異なったものにする」→「～を…と区別する」の意味。

② But recent studies have shown that this may not be the case.

▶ may not be ～は「～ではないかもしれない」。caseは「事実」の意味。

③ Julie started a fashion fad.

▶ a fashion fadは「(一時的な) ファッションの流行」。

④ The 18-year-old chimpanzee stuck blades of grass into her ears and went around a wildlife sanctuary in Zambia

showing off her new accessories.

▶ stick ～ into ... は「～を…に突き刺す」、blade of grass は「草の葉」。

▶ a wildlife sanctuary は「野生動物保護区」。

▶ showing ～は〈付帯状況〉の分詞構文。show off ～は「～を見せびらかす」。

⑤ The other chimpanzees couldn't take their eyes off her.

▶ The other chimpanzees は「ほかのすべてのチンパンジー」の意味で、Julie以外のチンパンジーのこと。

▶ take *one's* eyes off ～は「～から目を離す」（≒ stop looking at ～）。

✍ 次の英文を日本語に直しなさい。

The movie was so exciting that I couldn't take my eyes off the screen.
その映画はとてもわくわくしたので、＿＿＿＿＿＿＿＿＿＿。

⑥ Eight out of the 10 in the group took up the fad.

▶ Eight out of the 10は「10頭のうちの８頭」。

▶ take up ～は「（興味のあることなど）を学び始める」（≒ learn to *do* ～）。

✍ 英文を完成させなさい。

彼は芸術の才能を開花させるために、絵画を学び始めることにした。
He decided to (　　　) (　　　) painting to develop his artistic talents.

⑦ Julie died soon after, but her grass-in-the-ear fashion trend still lives on among her followers.

▶ grass-in-the-ear fashion trend は「草の葉を耳に突き刺すファッションの流行」、live on は「生き続ける」（≒ continue to exist）。

✍ 次の英文を日本語に直しなさい。

The traditions of the indigenous people still live on in their customs.
先住民の伝統は、＿＿＿＿＿＿＿＿＿＿。

▶ follower「信奉者、支持者」とは、ここではJulieのファッションを受け継いだチンパンジーのこと。

⑧ The tradition arose spontaneously and spread through social networks, very much like a human fad.

▶ arise spontaneously は「自然発生的に起こる」。arose は arise の過去形。

▶ very much like ～は「～とまさに同じように」。

⑨ This is just one of many surprising examples of animal behavior that lead animal researchers to talk about animal "culture."

▶ just one of ～は「～の１つにすぎない」。

▶ that 以下は、many ～ behavior を先行詞とする関係代名詞節。

▶〈lead ＋人＋ to *do*〉は「（人）に～させる」。

このセクションの内容 の答え→ A. チンパンジー　B. 耳　C. 文化

教科書pp.132～133 *ll*.16～43 Ⅱ

Definition of "Culture"

①It was once thought that only human beings have culture. We have art, science, and music; animals have only instinct. ②But that belief turns out to be misguided. ③Many new findings about animal behavior tell us that "culture," as many biologists now understand it, is not exclusive to humans.

④The idea that animals have culture may seem like nonsense. ⑤If "culture" means symphony orchestras, novels like *The Tale of Genji*, and museums like the Louvre, it is obvious that animals do not have culture. ⑥But that is not how these scientists define culture.

⑦Andrew Whiten, an evolutionary psychologist, defines culture as behavior that can be passed from one individual in a group to another individual, and which then spreads across the group and can be passed down through generations.

⑧If we use that definition, evidence is mounting that some animals—like Julie the chimp *fashionista* and her followers—also have culture.

Dressing Up

⑨Chimps and humans are not the only creatures who like to dress up. ⑩Some birds add material to their feathers to change their appearance, much like humans use makeup. ⑪Some vultures rub their heads, necks, and bodies in iron-rich soil, which gives them a reddish-brown hue.

⑫Bowerbirds in Australia and New Guinea build elaborately-decorated nests. ⑬Male bowerbirds make entrances (or bowers) leading to their nests, decorated with shiny stones, charcoal, and colorful objects of all sorts, including bottle caps. ⑭The bowers attract females, so, after all, building them may be a matter of instinct. ⑮However, each bower is unique and the design changes year by year.

このセクションの内容

文化が（A.　　　　　）に限られたものだとは言えない発見が数多くある。ある学者は、文化とは、ある（B.　　　　　）が個人から別の個人、さらには集団全体に広がり次世代に受け継がれることだと定義している。これはチンパンジーのジュリーの例に当てはまる。また、鳥の中には（C.　　　　　）をする鳥や、精巧に装飾された巣をつくる鳥がいる。

① It was once thought that only human beings have culture.

▶ It was once thought that ～は「～だとかつて考えられていた」。Itはthat以下を指す形式主語。

② But that belief turns out to be misguided.

▶ that beliefは、①の文のthat以下の内容を指し、人間だけが文化を持つという考えや信念のこと。

▶ turn out (to be) ～は「～だとわかる、～になる」、misguidedは「見当違いの、誤った」。

✍ 次の英文を日本語に直しなさい。

The book seemed boring, but it turned out to be interesting.

その本はつまらなさそうだったが、＿＿＿＿＿＿＿＿＿＿＿＿＿＿。

③ Many new findings about animal behavior tell us that "culture," as many biologists now understand it, is not exclusive to humans.

▶ 〈S + V + O (= 人) + O (= that節)〉の文。Many ～ behaviorが文全体の主語。

▶ as many biologists now understand itは挿入節で、「多くの生物学者が今日理解しているように」の意味。

▶ exclusive to ～は「～に限られた」。

④ The idea that animals have culture may seem like nonsense.

▶ The idea that ～は「～という考え」。thatの前後は同格の関係。

▶ may seem like nonsenseは「ばかげた考え[ナンセンス]に思えるかもしれない」。

⑤ If "culture" means symphony orchestras, novels like *The Tale of Genji*, and museums like the Louvre, it is obvious that animals do not have culture.

▶ it is obvious that ～は「～ということは明らかだ」。itは、that以下を指す形式主語。

⑥ But that is not how these scientists define culture.

▶ thatは、⑤の文で述べられたように、文化を交響楽団や小説や美術館のように考えることを指す。

▶〈how + S + V〉は「〜する方法」の意味で、howは先行詞を含む関係副詞（≒ the way in which）。

▶ these scientistsの具体的な科学者はこのあとに述べられる。

⑦ Andrew Whiten, an evolutionary psychologist, defines culture as behavior that can be passed from one individual in a group to another individual, and which then spreads across the group and can be passed down through generations.

▶ define 〜 as ... は「〜を…と定義する」。

▶ behavior「行為」を先行詞として、that 〜 another individualとwhich 〜 generationsの２つの関係代名詞節が並列している。

▶ be passed from 〜 to ... は「〜から…へ伝えられる」。

▶ spread across 〜は「〜の全体に広がる」、pass down 〜は「（伝統・知識など）を次の世代へ伝える」。

次の英文を日本語に直しなさい。

The antique chair has been passed down in my family for generations.

そのアンティークの椅子は、＿＿＿＿＿＿＿＿＿＿＿＿＿＿＿＿。

⑧ If we use that definition, evidence is mounting that some animals—like Julie the chimp *fashionista* and her followers—also have culture.

▶ that definition「その定義」とは、⑦の文での文化の定義のこと。

▶ 後半のthat以下は、evidenceの内容を説明している（同格）。evidence that 〜 is mountingのように主語が長くなるのを避け、that節を後ろに置いている。evidence is mounting that 〜で「〜という証拠が増えている」の意味。mountは「増える」。

▶ Julie the chimp *fashionista*は「おしゃれなチンパンジーのJulie」。

⑨ Chimps and humans are not the only creatures who like to dress up.

▶ are not the only 〜は「唯一の〜ではない」。

▶ dress upは「着飾る」（≒ put on special clothes）。

英文を完成させなさい。

私たちは正式な夕食会のために着飾る必要がある。

We need to (　　　) (　　　) for the formal dinner event.

⑩ Some birds add material to their feathers to change their appearance, much like humans use makeup.

このセクションの内容 の答え→　A. 人間　B. 行為[ふるまい]　C. 化粧

▶ add ～ to ... は「～を…に加える」、material は「素材、物質」、feather は「羽根」。*cf.* wing「翼、(昆虫の) 羽」

▶ much like ～は「～とほぼ同じように」、makeup は「化粧品」。

⑪ Some vultures rub their heads, necks, and bodies in iron-rich soil, which gives them a reddish-brown hue.

▶ vulture は「ハゲワシ」、rub は「～をこする、すり合わせる」、iron-rich soil は「鉄分が豊富な土壌」。

▶〈, which〉は非制限用法の関係代名詞。ここでは「そうすることは」の意味で、直前のハゲワシの動作を指す。

▶ give them a reddish-brown hue は「それら (＝頭と首と胴体) を赤茶色にする」。hue「色」は主に中間色を表す語。

⑫ Bowerbirds in Australia and New Guinea build elaborately-decorated nests.

▶ Bowerbird は「ニワシドリ、アズマヤドリ」、elaborately-decorated nests は「精巧に装飾された巣」。

⑬ Male bowerbirds make entrances (or bowers) leading to their nests, decorated with shiny stones, charcoal, and colorful objects of all sorts, including bottle caps.

▶ entrances leading to ～は「～に通じる入口」。

▶ bower は公園などにある日陰をつくる休憩所で、木々の葉で覆われたものや、小屋のようなものがある。

▶ decorated 以下は過去分詞で始まる句で、nests を補足説明する。

▶～ of all sorts は「あらゆる種類の～」、including ～は「～を含む」。

⑭ The bowers attract females, so, after all, building them may be a matter of instinct.

▶ attract は「～を魅了する、(注意など) を引く」、after all は「結局」。

▶ a matter of instinct は「本能の問題、本能に関わること」の意味で、つまり bower をつくること (自体) は文化的な行為ではないということ。

⑮ However, each bower is unique and the design changes year by year.

▶⑭の文を受けて、bower をつくることが、単に本能的な行為とは言い切れないことを述べている。

▶ year by year は「年々、年ごとに」。*cf.* each year「毎年」

教科書pp.134～135 *ll*.44～67 Ⅲ

Lobtail Feeding

①A long way away, in the North Atlantic Ocean, whales also exhibit a kind of culture. ②Ed Yong, a science journalist, writes about social learning among whales:

> ③In 1980, a humpback whale in the Gulf of Maine started doing something different. ④All its neighbors would catch small fish by swimming in circles below them, blowing curtains of bubbles, and then plunging straight up. ⑤Then one individual, out of the blue, started smacking the water surface with its tail before diving down and blowing bubbles.
>
> ⑥This behavior is called "lobtail feeding," and no one knows why it works. ⑦Whatever the benefit, it went viral. ⑧Just eight years after the first innovative whale started doing it, 20 percent of the Maine humpbacks had picked up the technique. ⑨Now, it's more like 40 percent. ⑩What began as one whale slapping the water is now a tradition. ⑪The obvious explanation is that the whales were learning from each other.

⑫Skeptics will argue that there could be other explanations. ⑬The lobtail technique may have a genetic basis and be passed down without social learning. ⑭Maybe environmental changes are responsible.

⑮But a group of researchers used the whale data to simulate the spread of lobtail feeding. ⑯The results were so clear that the leader of the research team concluded that social learning was important in the spread of the behavior.

このセクションの内容

北大西洋では、クジラの（A.　　　　　）的学習が確認されている。あるザトウクジラが、（B.　　　　　）をとる前に、尾びれを水面にたたきつけ始めた。この行為はほかのクジラにも広がり、今では（C.　　　　　）となっている。ここから、クジラ同士が学び合っていたと考えられる。

① A long way away, in the North Atlantic Ocean, whales also exhibit a kind of culture.

▶ a long way away は「遠く離れて」。

▶ exhibit は「(特質など) を見せる[表す]」。

② Ed Yong, a science journalist, writes about social learning among whales:

▶ social learning は「社会的学習」の意味で、他者を観察したり模倣したりして学習すること。

③ In 1980, a humpback whale in the Gulf of Maine started doing something different.

▶ ③～⑪の文は、Ed Yong の記事からの引用。文章の一節を引用する場合は、引用符 (“ ”) を使わずにインデント[字下げ]を入れて示す。

▶ a humpback whale in the Gulf of Maine は「メイン湾のザトウクジラ」。

▶ start doing something different は「変わったことをし始める」。

④ All its neighbors would catch small fish by swimming in circles below them, blowing curtains of bubbles, and then plunging straight up.

▶ its neighbors とは、③の文の a humpback whale と行動を共にしているザトウクジラたちを指す。

▶ would *do* は「～したものだ、～していた」の意味で、過去の習慣を表す。

▶ by ～は手段を表し、swimming、blowing、plunging と動名詞が続く。

▶ by 以下は、小さな魚 (＝餌) の下で円を描くように泳いで、泡を吹き出してカーテンをつくり、それからまっすぐ上に向かって泳ぐということ。

⑤ Then one individual, out of the blue, started smacking the water surface with its tail before diving down and blowing bubbles.

▶ individual はザトウクジラの個体のこと。

▶ out of the blue は「突然」(≒ unexpectedly)、smack は「～をぴしゃりと打つ、強打する」。

✍ 英文を完成させなさい。

車が突然故障して、私たちは置き去りにされた。

The car broke down (　　　) of the (　　　), leaving us abandoned.

⑥ This behavior is called “lobtail feeding,” and no one knows why it works.

▶ This behavior は、⑤の文の水面を尾びれでたたいてから潜ることを指す。lobtail はこの動作を表す動詞。

このセクションの内容 の答え→ A. 社会 B. 餌[小魚] C. 伝統

▶ no one knowsは「誰も知らない」、why it worksは「なぜそれ(＝ロブテイルフィーディング)が機能するのか[捕食に効果があるのか]」。

例 A new teaching method seems to be *working* for the students.
「新しい教授法は、生徒たちに効果が出ているようだ」

⑦ Whatever the benefit, it went viral.

▶ Whatever the benefitは「その利点が何であれ」。benefitのあとにbe動詞のwasが省略されている(≒ No matter what the benefit was)。

✍ 次の英文を日本語に直しなさい。

Whatever they say, you should not give up.

▶ go viralは「急速に広がる、大流行する」。viralは「ウイルスの、拡散した」の意味で、virus「ウイルス」の形容詞形。

⑧ Just eight years after the first innovative whale started doing it, 20 percent of the Maine humpbacks had picked up the technique.

▶ Just eight years after ～は「～からわずか8年後には」。

▶ the first innovative whale started doing itは「最初の革新的なクジラがそれ(＝ロブテイルフィーディング)を始めた」。

▶ had picked upは「(すでに)身につけていた、取り入れていた」。pick up ～は「(習慣など)を身につける」(≒ learn ～)。

⑨ Now, it's more like 40 percent.

▶ itは、ロブテイルフィーディングを身につけたメイン湾のザトウクジラの割合のこと。

▶ more like ～は「～により近い」。

⑩ What began as one whale slapping the water is now a tradition.

▶ What ～ waterが文の主語で、whatは関係代名詞。

▶ one whale slapping the waterは「一頭のクジラが水を叩くこと」。one whaleはslappingの意味上の主語。

⑪ The obvious explanation is that the whales were learning from each other.

▶ The obvious explanation is that ～は「明らかな説明は～ということだ」→「～ということが明らかだ」。

✍ 次の英文を日本語に直しなさい。

The obvious explanation is that the wet ground means it rained this morning.

---

⑫ Skeptics will argue that there could be other explanations.

▶ skepticは「懐疑論者、疑い深い人」の意味。「懐疑論」「懐疑主義」とは、人間の認識を主観的なものと考え、客観性や普遍性を否定しようとする思想や態度のこと。

▶ argue that ～は「～だと主張する」、couldは〈可能性・推量〉を表し、「～かもしれない、～があり得る」の意味。

⑬ The lobtail technique may have a genetic basis and be passed down without social learning.

▶ have a genetic basisは「遺伝的な根拠がある」。geneticは「遺伝子の」の意味で名詞形はgene「遺伝子」。

▶ be passed downはpass down ～「(伝統・知識など)を次の世代へ伝える」の受け身。

▶ 文全体で、ロブテイルの技術は、社会的学習ではなく、遺伝によって受け継がれてきたものであるかもしれないという意味。

⑭ Maybe environmental changes are responsible.

▶ environmental changesは「環境の変化」。

▶ responsibleは「(～の)原因である」。ここでは、ロブテイルの技術が広まったことの原因が、環境の変化にあるかもしれないということ。

⑮ But a group of researchers used the whale data to simulate the spread of lobtail feeding.

▶ to simulate ～は目的を表す副詞的用法の不定詞。

▶ simulate the spread of lobtail feedingは「ロブテイルフィーディングの広がり[広がる様子]を模擬実験[シミュレート]する」。

⑯ The results were so clear that the leader of the research team concluded that social learning was important in the spread of the behavior.

▶ The resultsは、⑮の文の模擬実験の結果。

▶ so ～ that ...は「とても～なので…、…なほど～」。

▶ importantは、ここでは「(重大な)影響力を持つ」の意味。

▶ the behaviorは、ロブテイルフィーディングのこと。

▶ 文全体で、「研究チームのリーダーがロブテイルフィーディングの広がりには、社会的学習が影響力を持っていると結論づけるほど、(模擬実験の)結果は明らかだった」となる。

教科書pp.135 *ll*.68～84 Ⅳ

Coat Hanger Nests

①Closer to home, since around 2005 Tokyoites have been watching a remarkable experiment in social learning among crows. Ordinarily, crows use twigs and natural material to build their nests. ②However, natural materials are hard to come by in the busy city, so the birds settle for the next best thing: coat hangers. ③The first photo of a coat hanger nest was posted in 2005. ④Just as lobtail feeding began with one humpback whale and then was passed on by social learning, so coat hanger nest-building has passed to another generation of crows. ⑤There are now so many coat hanger nests that they are becoming a problem. ⑥When the crows build nests on power poles, it can cause electrical shorts. ⑦The electric company has to send out crews to take down the nests.

このセクションの内容

カラスはふつう、（A.　　　　）や自然の素材を使って巣をつくるが、都市では入手が難しいため、（B.　　　　）を使って巣づくりを始めた。クジラの例と同様に、カラスのこの巣づくりも次の（C.　　　　）に伝えられている。今日では、このような巣が多くなりすぎて社会問題になっている。

① Closer to home, since around 2005 Tokyoites have been watching a remarkable experiment in social learning among crows.

▶ Closer to homeは「より身近なところでは」。

▶ have been watchingは現在完了進行形で、習慣の継続を表す。

▶ Tokyoiteは「東京都民」(≒ citizen of Tokyo)。*cf.* Muscovite「モスクワ人」

▶ remarkableは「注目すべき」、experiment in ～は「～に関する実験」。

② However, natural materials are hard to come by in the busy city, so the birds settle for the next best thing: coat hangers.

▶ be hard to *do*は「～するのが難しい」、come by ～は「(努力して) 手に入れる」(≒ find ～)。

▶〈S + be + 形容詞 + to *do*〉の形で、主語のnatural materials「自然の素材」についての評価を表す (≒ it is hard to come by natural materials)。

✍ 次の英文を日本語に直しなさい。

Affordable housing is hard to come by in the city center.

手頃な住居は、＿＿＿＿＿＿＿＿＿＿＿＿＿＿＿＿＿＿。

▶ the birdsはthe crowsのこと。

▶ settle for ～は「～でがまんする」、the next best thingは「(小枝の) 次によいもの、次善の策」。

▶ coat hangerは「(衣服の) ハンガー」。clothes[dress] hangerまたはhangerとだけ言うこともある。*cf.* hang「～をつるす[かける]、ぶら下がる、～を絞首刑にする」

③ The first photo of a coat hanger nest was posted in 2005.

▶ coat hanger nestは「ハンガーの[ハンガーでつくられた]巣」。

▶ postは「(インターネットなどに) ～を投稿[掲載]する」。

④ Just as lobtail feeding began with one humpback whale and then was passed on by social learning, so coat hanger nest-building has passed to another generation of crows.

▶ (just) as ～, so ...は「～と(まさに)同様に…」。lobtail feedingとcoat hanger nest-buildingを対比する文。

▶ begin with ～は「～で[から]始まる」、pass on ～は「～を伝える」。

▶ has passedは現在完了で、pass to ～は「～に伝わる」の意味 (≒ be passed on to ～)。

✍ ほぼ同じ意味を表すように、英文を完成させなさい。

The secret recipe has been passed on to a chef in the village.

The secret recipe has (　　　) (　　　) a chef in the village.

▶ another generationは「別の[次の]世代」。

⑤ There are now so many coat hanger nests that they are becoming a problem.

▶ so ～ that ...は「とても～なので…」。theyはcoat hanger nestsを指す。

▶ 文全体で、「ハンガーの巣がとても多いので、それら (＝巣) が問題になってきている」という意味。

⑥ When the crows build nests on power poles, it can cause electrical shorts.

▶ power poleは「電柱」。itは「カラスが電柱に巣をつくること」を指す。

▶ causeは「～を引き起こす」、electrical shortは「電気回路のショート」。

⑦ The electric company has to send out crews to take down the nests.

▶ send out ～は「～を派遣する」、take down ～は「～を撤去する」。

このセクションの内容の答え→ A. 小枝　B. ハンガー　C. 世代

教科書pp.135～136 *ll*.85～108 V

Migration

①More evidence of social learning comes from the study of animal migration, which for a long time was thought to be instinctive.

Peter Richerson, a researcher on human cultural evolution, studies migration. ②Recent observations appear to show that migratory animals, birds, and even butterflies plan their routes and adjust them for changing circumstances. ③Young members of the group have to learn the route from adults.

④One dramatic example of social learning among migratory creatures involves whooping cranes. ⑤In the late 20th century, whooping cranes became almost extinct. ⑥To save the species, a small flock of cranes was introduced in Wisconsin. ⑦Cranes must migrate to a warmer climate in winter, and there were no experienced cranes to teach the young chicks the route. ⑧The flock was saved by a man in a crane suit flying a light airplane. ⑨The birds quickly learned to follow their human guide. ⑩He led them on a month-long 1,250-mile flight to Florida.

Is there culture in the animal kingdom?

⑪Whiten says, “Other species were thought to live by instinct and some ability to learn, but only humans had culture. ⑫Over recent decades, a rapidly growing body of research has increasingly revealed a very different picture.”

⑬Richerson was once reluctant to talk about animal “culture” at all. ⑭However, he has changed his mind. ⑮He says, “This is a golden age of animal culture and nonhuman learning studies.”

このセクションの内容

社会的学習は、動物の（A.　　　　　）にも見られる。渡りをする動物は、ルートを計画し、（B.　　　　　）の変化に応じて調整する。群れの若いメンバーは大人からそのことを学ぶ。近年急速に増えている（C.　　　　　）によって、これまでとは異なる動物像が明らかになってきている。

① More evidence of social learning comes from the study of animal migration, which for a long time was thought to be instinctive.

▶ More evidence of 〜は「〜のさらに多くの証拠」。

▶〈, which〉は非制限用法の関係代名詞で、先行詞のanimal migrationを補足説明する。

▶ be thought to be instinctiveは「本能的なものと考えられている」。think 〜 (to be) ...「〜を…と思う[みなす]」の受け身。

✍ 次の英文を日本語に直しなさい。

The planet found by the astronomers is thought to be habitable.

天文学者が発見したその惑星は、＿＿＿＿＿＿＿＿＿＿＿＿＿＿＿＿。

② Recent observations appear to show that migratory animals, birds, and even butterflies plan their routes and adjust them for changing circumstances.

▶ appear to *do* は「〜であるようだ」。

▶ migratoryは「移住性の、定期的に移動する」。migratory animals「渡り[移動]をする動物」として、ほ乳類ではトナカイやバイソンがいる。

▶ routeは「(移動) ルート」。

▶ adjust 〜 for ...「〜を…に合わせて調整する」。themは「動物や鳥や蝶が計画した移動ルート」を指す。

✍ 次の英文を日本語に直しなさい。

The pilot had to adjust the flight route for the storm.

＿＿＿＿＿＿＿＿＿＿＿＿＿＿＿＿＿＿＿＿＿＿＿＿＿＿＿＿＿＿＿

▶ changing circumstancesは「変化する状況[状況の変化]」。

③ Young members of the group have to learn the route from adults.

▶ Young members of the groupとは、群れの若いメンバーのこと。

④ One dramatic example of social learning among migratory creatures involves whooping cranes.

▶ One 〜 creaturesが文の主語。

▶ One dramatic example of 〜は「〜の劇的な一例」、social learning among migratory creaturesは「渡り[移動]をする生き物の社会的学習」。

▶ involveは「〜を必ず含む」、whooping craneは「アメリカシロヅル」。ここでは、(劇的な一例には) アメリカシロヅルの例があるということ。

⑤ In the late 20th century, whooping cranes became almost extinct.

このセクションの内容 の答え→ A. 渡り[移動] B. 状況 C. 研究

▶ the late 20th century は「20世紀後半」。

▶ almost extinct は「ほぼ絶滅して」。*cf.* extinction「絶滅」

例 Orangutans are almost *extinct.*

≒ Orangutans are in danger of *extinction.*

「オランウータンは絶滅の危機にある」

⑥ To save the species, a small flock of cranes was introduced in Wisconsin.

▶ species は「(分類上の) 種」(複数形も species) の意味で、the species とはアメリカシロヅルの種のこと。

▶ a flock of ～は「～の群れ」、introduce は「～を持ち込む」。

▶ Wisconsin「ウィスコンシン州」はアメリカ北中部の州。

⑦ Cranes must migrate to a warmer climate in winter, and there were no experienced cranes to teach the young chicks the route.

▶ migrate to ～は「～へ移動する[渡る]」、warmer climate は「より暖かい地方」。climate は、ここでは「(気候に関する) 地方、気候帯」の意味。

✍ 次の英文を日本語に直しなさい。

These plants grow in tropical climates.

____

▶ experienced は「経験のある、経験豊富な」。experienced cranes とは、渡り[移動]の経験があるツルのこと。

▶ to teach は形容詞的用法の不定詞で、experienced cranes が意味上の主語。

▶ the young chicks は「若いひな鳥」。the route は飛行ルートのこと。

⑧ The flock was saved by a man in a crane suit flying a light airplane.

▶ The flock は、⑥の文で述べたウィスコンシン州に持ち込まれたアメリカシロヅルの群れのこと。

▶ a man in a crane suit は「ツルのスーツ (着ぐるみ) を着た男性」。

▶ fly は他動詞で、「～を (操縦して) 飛ばす」の意味。ここでは、a man in a crane suit を修飾する現在分詞になっている。

⑨ The birds quickly learned to follow their human guide.

▶ The birds は、⑧の文と同じアメリカシロヅルのこと。

▶ learn to *do* は「～することを学ぶ」。

▶ their human guide は「彼ら (＝アメリカシロヅル) の人間の案内役」の意味で、⑧の文の男性のこと。

⑩ He led them on a month-long 1,250-mile flight to Florida.

▶ ledはlead「～を導く」の過去形。

▶ a month-long 1,250-mile flight to Floridaは「フロリダまでの1か月間に及ぶ1,250マイルの飛行」。フロリダ州はアメリカ南東部のフロリダ半島を占める州で、1年を通して温暖な気候で知られる。

⑪ Whiten says, "Other species were thought to live by instinct and some ability to learn, but only humans had culture.

▶ Other speciesとは、「人間以外の種」のこと。

▶ be thought to *do*は「～すると考えられている」、live by instinct and some ability to learnは「本能といくらかの学習能力を使って生きる」。

⑫ Over recent decades, a rapidly growing body of research has increasingly revealed a very different picture."

▶ Over recent decadesは「最近の[ここ]数十年にわたり」。

▶ a rapidly growing body of researchは「急速に増えている一連の研究」。ここでは、動物の社会的学習に関する研究のことを指す。

▶ revealは「(知られていないことなど)を明らかにする」。

▶ a very different pictureは「まったく異なる像[描写]」。ここでのpictureは、対象(＝動物)がどのようなものかを説明する描写のこと。

例 Her diary has presented a clear *picture* of her experiences.
「彼女の日記は、彼女の経験をはっきりと描写している」

⑬ Richerson was once reluctant to talk about animal "culture" at all.

▶ be reluctant to *do*は「～したくない、～する気がおきない」(≒be not willing to *do*)、at allは「まったく」。

✍ 英文を完成させなさい。

彼は一人で外国を旅行したがらなかった。

He was (　　　) (　　　) travel alone to a foreign country.

⑭ However, he has changed his mind.

▶ change *one's* mindは「考えを変える」。

⑮ He says, "This is a golden age of animal culture and nonhuman learning studies."

▶ a golden ageは「黄金時代」(≒the most flourishing period)。

✍ 次の英文を日本語に直しなさい。

We are now experiencing the golden age of the internet.

____

▶ nonhuman learning studiesは「非人間(＝動物)の学習の研究」(≒studies of nonhuman learning)。

確認問題

語彙

1 次の語を（　）内の指示にしたがって書きかえなさい。

(1) define（名詞形に）
(2) appear（名詞形に）
(3) evolution（形容詞形に）
(4) instinct（形容詞形に）
(5) migrate（名詞形に）
(6) exclude（形容詞形に）

2 次の各組でアクセントの位置が同じなら○、異なるなら×を書きなさい。

(1) (skep-tic　ex-tinct)
(2) (bi-ol-o-gist　fash-ion-ist-a)
(3) (cir-cum-stance　or-ches-tra)
(4) (ac-ces-so-ry　sanc-tu-ar-y)

文法・表現

1 日本語に合うように、（　）内に適切な語を入れなさい。

(1) まさにあたたかい毛布のように、その部屋は快適な雰囲気だった。
The room had a cozy atmosphere, very (　　　) (　　　) a warm blanket.

(2) 祖母の知恵は、私の中に生き続けるだろう。
The wisdom of my grandmother will (　　　) (　　　) in my heart.

(3) 参加者はパーティーでコスチュームを着飾っていた。
Participants (　　　) (　　　) in costumes at the party.

(4) 日本の人口は年々減少している。
Japan's population is declining (　　　) by (　　　).

(5) 古い友人が突然、私に電話をかけてきた。
An old friend of mine gave me a phone call (　　　) (　　　) the (　　　).

(6) 事故が原因で交通渋滞が起きたことは明らかだ。
The (　　　) (　　　) is that the traffic jam occurred due to the accident.

2 各組の文がほぼ同じ意味になるように、（　）内に適切な語を入れなさい。

(1) I couldn't stop looking at the sight.
I couldn't (　　　) (　　　) (　　　) off the sight.

(2) No matter what happens, be sure to keep calm.
(　　　) (　　　), be sure to keep calm.

(3) She was not willing to admit that it was her fault.
She was (　　　) (　　　) admit that it was her fault.

3 日本語に合うように、( )内の語句を並べかえなさい。

(1) サリーは退職を機に編み物を始めることに決めた。
Sally (up / to / knitting / take / decided) when she retired.
Sally ______________________________ when she retired.

(2) その技術は若い世代へ受け継がれてきた。
(been / to / passed / the technique / down / has) younger generations.
______________________________ younger generations.

(3) 最後に実験は大成功だとわかった。
In the end, (be / turned / the experiment / a great success / to / out).
In the end, ______________________________.

総合

次の文を読んで、あとの問いに答えなさい。

Closer to home, since around 2005 Tokyoites have been watching a remarkable experiment in ①social learning among crows. Ordinarily, crows use twigs and natural material to build their nests. However, natural materials are hard to (②) by in the busy city, so the birds (③) for the next best thing: coat hangers. The first photo of a coat hanger nest was posted in 2005. ④(one humpback whale / and then / just as / with / passed on / was / lobtail feeding / began) by social learning, so coat hanger nest-building has passed to another generation of crows. ⑤There are now so many coat hanger nests that they are becoming a problem. When the crows build nests on power poles, it can cause electrical shorts. The electric company has to send out crews to take down the nests.

問1 下線部①について、カラスが社会的学習により受け継いだものは何か、日本語で説明しなさい。

問2 (②)(③)に適する語を下から選んで入れなさい。
〔find settle make come〕

問3 下線部④が、「ロブテイルフィーディングが一頭のザトウクジラから始まり、その後社会的学習によって受け継がれたのとまさに同様に」という意味になるように、( )内の語句を並べかえなさい。

問4 下線部⑤を日本語に直しなさい。

Lesson 10 Does Money Make You Mean?

教科書p.146 *ll*.1～15 I

①If the rich would share their wealth with the poor, inequality might be solved. ②But this does not seem to be happening. ③Paul Piff, an American social psychologist, wanted to find out why.

④Do rich people think and act differently from poor people? ⑤Paul Piff has explored this question in dozens of experiments. ⑥His findings suggest that as people's wealth increases, so do their feelings of entitlement and their self-interest, but their empathy and compassion decrease. ⑦Piff worries that as economic inequality increases, the idea that everyone has an equal opportunity to succeed and prosper will suffer.

このセクションの内容

裕福な人と貧しい人では、考え方や行動に（A.　　　　）はあるのだろうか。調査の結果、（B.　　　　）が増えるにつれて、権利意識や利己心が高まる一方で、（C.　　　　）や思いやりは減少することがわかった。

① If the rich would share their wealth with the poor, inequality might be solved.

▶仮定法過去の文で、「もし～なら、…かもしれない」の意味。wouldは〈意志〉を表す。

▶〈the＋形容詞〉は「～な人々」の意味で、the richはrich people、the poorはpoor peopleを表す。

▶share ～ with ... は「～を…と分かち合う」、inequalityは「不平等」。

② But this does not seem to be happening.

▶thisは、①の文の内容を指す。

▶seem to be V-ingは「～しているようだ、～しているように思われる」。

③ Paul Piff, an American social psychologist, wanted to find out why.

▶挿入句のan American social psychologistはPaul Piffの補足説明（同格）。

▶find out ～は「～を見つけ出す、～を知る」。

▶whyの後ろにit does not seem to be happeningが省略されている。

④ Do rich people think and act differently from poor people?

▶ differently from ～は「～とは違うように」(≒ in a different way from ～)。

✍ ほぼ同じ意味を表すように、英文を完成させなさい。

The cat greets in a different way from the dog.

The cat greets (　　　) (　　　) the dog.

⑤ Paul Piff has explored this question in dozens of experiments.

▶ exploreは「～を調査[分析]する」。

▶ this questionは、④の文の「裕福な人は、貧しい人とは考え方や行動が異なるか」という問いのこと。

▶ dozens of ～は「多くの～」(≒ many ～)。*cf.* dozen「ダース(12個)」

✍ 次の英文を日本語に直しなさい。

The flood has destroyed dozens of houses in the town.

____

⑥ His findings suggest that as people's wealth increases, so do their feelings of entitlement and their self-interest, but their empathy and compassion decrease.

▶ findingは「発見したもの」→「調査結果」。

▶ as ～, so ...は「～と同様に…、～につれて…」。so以下は〈so + V + S〉の語順(倒置)になっている。doはincreaseの言いかえで、主語はtheir feelings of entitlement and their self-interest「権利[特権]意識と利己心[自己利益]」。

✍ 次の英文を日本語に直しなさい。

As the population in the city increases, so does the need for housing.

市の人口が増えるにつれて、________________________。

▶ empathyは「共感」、compassionは「思いやり」。

⑦ Piff worries that as economic inequality increases, the idea that everyone has an equal opportunity to succeed and prosper will suffer.

▶ worry that ～は「～ということを心配[懸念]している」。文末までがthat節の内容になる。

▶ as economic inequality increasesは「経済格差が広がるにつれて」。

▶ the idea that ～は「～という考え」の意味で、that ～ prosperがthe ideaの内容になる(同格)。the idea ～ prosperは「誰もが成功して栄える平等な機会をもつという考え」の意味。

▶ sufferは「損なわれる、危うくなる」。

このセクションの内容 の答え→ A. 違い B. 富 C. 共感

教科書pp.146～147 ll.16～61 II

A Rigged Game

①In one interesting experiment, people played a board game in which two players compete in buying and selling land, buildings, and houses. ②The goal is to see who ends up with the most money and property. ③Each player begins with the same amount of money (of course, it is play money) and each must follow the same rules.

Piff decided to change the game. ④He wanted to see what would happen if the game were rigged so that one player got twice as much money as the other player and the rules also worked in favor of the "rich" player. ⑤More than 100 pairs of strangers were asked to be either a "rich" player or a "poor" player in a rigged game. ⑥Through hidden cameras, Piff watched what happened.

⑦As the game went on, dramatic differences appeared between the two players. ⑧The rich players began to show signs of power and celebration. ⑨They became loud and slapped their pieces down on the board. ⑩They took more than their share of the pretzels which the researchers had provided. The rich players became more boastful. ⑪They were less and less sensitive to the plight of the poor players. In some cases, they were actually rude.

⑫According to Piff, the rigged game can be used as a metaphor for understanding a society in which a few people have a lot more wealth and status than the rest of the people.

⑬In dozens of studies involving thousands of participants, Piff is finding that as people get richer, they lose their sense of compassion and they feel an increased sense of entitlement. ⑭Wealthier individuals are actually more likely to feel that greed is good and that the pursuit of self-interest is good and moral.

このセクションの内容

「金持ち」のプレーヤーが有利になるよう操作された（A.　　　　　）を使った実験では、「金持ち」は自慢げで失礼な態度になり、「貧乏」なプレーヤーの（B.　　　　　）には敏感ではなくなった。人は（C.　　　　　）になると、思いやりが失われ、権利意識が強まることがわかってきている。

① In one interesting experiment, people played a board game in which two players compete in buying and selling land, buildings, and houses.

▶ play a board gameは「ボードゲームをする」。

▶ in which ～は〈前置詞＋関係代名詞節〉で、先行詞のa board gameを修飾する。a board game in which two players competeで「２人のプレーヤーが競うボードゲーム」の意味。

▶ compete in buying and selling ～は「～を売買することで競う」。

② The goal is to see who ends up with the most money and property.

▶ The goal is to *do*は「目的は～することだ」、seeは「～を調べる」。

▶ who ～は間接疑問で、seeの目的語。

✍ 次の英文を日本語に直しなさい。

The goal is to see whether dogs like the new toy.

________________________________ を調べることだ。

▶ end up with ～は「～で終わる」。who以下は「最終的に誰が最も多くのお金と財産を手にするか」という意味。

③ Each player begins with the same amount of money (of course, it is play money) and each must follow the same rules.

▶ begin with ～は「～から始める」、the same amount of ～は「同じ量の～」。

▶ play moneyは「(本物ではない) ゲーム用のお金」のこと。

④ He wanted to see what would happen if the game were rigged so that one player got twice as much money as the other player and the rules also worked in favor of the "rich" player.

▶ what ～は間接疑問で、文末までがwhat節になる。

▶ what would happen if ～は「もし～なら、何が起こるだろうか」の意味で、仮定法過去の文。仮定法過去は主節の時制 (wanted) の影響を受けない。

例 She thought that she *would* go shopping if the weather *were* good.
「彼女は、もし天気がよければ買い物に行くだろうにと思った」

▶ rigは「～を (不正に) 操作する」の意味で、ここでは受け身の形で使われている。so that ～は「～するように」(目的)。

▶ twice as much ～ as ...は「…の２倍の～」。

✍ 英文を完成させなさい。

私は起きているために普段の２倍のコーヒーを飲んだ。

I drank (　　　) (　　　) (　　　) coffee as I usually do to stay awake.

▶ and the rules ～はand *if* the rules ～のことで、２つ目の条件を表す。

このセクションの内容 の答え→ A. ボードゲーム B. 苦境 C. 裕福［金持ち］

▶ in favor of ～は「～に有利に」(≒ to the advantage of ～)。the "rich" playerとは、お金を2倍受け取るように操作されたプレーヤーのこと。つまり、ルール自体も、お金を持っているプレーヤーが有利になるようにできていたということ。

⑤ More than 100 pairs of strangers were asked to be either a "rich" player or a "poor" player in a rigged game.

▶ a pair of ～は「1組の～」で、2人[2つ]から成る場合に使われる。

▶ strangerは「見知らぬ人」、be asked to *do*は「～するように依頼される」。

▶ either ～ or ... は「～か…のどちらか」。

✍ 英文を完成させなさい。

顧客は現金またはクレジットカードでの支払いを選ぶことができる。

Customers can choose to pay with (　　　) cash (　　　) a credit card.

⑥ Through hidden cameras, Piff watched what happened.

▶ hidden cameraは「隠しカメラ」。

▶ what happenedは「何が起こるか[起こること]」。

⑦ As the game went on, dramatic differences appeared between the two players.

▶ As the game went onは「ゲームが進むにつれて」。go onは「進み続ける」。

▶ the two playersは、⑤の文の「『金持ち』プレーヤーと『貧乏人』プレーヤー」のこと。

⑧ The rich players began to show signs of power and celebration.

▶ sign of power and celebrationは「権力と祝賀の兆候」。

⑨ They became loud and slapped their pieces down on the board.

▶ Theyは、⑧の文のThe rich playersを指す。

▶ become loudは「声が大きくなる、大声になる」。

▶ slap ～ downは「～を乱暴に置く、～をたたきつける」、pieceは「(ゲームに使われている)駒」。

✍ 英文を完成させなさい。

彼はゲームに負けたあと、コントローラーをたたきつけた。

He (　　　) the controller (　　　) after losing the game.

⑩ They took more than their share of the pretzels which the researchers had provided.

▶ shareは「分け前、取り分」、pretzelは「(焼き菓子の)プレッツェル」。

▶ whichはthe pretzelsを先行詞とする関係代名詞。had providedは過去完了で、tookよりも前のことを表す。

⑪ They were less and less sensitive to the plight of the poor

players.

▶ less and less ～は「だんだん～でなくなる」。*cf.* more and more ～「ますます～」

✍ 次の英文を日本語に直しなさい。

Students are spending less and less time reading books.

___

▶ sensitive to ～は「～に敏感な」、plightは「悪い状態、苦境」。

⑫ **According to Piff, the rigged game can be used as a metaphor for understanding a society in which a few people have a lot more wealth and status than the rest of the people.**

▶ According to ～は「～によれば」。

▶ can be used as ～は「～として使うことができる」。

▶ metaphorは「象徴（のようなもの）、代表例」。

▶ in which ～は〈前置詞＋関係代名詞節〉で、先行詞のa societyを修飾する。

▶ a lot more ～は「ずっと多くの～」。in which以下は、「少数の人々が、その他の人々よりもはるかに多くの富と地位をもつ（社会）」となる。

⑬ **In dozens of studies involving thousands of participants, Piff is finding that as people get richer, they lose their sense of compassion and they feel an increased sense of entitlement.**

▶ dozens of ～は「多くの～」。

▶ involving thousands of participantsは「何千もの［多くの］参加者を巻き込んでいる［参加者が関わっている］」という現在分詞の句で、直前のstudiesを修飾する。

▶ is findingと進行形になっているのは、現在も研究が続いているから。

▶ as people get richerは「人は裕福になるにつれて」。

▶ lose *one's* sense of ～は「～の感覚を失う」。

⑭ **Wealthier individuals are actually more likely to feel that greed is good and that the pursuit of self-interest is good and moral.**

▶ wealthierはwealthy「裕福な」の比較級。

▶ be more likely to *do*は「より～しそうだ、より～する傾向がある」。

▶ feelの目的語のthat節が２つ並列している。

▶ greedは「貪欲」、pursuit of self-interestは「自己利益の追求」、moralは「道徳的な、道徳上正しい」。

教科書pp.147〜148 *ll*.62〜108 Ⅲ

Other Experiments

①Piff set up other experiments. ②He asked people about their family income, level of education, financial security, and how much they valued the way they look. ③Piff even tested how much time participants spent looking at themselves in the mirror. ④He found that rich people looked at themselves more often and were more narcissistic.

⑤Piff also looked at helping behavior. ⑥He was interested in who is more likely to offer help to another person. Rich and poor members of the community were each given $10. ⑦They were told that they could keep it all for themselves or share a portion of it with a stranger. ⑧The researchers monitored how much people gave. ⑨The poorer people, who had incomes between $15,000 and $25,000 a year, gave 44 percent more of their money to the stranger than did people making between $150,000 and $200,000 a year.

⑩Another study examined whether anybody would take candy that was reserved for children who were participating in a developmental program. ⑪People who felt rich took twice as much candy as those who felt poor.

⑫Of course, it is not only wealthy people who show these patterns of behavior. ⑬In fact, most of us in our regular daily lives struggle to decide when or whether to put our own interests above the interests of other people. ⑭This is understandable because most people like to think that we all have an equal opportunity to succeed and prosper as long as we apply ourselves and work hard. Sometimes we need to put our own interests first. ⑮But Piff's studies show that the wealthier people are, the more likely they are to pursue personal success without thinking about others.

このセクションの内容

ほかの実験では、裕福な人が頻繁に（A.　　　　　）で自分を見ることや、貧しい人よりも見知らぬ人を援助する金額が（B.　　　　　）ことなどがわかった。私たちは、時に自分の（C.　　　　　）を優先しなければならないが、裕福な人ほど他人のことを考えずに自分の成功を追い求める傾向が強い。

① Piff set up other experiments.

▶ set up ～は「～の準備をする」。このsetは過去形。

② He asked people about their family income, level of education, financial security, and how much they valued the way they look.

▶ aboutの目的語が4つ並列する文。

▶ financial securityは「財務[資金]の安定(性)」の意味で、ここでは個人の十分な金融資産を表す。

▶ how much they valued ～は「彼らが～をどれだけ評価しているか」(間接疑問)。

▶ the way they lookは、「自分の見え方[外見]」。

③ Piff even tested how much time participants spent looking at themselves in the mirror.

▶ how much ～は間接疑問。participantsは実験の参加者のこと。

▶ 〈spend + 時間 + V-ing〉は「～することに(時間)を費やす」。

✍ 英文を完成させなさい。

彼らは数週間かけてヨーロッパを旅行した。

They (　　　) a few (　　　) traveling through Europe.

▶ look at *oneself* in the mirrorは「鏡で自分の姿を見る」。

④ He found that rich people looked at themselves more often and were more narcissistic.

▶ narcissisticは「自己愛の強い」。*cf.* narcissism「(過度な)自己愛、ナルシシズム」、narcissist「自己愛の強い人」

⑤ Piff also looked at helping behavior.

▶ look at ～は、ここでは「～に注目する、～を取り上げる」。

▶ helping behaviorは「援助行為」。

⑥ He was interested in who is more likely to offer help to another person.

▶ who以下は間接疑問で、「誰が～か」の意味。

▶ be more likely to *do*は「より～しそうだ、より～する傾向がある」。

▶ offer ～ to ...は「～を…に申し出る[提供する]」。

⑦ They were told that they could keep it all for themselves or share a portion of it with a stranger.

▶ Theyは、直前の文のRich and poor members of the communityを指す。

▶ keep it all for themselvesは「それをすべて自分のために取っておく」。itは直前の文の10ドルのお金を指す。

▶ share ～ with ...は「～を…と分け合う」、a portion of itは「それ(＝10ドル)

このセクションの内容 の答え→ A. 鏡 B. 少ない C. 利益

の一部」。

⑧ The researchers monitored how much people gave.

▶ monitorは「～を監視する」、how much people gaveは「人がどれだけ（見知らぬ人に）与えるか」（間接疑問）。

⑨ The poorer people, who had incomes between $15,000 and $25,000 a year, gave 44 percent more of their money to the stranger than did people making between $150,000 and $200,000 a year.

▶ 関係代名詞whoで始まる節が挿入されている。

▶ thanのあとは、〈動詞（did）＋主語〉の語順になっている（倒置）。didはgave their money to the strangerということ。

▶ makingはpeopleを修飾する現在分詞。

⑩ Another study examined whether anybody would take candy that was reserved for children who were participating in a developmental program.

▶ whether ～ programがexaminedの目的語。whether ～は「～かどうか」。

▶ that以下はcandyを先行詞とする関係代名詞節で、さらに節内にchildrenを先行詞とする関係代名詞whoが続く。that以下は、「発達プログラムに参加している子どもたちのために用意された（キャンディ）」の意味。

▶ participate in ～は「～に参加する」（≒ take part in ～）。

⑪ People who felt rich took twice as much candy as those who felt poor.

▶ People who felt richは「自分が金持ちだと思う（大人の）人々」。

▶ twice as much ～ as ...は「…の2倍の～」、those who ～は「～する人々」（≒ people who ～）。

✍ 次の英文を日本語に直しなさい。

People who ask questions usually gain twice as much knowledge as those who stay quiet.

質問をする人はたいてい ＿＿＿＿＿＿＿＿＿＿＿＿＿＿＿＿＿＿＿＿＿＿＿＿＿＿＿＿＿＿。

⑫ Of course, it is not only wealthy people who show these patterns of behavior.

▶ it is ～ who ...は強調構文。not only wealthy people「裕福な人々だけではない」が強調されている。

✍ 次の英文を完成させなさい。

よく友人から支援を受けるのは親切な人だ。

(　　　) is kind people (　　　) often get support from their friends.

▶ these patterns of behavior「こうした行動パターン」とは、直前の3段落で述べられてきた裕福な人々にみられる行動のこと。

⑬ In fact, most of us in our regular daily lives struggle to decide when or whether to put our own interests above the interests of other people.

▶ In factは「実際に」、in our regular daily livesは「私たちの普段の日常生活での」。

▶ struggle to *do*は「苦労して～する」。

▶ when or whether to *do*は「いつ～すべきか、あるいは～すべきかどうか」。

▶ put ～ above ...は「…より～を優先する」(≒ treat ～ as more important than ...)、interestsは「利益」(≒ benefit)。

✍ 次の英文を日本語に直しなさい。

I want to put helping my classmates above competing with them.
私はクラスメイトと競争するより、＿＿＿＿＿＿＿＿＿＿＿＿。

▶ struggle以下は、「他人の利益より自分の利益をいつ優先すべきか、あるいは優先すべきかどうかを苦労して決める」という意味。

⑭ This is understandable because most people like to think that we all have an equal opportunity to succeed and prosper as long as we apply ourselves and work hard.

▶ Thisは⑬の文の内容を指している。

▶ equal opportunity to succeed and prosperは「成功して栄える平等な機会」。

▶ as long as ～は「～である限り、～さえすれば」(≒ only if ～)、apply *oneself*は「一生懸命やる、専念する」(≒ work hard)。

✍ 次の英文を日本語に直しなさい。

You can play music, as long as it's not too loud.
＿＿＿＿＿＿＿＿＿＿＿＿＿＿＿＿音楽をかけていいですよ。

⑮ But Piff's studies show that the wealthier people are, the more likely they are to pursue personal success without thinking about others.

▶ that以下は〈the＋比較級～, the＋比較級 ...〉「～すればするほどますます…」の文。

▶ be likely to *do*「～する傾向がある」のlikelyがthe moreと共に主語theyの前に置かれている。

▶ pursueは「～を追求する」、without V-ingは「～することなしに」。

教科書pp.148～149 *ll*.109～140 Ⅳ

Economic Inequality

①Today, the world is experiencing unprecedented levels of economic inequality. ②In America, the top 20 percent of the population owns close to 90 percent of the total wealth in the country. ③The dream that hard work and honesty will lead to success is increasingly out of reach for many. ④This pattern will never change if the wealthy feel that they are free to do whatever will serve their self-interest. ⑤There's every reason to think that things will only get worse.

⑥Economic inequality is something everyone should be concerned about. ⑦Social mobility, physical health, and social trust all decline as inequality increases. ⑧Not only that, violence and crime increase as economic inequality increases. ⑨These outcomes are felt across all levels of society. ⑩Even people at the top experience these outcomes.

⑪To sum up, economic inequality is not just a personal issue, or even a national issue. ⑫It is a matter of great international concern. ⑬In 2021, research showed that just the 10 richest individuals in the world owned a greater amount of wealth than the bottom 3.1 billion people. ⑭And inequality is expected to increase.

このセクションの内容

今日、経済的不平等はこれまでにないほど拡大し、勤勉さや誠実さが（A.　　　　　）につながるという夢はますます遠のいている。不平等が拡大すれば、社会的移動、身体的健康、社会的信頼が低下し、暴力や（B.　　　　　）が増えて、社会全体に影響を及ぼす。経済的不平等は今や国際的な関心事で、この不平等はさらに（C.　　　　　）するだろう。

① Today, the world is experiencing unprecedented levels of economic inequality.

▶ unprecedentedは「先例のない、空前の」。*cf.* precedent「先行する」

✍ 次の英文を日本語に直しなさい。

They experienced unprecedented economic growth.

____

▶ inequalityは「不平等」。つまり、世界では先例がないほどに不平等が拡大してきているということ。

② In America, the top 20 percent of the population owns close to 90 percent of the total wealth in the country.

▶ the top 20 percent of ～は「～の上位20パーセント」、close to ～は「およそ[だいたい]～」(≒ nearly ～)。

▶ アメリカの人口の上位20パーセントが、(アメリカ)国内の富全体のおよそ90パーセントを所有しているということ。

③ The dream that hard work and honesty will lead to success is increasingly out of reach for many.

▶ that以下はthe dreamの内容を説明する節(同格)で、successまでが文全体の主語。

▶ hard work and honestyは「勤勉さと誠実さ」、lead to ～は「～に通じる、～につながる」。

▶ be out of reachは「手の届かないところにある[不可能な]」(≒ be impossible)。

✍ 英文を完成させなさい。

宇宙旅行はほとんどの人にとって不可能なままだ。

Space travel remains out (　　　) (　　　) for most people.

▶ for manyはfor many peopleのこと。

④ This pattern will never change if the wealthy feel that they are free to do whatever will serve their self-interest.

▶ This pattern「この傾向」は、③の文の内容を指している。

▶ the wealthyは〈the＋形容詞〉の形で、wealthy peopleを表す。

▶ be free to *do*は「自由に～できる、～することは自由だ」。

▶ whatever ～は複合関係代名詞の節で、「～(するもの)は何でも」の意味の名詞節をつくる。なお、副詞節をつくる場合は「何[どんな…]が～しても」という意味になる。

例 You can buy *whatever* you need.
「あなたが必要なものは何でも買っていいですよ」
Stay positive *whatever* challenges you face.
「どんな困難に直面しても、前向きでいなさい」

▶ serve *one's* self-interestは「自分の利益になる[役立つ]」。

▶ if節は「もし裕福な人々が、自分の利益になることなら何でも自由にできると感じているなら」という意味になる。

⑤ There's every reason to think that things will only get worse.

このセクションの内容 の答え→ A. 成功 B. 犯罪 C. 拡大

▶ There is every reason to *do* は「～するのはもっともだ、～する理由は十分にある」(≒ There's very good reason to *do*)。

✍ 英文を完成させなさい。

嵐の間は、屋内にいる理由は十分にある。

During a thunderstorm, there is (　　　) (　　　) to stay indoors.

▶ things will only get worse は「事態はより悪くなるだけだろう」。ここでは、不平等や格差が大きくなることを表す。

⑥ Economic inequality is something everyone should be concerned about.

▶ be something ～は「～なほどの(重要な)こと[もの]」の意味で、重要性や価値などが高いことを伝える。something のあとに関係代名詞の that が省略されている。

▶ be concerned about ～は「～に関心を向ける、～を真剣に考える」(≒ think seriously about ～)。

✍ 英文を完成させなさい。

彼らは近隣で増加する犯罪率を真剣に考えている。

They are (　　　) (　　　) the rising crime rates in the neighborhood.

⑦ Social mobility, physical health, and social trust all decline as inequality increases.

▶ Social mobility, physical health, and social trust「社会的移動[流動性]、身体的健康、社会的信頼」が文の主語。social mobility とは、家族や個人が低所得層から中所得層に移動するような、社会階層間の移動を表す。階層間の移動がしやすい社会とは、努力が報われやすい社会とみなされる。

▶ decline は「低下する」、as ～は「～するにつれて」。ここでは、as 以下の内容と主節の内容は反比例の関係を表す。

✍ 次の英文を日本語に直しなさい。

As the temperature goes down, energy consumption rises.

＿＿＿＿＿＿＿＿＿＿＿＿＿＿＿＿＿＿電力の消費量は上がる。

⑧ Not only that, violence and crime increase as economic inequality increases.

▶ Not only that は「それだけではなく」。that は⑦の文の「社会的移動、身体的健康、社会的信頼の低下」を指している。

▶ violence and crime は「暴力と犯罪」。

⑨ These outcomes are felt across all levels of society.

▶ These outcomes「これらの結果」とは、⑦と⑧の文の不平等が拡大して起こることを指している。

▶ feelは、ここでは「〜の影響を受ける、〜を体感する」の意味。≒ People across all levels of society feel these outcomes.

✍ 次の英文を日本語に直しなさい。

Advances in technology are felt in various industries.

技術の進歩は、＿＿＿＿＿＿＿＿＿＿＿＿＿＿＿＿＿＿＿＿。

▶ across all levels of societyは「社会のすべての階層で」。

⑩ Even people at the top experience these outcomes.

▶ Evenは「〜でさえ」、at the topは「最上部の」(≒ at the highest point)。*cf.* people at the bottom「最下層の人々」

⑪ To sum up, economic inequality is not just a personal issue, or even a national issue.

▶ To sum upは「要約すれば」。

▶ not just 〜, or even ...は「単なる〜ではなく、…でさえない」。

⑫ It is a matter of great international concern.

▶ Itはeconomic inequalityを指す。

▶ a matter of 〜は「〜の事がら[問題]」。a matter of great international concernで「重大な国際的関心事」の意味。

✍ 英文を完成させなさい。

デザインの違いは、単に好みの問題だ。

The difference in design is just a (　　　) (　　　) taste.

⑬ In 2021, research showed that just the 10 richest individuals in the world owned a greater amount of wealth than the bottom 3.1 billion people.

▶ research showed that 〜は「調査は〜ということを示した」。

▶ a greater amount of wealth than 〜は「〜より多くの富」。

▶ the bottom 3.1 billion peopleは「最下層の31億の人々(が所有する富の量)」の意味。

⑭ And inequality is expected to increase.

▶ be expected to *do*は「〜すると予想される」。expectはよい意味(期待)でも悪い意味(懸念)でも使われる。

例 Over twenty million tourists *are expected to* come to Japan this year.
「今年は2,000万人以上の観光客が来日することが期待されている」

教科書pp.149～150 *ll*.141～187 V

Little Nudges

①So what can we do? ②It seems that the situation is out of control and there is nothing we can do about it. ③But, in fact, laboratory research has been finding that small nudges in certain directions, small changes in people's values, can restore levels of empathy. ④Reminding people of the benefits of cooperation, or the advantages of community, can lead wealthier individuals to be just as generous and empathetic as poor people.

⑤In one study, people were asked to watch a short video about childhood poverty that served as a reminder of the needs of others. ⑥After watching the video, researchers looked at how willing people were to help a stranger. ⑦Rich people became just as generous and willing to help out a stranger as poor people. ⑧This finding suggests that these differences in empathy and fellow feeling are not innate but are easily influenced by slight changes in people's values and by little nudges toward compassion and empathy.

⑨Beyond the walls of his lab, Piff feels he is beginning to see signs of change in society. ⑩Bill Gates, one of the world's wealthiest people, has called inequality the greatest challenge of our time. ⑪He has talked about what must be done to combat it, saying, "Humanity's greatest advances are not in its discoveries—but in how those discoveries are applied to reduce inequity." ⑫And there's the Giving Pledge, in which more than 100 of America's wealthiest people are pledging half of their fortunes to charity. ⑬They are using their own economic resources to combat inequality. ⑭In the end, they hope to restore people's faith that hard work and honesty will lead to a better life for themselves and their children.

このセクションの内容

不平等が拡大する社会で、私たちに何ができるだろうか。ある研究では、小さな働きかけと小さな（A.　　　　　）の変化で、共感のレベルが（B.　　　　　）することがわかってきている。さらに、大富豪のビル・ゲイツが不平等の解消を訴え、富裕層が多くの財産を（C.　　　　　）に寄付するなど、社会に不平等と戦うきざしが見え始めている。

① So what can we do?

▶前のセクションの「不平等はさらに拡大すると予想されている」ことを受けて、私たちに何ができるかと疑問を投げかけている。

② It seems that the situation is out of control and there is nothing we can do about it.

▶It seems that ～は「～だと思われる」。Itはthat節を指す形式主語。

▶be out of controlは「制御不能な」(≒be impossible to control)。

✍英文を完成させなさい。

物価の上昇は、制御できないようだ。

Rising prices seems to be (　　　) of (　　　).

▶there is nothing we can do about itは「それ(＝現状)について私たちにできることは何もない」。we ～ itはnothingを修飾する節で、itはthe situationを指す。

③ But, in fact, laboratory research has been finding that small nudges in certain directions, small changes in people's values, can restore levels of empathy.

▶in factは「実際は」、laboratory researchは「実験室での調査」。

▶has been finding that ～は「～を(継続的に)見つけてきた」。

▶small nudges in certain directionsは「ある方向への小さな働きかけ」。nudgeは「軽く押すこと」→「そっと促すこと」の意味。

▶small changes in people's valuesは「人々の価値観の小さな変化」。直前の働きかけによって引き起こされた変化のこと。

▶restoreは「～を回復する」。

④ Reminding people of the benefits of cooperation, or the advantages of community, can lead wealthier individuals to be just as generous and empathetic as poor people.

▶Reminding ～は動名詞句で文の主語。〈remind＋人＋of ～〉は「(人)に～を思い出させる」の意味で、Reminding people of the benefits of cooperationは「協力の利益[利点]を思い出させること」。

▶挿入句のor the advantages of community「または地域社会の利点」はthe benefits of cooperationの言いかえ。

▶〈lead＋人＋to *do*〉は「(人)に～させる[するように仕向ける]」。

▶just as ～ as ...は「ちょうど…と同じくらい～」。

▶generousは「寛大な、気前のよい」、empatheticは「共感力のある」。

⑤ In one study, people were asked to watch a short video about childhood poverty that served as a reminder of the

このセクションの内容 の答え→ A. 価値観 B. 回復 C. 慈善事業[活動]

needs of others.

▶ be asked to *do* は「～するように依頼される」。

▶ childhood poverty は「子どもの貧困」。

▶ that は a short video about childhood poverty を先行詞とする関係代名詞。

▶ serve as ～は「～として役立つ、～になる」、a reminder of ～は「～を思い出させるもの」。

▶ that 以下は「他人が必要としているものを思い出させてくれる（ビデオ）」の意味。

⑥ **After watching the video, researchers looked at how willing people were to help a stranger.**

▶ look at how ～は「どれだけ～かを調べる」。how 以下は間接疑問。

▶ be willing to *do* は「～するのをいとわない、喜んで～する」。

▶ how 以下は「人々がどれだけ喜んで見知らぬ人を助けるか」の意味。

⑦ **Rich people became just as generous and willing to help out a stranger as poor people.**

▶ just as ～ as ... は「ちょうど…と同じくらい～」。

▶ help out ～は「（困難な状況から）～を助け出す」（≒ help ～ who is in a difficult situation）。

✍ 次の英文を日本語に直しなさい。

The volunteers helped out the families affected by the natural disaster.

ボランティアは、＿＿＿＿＿＿＿＿＿＿＿＿＿＿＿＿＿＿＿＿。

⑧ **This finding suggests that these differences in empathy and fellow feeling are not innate but are easily influenced by slight changes in people's values and by little nudges toward compassion and empathy.**

▶ This finding とは、⑦の文の内容を指す。

▶ these differences in empathy and fellow feeling は「共感や仲間意識におけるこうした違い」。

▶ innate は「生まれつきの」。

▶ be influenced by ～は「～によって影響される」。by slight changes ～と by little nudges ～が並列している。

⑨ **Beyond the walls of his lab, Piff feels he is beginning to see signs of change in society.**

▶ Beyond the walls of ～は「～の壁を越えて、～の外では」（≒ outside of ～）。

▶ lab は laboratory「実験室」の略語。

▶ signs of change in society は「社会での変化のきざし」。

⑩ Bill Gates, one of the world's wealthiest people, has called inequality the greatest challenge of our time.

▶ one of the world's wealthiest people「世界的大富豪の一人」は、Bill Gates「ビル・ゲイツ」の補足説明(同格)。

▶〈call + O + C〉は「OをCと呼ぶ」。

▶ the greatest challenge of our timeは「私たちの時代の最大の課題」。

⑪ He has talked about what must be done to combat it, saying, "Humanity's greatest advances are not in its discoveries—but in how those discoveries are applied to reduce inequity."

▶ what must be done to combat itは「それ(=不平等)と戦うために何がなされなければならないか[なされなければならないこと]」。

▶ saying ～は〈付帯状況〉を表す分詞構文で、「そして～と言った」の意味。

▶ not in ～ but in ... は「～にあるのではなく…にある」。

▶ its discoveriesのitsはhumanityを指す。

▶ be applied to *do*は「～することに利用される」。

▶引用符(" ")内は「人類の偉大な進歩は、発見にあるのではなく、その発見を不平等の解消のためにどうやって利用するかにある」という意味。

⑫ And there's the Giving Pledge, in which more than 100 of America's wealthiest people are pledging half of their fortunes to charity.

▶ the Giving Pledgeは、ビル・ゲイツを含めた富裕層たちの慈善活動。

▶〈, in which〉は非制限用法の関係代名詞節で、the Giving Pledgeについて補足説明している。

▶ pledge ～ to ... は「(寄付など) ～を…に与えることを誓う」。

▶ fortuneは「財産、富」。

⑬ They are using their own economic resources to combat inequality.

▶ Theyとtheirは、⑫の文のmore than 100 of America's wealthiest peopleを指している。

▶ economic resourcesは「財産、経済資源」(≒ fortune)。

⑭ In the end, they hope to restore people's faith that hard work and honesty will lead to a better life for themselves and their children.

▶ In the endは「最終的には、最後には」。

▶ people's faith that ～は「～という人々の信念」で、that以下はpeople's faithの内容を説明している(同格)。

確認問題

語彙

1 次の文の意味が通るように、( )内の語を適する形にしなさい。

(1) The (economy) situation is serious in that country.
(2) Are you sure of his (honest)?
(3) Music and dancing are the essence of (celebrate).
(4) The (pursue) of happiness is one of the most basic human rights.

2 次の各組でアクセントの位置が同じなら○、異なるなら×を書きなさい。

(1) (pros-per in-nate)
(2) (out-come for-tune)
(3) (met-a-phor gen-er-ous)
(4) (em-pa-thet-ic par-tic-i-pate)

文法・表現

1 日本語に合うように、( )内に適切な語を入れなさい。

(1) 練習が完璧を生む[継続は力なり]と信じるのはもっともだ。
There is every (　　　) (　　　) believe that practice makes perfect.
(2) 結局、彼女は一人暮らしをすることに決めた。
(　　　) (　　　) (　　　), she decided to live alone.
(3) 私たちは自分の命を何よりも優先するべきだ。
We must (　　　) our lives (　　　) everything.
(4) 静かにしている限り、この部屋にいてもいいですよ。
You can stay in this room as (　　　) (　　　) you keep quiet.
(5) 私はプロのダンサーになるのが不可能だとわかった。
I found that becoming a professional dancer was (　　　) of (　　　).
(6) 手紙を書くことはだんだん人気がなくなってきている。
Writing letters is becoming (　　　) (　　　) (　　　) popular.

2 日本語に合うように、( )内の語句を並べかえなさい。

(1) その新ルールは私たちのチームに有利に働いた。
The new rule (of / in / worked / favor / our team).
The new rule ____.
(2) 科学者は、新しいワクチンの開発に打ち込んできた。
Scientists (themselves / have / new vaccines / developing / applied / to).
Scientists ____.

(3) 天才の物の見方はふつうの人とは異なると思う。
I think (see / differently / things / ordinary people / from / geniuses).
I think ________________________________.

(4) 人々は飲料水の汚染を心配している。
People (about / are / drinking water / the pollution / of / concerned).
People ________________________________.

総合

次の文を読んで、あとの問いに答えなさい。

So what can we do? ①It (out / that / control / seems / is / of / the situation) and there is nothing we can do about it. But, in fact, laboratory research has been finding that small nudges in certain directions, small changes in people's values, can restore levels of empathy. Reminding people (②) the benefits of cooperation, or the advantages of community, can lead wealthier individuals to be just as generous and empathetic as poor people.

In one study, people were asked to watch a short video about childhood poverty that served as a reminder of the needs of others. ③After watching the video, researchers looked at how willing people were to help a stranger. Rich people became just as generous and willing to help out a stranger as poor people. ④This finding suggests that these differences in empathy and fellow feeling are not innate but are easily influenced by slight changes in people's values and by little nudges toward (⑤) and empathy.

Beyond the walls of his lab, Piff feels he is beginning to see signs of change in society. Bill Gates, one of the world's wealthiest people, has called inequality the greatest (⑥) of our time.

問1 下線部①が、「状況は制御できず、私たちにできることは何もないように思われる」という意味になるように、( )内の語句を並べかえなさい。
問2 (②)に入る最も適切な前置詞を書きなさい。
問3 下線部③を日本語に直しなさい。
問4 下線部④の内容を具体的に日本語で説明しなさい。
問5 (⑤)(⑥)に適する語を下から選んで入れなさい。
〔challenge portion compassion concern〕

Story 1 The Silent Miaow

教科書pp.158～159 *ll*.1～31 I

①When I was a very young kitten I had the bad luck to lose my mother and find myself alone in the world at the age of six weeks. ②After a week or so in the country living off a most revolting diet of grubs and insects, I determined to take over a family and become a house cat, and I set about immediately to achieve my ends.

③I emerged from the woods, hungry and disgusted with nature in the raw, to see, standing in a clearing, a small, white house with green-painted shutters. ④There was a barn nearby, a flower and vegetable garden, a small grape arbor, a fish pond, etc. ⑤The house and the grounds were neat and well-kept, and obviously belonged to persons of some affluence.

⑥I went to the back door of the house and looked around. A man and his wife were having breakfast inside. ⑦This pair looked exactly like the family I wanted, so I jumped onto the screen door, clung there, and cried piteously. They looked up at me from their breakfast.

The woman said, "Oh, look! ⑧The poor little thing, it wants to come in. Maybe it's hungry. I'll give it some milk."

⑨Just as I expected! ⑩I had her. ⑪All I needed was to get one paw inside the door.

⑫However, it wasn't going to be all that simple. The man! ⑬He began to shout, bellowing that he hated cats and he wouldn't have one in the house.

⑭"Oho!" I said to myself. ⑮"This man is trouble, but I can handle him."

⑯The woman opened the door and picked me up, saying to him, "Oh, don't make such a fuss, darling. ⑰I'll just give her some milk. We'll put her out afterward." ⑱And, of course, the more she fussed over me the angrier he got until finally he shouted, "Okay now, that's enough! ⑲Come on, get it out of here."

このセクションの内容

生後６週間で身寄りをなくした子猫は、（A.　　　　　）になることにした。林から出た猫は小ぎれいな白い家を見つけ、中では（B.　　　　　）が朝食をとっていた。女性は猫に（C.　　　　　）をやろうとするが、猫が嫌いな男性は怒り、家から出すように言った。

① **When I was a very young kitten I had the bad luck to lose my mother and find myself alone in the world at the age of six weeks.**

▶ When節はkittenまで。物語は子猫の視点で描かれる。

▶ the bad luck to *do*は「〜するという運の悪さ」。to以下は、lose 〜とfind 〜が並列している。

▶ find *oneself* 〜は「(気がつくと) 〜 (の状態) にある[いる]」。find myself aloneで「一人になる」。

▶ at the age of six weeksは「生後6週間で」。

② **After a week or so in the country living off a most revolting diet of grubs and insects, I determined to take over a family and become a house cat, and I set about immediately to achieve my ends.**

▶〜 or soは「〜かそこら、〜ほど」。

▶ live off 〜は「〜に頼って生きる」。living 〜は分詞構文で、「〜したあと」と動作の連続を表す。*cf.* live on 〜「〜を食べて生きる」

▶ a most revolting dietは「非常に不快な食事」。

▶ determine to *do*は「〜しようと決心する」、take over 〜は「〜を乗っ取る、〜を支配する」(≒ get control of 〜)。

✍ 次の英文を日本語に直しなさい。

The pirates took over the ship and stole its treasures.

海賊は＿＿＿＿＿＿＿＿＿＿＿＿＿＿＿＿＿＿＿＿＿＿＿＿。

▶ set about 〜は「〜に着手する[とりかかる]」(≒ begin 〜)。aboutのあとの目的語は直前のto take over 〜になるため、省略されている。

▶ to achieve *one's* endsは「目的を達成するために」。

③ **I emerged from the woods, hungry and disgusted with nature in the raw, to see, standing in a clearing, a small, white house with green-painted shutters.**

▶ emerge from 〜は「〜から出てくる」、woodsは「小さな森、林」。

▶ hungry 〜 rawは、主語の状態を補足説明している。

▶ disgusted with nature in the rawは「ありのままの自然にうんざりして」。in the rawは「自然の[ありの]ままの、むき出しの」(≒ uncontrolled)。

▶ to see 〜は結果を表す不定詞で、「林を出たら〜が見えた」という意味。

✍ 英文を完成させなさい。

彼女は成長して、有名なバイオリニストになった。

She (　　　) up (　　　) (　　　) a famous violinist.

このセクションの内容 の答え→ A. 家猫 B. 夫婦[男女] C. ミルク

▶ a small, white house with green-painted shuttersがseeの目的語。挿入句のstanding in a clearing「開拓地に建っている」は現在分詞の句で、a small, white houseについて補足説明する。

④ There was a barn nearby, a flower and vegetable garden, a small grape arbor, a fish pond, etc.

▶ nearbyは「近くに」、grape arborは「ブドウ棚」。

▶ etc.は「その他の種々のもの」の意味で、ラテン語のet ceteraの略。

⑤ The house and the grounds were neat and well-kept, and obviously belonged to persons of some affluence.

▶ neatは「きちんとした、小ぎれいな」、well-keptは「手入れの行き届いた」。

▶ persons of some affluenceは「かなり裕福な人たち」。of ～は「～の性質[特徴]を持つ」の意味。*cf.* a person of importance「重要人物」

⑥ I went to the back door of the house and looked around.

▶ back doorは「裏口」、look aroundは「周囲を見回す、見て回る」。

⑦ This pair looked exactly like the family I wanted, so I jumped onto the screen door, clung there, and cried piteously.

▶ This pairは、直前の文のA man and his wifeを指す。

▶ exactly like ～は「ちょうど～のような」。

▶ screen doorは「網戸」。アメリカの戸建ての家では、入り口のドアに網戸が付いていることがある。

▶ clungはcling「しがみつく」の過去形。

▶ piteouslyは「哀れに、悲しそうに」。*cf.* pity「哀れみ、残念なこと」

⑧ The poor little thing, it wants to come in.

▶ The poor little thing「かわいそうなおチビちゃん」とは猫のこと。

⑨ Just as I expected!

▶ as I expectedは「予想[期待]したように」(様態)。justは強調。ここでは、女性が猫を気にかけてミルクを与えようとしたことが、猫にとって予想通りだったということ。

⑩ I had her.

▶ haveは「～を自分のものにする、～をつかまえる」で、文全体で「私は彼女をものにした」の意味。

⑪ All I needed was to get one paw inside the door.

▶ All I needed was to *do*は「私は～しさえすればよかった」。

▶ 〈get + O + C〉は「OをCの状態にする」。get one paw inside the doorで「片足をドアの内側に入れる」の意味。

⑫ However, it wasn't going to be all that simple.

▶ itは猫が夫婦をものにしようとしている状況を指す。

▶ all that ～はnotを伴って「それほど～（ではない）」。⑪の文を受けて、片足を入れるだけでうまくいくほど簡単にいきそうではなかったということ。

⑬ He began to shout, bellowing that he hated cats and he wouldn't have one in the house.

▶ bellowing that～は〈付帯状況〉の分詞構文で、「～だとどなって言いながら」の意味。

▶ wouldn't *do*は「～するつもりはない」（意志）。

⑭ "Oho!" I said to myself.

▶ say to *oneself*は「（心の中で）考える［思う］」。

✍ 英文を完成させなさい。

彼女は「絶対にあきらめない」と心の中で思った。

She (　　　) (　　　) (　　　), "I'll never give up."

⑮ "This man is trouble, but I can handle him."

▶ troubleは「面倒（なこと）」、handleは「～を（うまく）扱う」。

⑯ The woman opened the door and picked me up, saying to him, "Oh, don't make such a fuss, darling.

▶ pick ～ upは「～を拾い［抱き］上げる」。

▶ saying ～は〈付帯状況〉の分詞構文で、「～と言いながら［そして～と言った］」の意味。

▶ make a fussは「大騒ぎをする」。

⑰ I'll just give her some milk.

▶ 女性は猫をitと言っていたが、ここでは親しみを込めて人称代名詞のherを使っている。

⑱ And, of course, the more she fussed over me the angrier he got until finally he shouted, "Okay now, that's enough!

▶ 〈the + 比較級～, the + 比較級 ...〉「～すればするほどますます…」の文。

▶ fuss over ～は「～をかわいがる［ちやほやする］」。

✍ 次の英文を日本語に直しなさい。

He fusses over his daughter as if she were a little girl.

____

▶ until finallyは「そしてついに」、that's enoughは「もう十分だ、いい加減にしろ」。

⑲ Come on, get it out of here."

▶ Come onは、ここでは女性をせかして「さあ、早く」の意味。

▶ get ～ out of ...は「～を…から（外に）出す」。

教科書pp.159〜161 *ll*.32〜66 Ⅱ

①The woman did this, but as soon as she turned around, I followed her back to the house. ②We did this three times, while the man came out of the house, got into his car, and watched us. ③The fourth time I just sat down in the woods and looked miserable. ④The man kissed his wife goodbye, but the last thing he did before he drove away was to turn around to see me sitting there, all alone, by myself. ⑤I was satisfied because I was sure that I had spoiled his day, and all he would be able to think of would be me.

⑥Of course, as soon as the car had disappeared down the road, the wife came out of the house, picked me up and carried me back inside, as I knew she would. ⑦I had her where I wanted her. We had a lovely day together.

⑧Just before evening the woman took me in her arms, kissed me, and said, "Now, Kitty, I'm afraid you must go. ⑨He'll be coming back." ⑩She put me out, and soon the headlights of the car came around the corner and the man came home.

⑪I stayed until it was quite dark and then, feeling sorry for myself, because I was lonely and hungry again, I sat outside the screen door and just cried and cried and cried.

The light was on in the dining room. ⑫Through the window I saw them eating their supper. I went and sat under the window and cried louder. ⑬I put everything I had into my miaows. ⑭They would have melted a heart of stone.

The woman said, "Oh, the poor little thing, she must be hungry again."

⑮The man shouted, "For heaven's sake then, why don't you let it in and feed it?" ⑯So the woman came out and fetched me and I had another good meal, and after dinner, instead of putting me out, she took me onto her lap, where she played with me, and I at once began to purr and make up to her. ⑰The man was reading his newspaper, but every so often he would put it down and throw us black looks.

⑱After a while the woman put me onto her chair and went out of the room. ⑲Then she called down from upstairs, "Oh, darling, I'm almost ready for bed. Will you put the cat out?"

このセクションの内容

男性が出かけると、女性は猫を抱き上げて家に入り、共に楽しく過ごしたが、男性が（A.　　　　　）する前に猫を外に出した。猫が（B.　　　　　）の下で鳴くと、男性は家に入れることを許して、猫は餌を与えられた。（C.　　　　　）時間になると、女性は男性に猫を外に出すように頼んだ。

① The woman did this, but as soon as she turned around, I followed her back to the house.

▶ did thisとは、直前の男性の指示で、猫を家の外に出すこと。

▶ as soon as ～は「～するとすぐに」。

▶ follow *one's* back to ～は「～まで…の後ろをついて行く」。

② We did this three times, while the man came out of the house, got into his car, and watched us.

▶ did thisは①の文の内容で、女性が猫を家の外へ出し、猫が家に入ろうとする女性の後ろをついて行くこと。

▶ whileは「一方で～」の意味で、女性と猫のやり取りのかたわらで、男性がしたことを伝える。

③ The fourth time I just sat down in the woods and looked miserable.

▶ The fourth timeとは、①の文の女性と猫のやり取りの４度目を表す。

▶ miserableは「みじめな」。

④ The man kissed his wife goodbye, but the last thing he did before he drove away was to turn around to see me sitting there, all alone, by myself.

▶ kiss ～ goodbyeは「～に別れのキスをする」。

▶ the last thing he didは「彼が最後にしたこと」。

▶ drive awayは「車で出かける」（≒ drive off）。

▶ to turn ～は名詞的用法の不定詞で文の補語、to see ～は副詞的用法の不定詞。

▶ 〈see + O + V-ing〉は「Oが～しているのを見る」。

▶ all aloneとby myselfはsittingを修飾する副詞句。

⑤ I was satisfied because I was sure that I had spoiled his day, and all he would be able to think of would be me.

▶ be sure that ～は「～だと確信している」。

▶ spoilは「～を台なしにする」で、had spoiledは過去完了。

▶ all he would be able to think ofは「彼が考えることができることのすべて」の意味で、and以下の節の主語にあたる。

▶ and以下は「彼が考えられるのは私のことだけだろう」の意味。

⑥ **Of course, as soon as the car had disappeared down the road, the wife came out of the house, picked me up and carried me back inside, as I knew she would.**

▶ down the roadは「道に沿って」。男性の車が道を通って出ていき、見えなくなったということ。

▶ carry ～ backは「～を戻す」。

▶ as I knew she wouldは「彼女がそうするだろうとわかっていた通りに」。wouldのあとにcome out of the house, pick me up and carry me back insideが省略されている。

⑦ **I had her where I wanted her.**

▶「私は彼女を、私の望むところで自分のものにした」とはつまり、「彼女は自分の思い通りになった」ということ。

▶ whereは接続詞で「～するところで」。

⑧ **Just before evening the woman took me in her arms, kissed me, and said, "Now, Kitty, I'm afraid you must go.**

▶ take me in her armsは「私を腕につかまえる[抱える]」。

▶ I'm afraid (that) ～は「残念ながら～のようだ」。

⑨ **He'll be coming back."**

▶ will be V-ingは未来進行形で、「～することになるだろう」の意味。

✍ 英文を完成させなさい。

バスは遅れているが、もうすぐ来るだろう。

The bus is late, but it (　　　) (　　　) (　　　) soon.

⑩ **She put me out, and soon the headlights of the car came around the corner and the man came home.**

▶ come around the cornerは「角を曲がってくる」。ヘッドライトを点けた車が(家の敷地に)入ってきた様子を描写した文。

⑪ **I stayed until it was quite dark and then, feeling sorry for myself, because I was lonely and hungry again, I sat outside the screen door and just cried and cried and cried.**

▶ feeling ～は〈付帯状況〉の分詞構文で、「～を感じながら」の意味。

▶ feel sorry for *oneself*は「自分を哀れむ、わが身を嘆く」。

⑫ **Through the window I saw them eating their supper.**

▶〈see + O + V-ing〉で「Oが～しているのを見る」。

このセクションの内容 の答え→ A. 帰宅 B. 窓 C. 寝る[就寝]

⑬ I put everything I had into my miaows.

▶ put ~ into ... は「~を…の中に入れる[込める]」。

▶ everything I had は「私が持っていたすべて」→「ありったけの思い」。

▶ miaows は「ミァオ」という猫の鳴き声の複数形。

⑭ They would have melted a heart of stone.

▶ They は⑬の文の my miaows を指す。

▶ would have melted a heart of stone は仮定法過去完了で、「石の(ように冷たい)心でも溶かしただろう」の意味。

⑮ The man shouted, "For heaven's sake then, why don't you let it in and feed it?"

▶ For heaven's sake は「お願いだから」(≒ For goodness(') sake)。いらだちや怒りを表して、頼みごとなどを強調する。

▶ let ~ in は「~を入れてやる」、feed は「(動物など)にえさをやる」。

⑯ So the woman came out and fetched me and I had another good meal, and after dinner, instead of putting me out, she took me onto her lap, where she played with me, and I at once began to purr and make up to her.

▶ fetch は「~を取ってくる」。

▶ 〈, where〉は関係副詞の非制限用法で、先行詞は her lap。

▶ purr は「(猫が喜んで)ゴロゴロとのどを鳴らす」、make up to ~は「~に取り入る、~にこびへつらう」。

✍ 次の英文を日本語に直しなさい。

The students tried to make up to their teacher by offering help.
手伝いを申し出ることで、＿＿＿＿＿＿＿＿＿＿＿＿＿＿＿＿。

⑰ The man was reading his newspaper, but every so often he would put it down and throw us black looks.

▶ every so often は「ときどき」(≒ sometimes)。

▶ would *do* は「(よく) ~した(ものだ)」と習慣的動作を表す。

▶ put ~ down は「~を置く[下ろす]」。it は his newspaper を指す。

▶ throw ~ black looks は「~に不機嫌な視線を向ける」(≒ look at ~ angrily)。

⑱ After a while the woman put me onto her chair and went out of the room.

▶ After a while は「しばらくして」、go out of ~は「~を出る」。

⑲ Then she called down from upstairs, "Oh, darling, I'm almost ready for bed.

▶ call は「呼びかける」、down from upstairs は「2階[階上]から階下に」。

教科書pp.161～163 *ll*.67～95 Ⅲ

①The man shouted, "All right!" and picked me up, got a flashlight, and carried me out. ②He was most awkward holding me, and when I got my head under his chin he said, "Cut it out, Kitty," and I knew I could have had him right then and there. ③But I wasn't in any hurry. ④I knew now that I could take him whenever I wanted. ⑤I made up my mind to soften him up so that when the time came he would become my absolute slave. ⑥So, when he went to put me down in the woods, I just fastened my claws into his shirt and screamed.

He unfastened me and put me down. ⑦I kept on yelling as he went off, and of course, as I knew he would, he turned around and turned on his flashlight to see whether I was following him, which of course I was. ⑧He picked me up, saying, "Kitty, stay there!" ⑨I anchored myself to his shirt again. ⑩We kept going through this routine. ⑪He said, "Don't kid yourself, Kitty," and marched off with me, but this time he took me to the barn, where he rummaged about until he found an old cardboard box, into which he dumped me. He said, "There! You can stay there, and for heaven's sake keep quiet!" ⑫Then he walked off again but couldn't resist turning around and putting the light on to see if I was going to follow him again. ⑬This time I didn't. ⑭I just sat there looking at him, with my head showing above the box, and he stood looking at me. And so I gave him the Silent Miaow. ⑮When I give the Silent Miaow I open my mouth as if I am going to miaow. But no sounds come out. ⑯I look so sad that people give me anything I ask for.

⑰The man came all unstuck. ⑱He stood there looking absolutely helpless, saying, "For heaven's sake, Kitty, what do you want now?"

I gave him the Silent Miaow again.

このセクションの内容

男性に（A.　　　　　）へ運ばれるとき、猫はいつでも男性をものにできるとわかっていた。何度森に置いてもついてくるので、男性は猫を納屋にあった（B.　　　　　）に放り込んだ。男性が振り返ると、猫は「（C.　　　　　）のミャオ」を鳴き、男性の心をつかんだ。

① The man shouted, "All right!" and picked me up, got a flashlight, and carried me out.

▶ flashlightは「懐中電灯」、carry ～ outは「～を（外へ）運び出す」。

② He was most awkward holding me, and when I got my head under his chin he said, "Cut it out, Kitty," and I knew I could have had him right then and there.

▶ mostは副詞で「とても、たいそう」、awkwardは「ぎこちない」。

▶ holding ～は〈付帯状況〉の分詞構文で「～を抱きかかえながら」の意味。

▶ get ～ under ... は「～を…の下に移動させる」。

▶ Cut it outは「やめろ」（≒ Stop it）。

▶ could have had himは仮定法過去完了で、「（そうしようと思えば）彼を自分のものにすることができた」（実際はそうしなかった）の意味。

✍ 次の英文を日本語に直しなさい。

This medicine could have saved her life.

____

▶ then and thereは「その場ですぐに」（≒ at that moment and in that place）。

③ But I wasn't in any hurry.

▶ be not in any hurryは「少しも急いでいない」（≒ have a lot of time）。

④ I knew now that I could take him whenever I wanted.

▶ 過去の文で使われるnowは「その時」の意味。

▶ whenever I wantedは「私が望むときにいつでも」。

⑤ I made up my mind to soften him up so that when the time came he would become my absolute slave.

▶ make up *one's* mind to *do*は「～しようと決心する」。

▶ soften ～ upは「～の態度を軟化させる、～を丸め込む」（≒ make ～ more sympathetic）。

✍ 次の英文を日本語に直しなさい。

I tried to soften her up before asking her a favor.

頼みごとをする前に、______________________________。

▶ so that ～は「～するように」（目的）。

▶ when the time cameは「その時が来れば」。

⑥ So, when he went to put me down in the woods, I just fastened my claws into his shirt and screamed.

▶ go to *do*は「～しに行く」、fasten ～ into ... は「～を…に食い込ませる」。

⑦ I kept on yelling as he went off, and of course, as I knew he would, he turned around and turned on his flashlight to see

このセクションの内容 の答え→ A. 外[森、林] B. 段ボール（箱） C. 無言

whether I was following him, which of course I was.

▶ keep on V-ingは「～し続ける」。

▶ as he went offは「彼が立ち去るとき」。go offは「立ち去る」(≒ go away)。

▶ as I knew he wouldは「彼がそうするだろうとわかっていた通りに」。wouldのあとは、主節の動作が省略されている。

▶ to see whether ～は「～かどうかを見る[確かめる]ために」。

▶〈, which〉はhimを先行詞とする非制限用法の関係代名詞。wasのあとにfollowingが省略されている。

⑧ **He picked me up, saying, "Kitty, stay there!"**

▶ saying ～は〈付帯状況〉の分詞構文で、「～と言いながら」の意味。

⑨ **I anchored myself to his shirt again.**

▶ anchor ～ to ...は「～を…にしっかり固定する」。ここでは、猫が男性のシャツにしがみついたということ。

⑩ **We kept going through this routine.**

▶ keep V-ingは「～し続ける」。

▶ go through this routineは「同じことを繰り返す」。ここでは、次の流れになる。男性がしがみつく猫をシャツから引き剥がして森の地面に下ろす→男性が立ち去ろうとすると猫は鳴き続ける→男性は振り返って猫がついてきていないか懐中電灯で確認する→猫はついてきている→男性は猫を抱え上げる→猫は男性にしがみつく。

⑪ **He said, "Don't kid yourself, Kitty," and marched off with me, but this time he took me to the barn, where he rummaged about until he found an old cardboard box, into which he dumped me.**

▶ kid *oneself*は「(都合のよいように考えて)思い違いをする、勘違いする」(≒ deceive *oneself*)。

✍ 次の英文を日本語に直しなさい。

You should not kid yourself about your abilities.

自分の能力について ______________________________ 。

▶ march offは「(足早に)去る」(≒ go away)。

▶ rummage about「引っかき回してさがす」(≒ rummage around)。*cf.* look around「見回す、さがす」

▶ さがしていたものはan old cardboard box「古い段ボール箱」。

▶〈, into which〉は〈前置詞＋関係代名詞〉の形(非制限用法)で、先行詞はan old cardboard box。

▶ dumpは「(ゴミなど)を捨てる」。

⑫ **Then he walked off again but couldn't resist turning around and putting the light on to see if I was going to follow him again.**

▶ walk offは「(怒りや不満などで)急に(黙って)去る」(≒ go away)。

▶ resist V-ingは「〜することに抵抗する」。couldn't resist turning around で「振り返らずにはいられなかった」の意味。

▶ put 〜 onは「(器具など)のスイッチを入れる」(≒ turn 〜 on)。

▶ to see if 〜は「〜かどうかを確かめるために」(≒ to see whether 〜)。

⑬ **This time I didn't.**

▶ didn'tのあとにfollow himが省略されている。

⑭ **I just sat there looking at him, with my head showing above the box, and he stood looking at me.**

▶ sit (there) V-ingは「〜しながら座っている」。

▶ with 〜 V-ingは〈付帯状況〉を表し、「〜を…しながら」の意味。

✍ 英文を完成させなさい。

彼女は涙を流しながら本を読んでいた。

She was reading a book (　　　) (　　　) (　　　) down her face.

▶ stand V-ingは「〜しながら立っている」。

⑮ **When I give the Silent Miaow I open my mouth as if I am going to miaow.**

▶ タイトルでもあるthe Silent Miaowは、それが唯一の方法または概念であるかのように文中でも大文字で書かれている。

▶ as if I am going to miaowは「いかにもミァオと鳴くように」。

⑯ **I look so sad that people give me anything I ask for.**

▶ so 〜 that ...「とても〜なので…」の構文。

▶ anything I ask forは「私が求めるものは何でも」。

⑰ **The man came all unstuck.**

▶ come unstuckは「(計画などが)失敗する、行き詰まる」。allは強調を表し、「まったく、完全に」の意味。

⑱ **He stood there looking absolutely helpless, saying, "For heaven's sake, Kitty, what do you want now?"**

▶ stand (there) V-ingは「〜しながら立っている」、look helplessは「無力に[お手上げ状態に]見える」。

▶ saying 〜は〈付帯状況〉の分詞構文で、「〜と言いながら」の意味。

教科書pp.163〜164 *ll*.96〜126 Ⅳ

①He came back into the barn looking confused, picked me up out of the box, and said, "What the hell are you after, Kitty?"

②His wife must have been waiting at the door for him, for I heard her say, "Darling, what on earth have you been doing? ③You've been ages," and his reply, "I thought maybe it might be going to rain. I put the cat in the barn. ④She can stay there."

Ha! Ha! Ha! ⑤Me stay there! ⑥That was a good one! ⑦I laughed myself to sleep.

⑧Of course, after that it didn't take long at all, and the very next night I thought it was time to take him.

It was a hot, sultry summer evening. ⑨I was sitting on the woman's lap interfering with her sewing and the man was reading his newspaper as usual. ⑩Just then there was a flash of lightning and a crashing of thunder and it began to rain hard.

⑪Some time later the thunder and lightning went away, but it kept on raining and the woman said, "Will you put the cat out?"

⑫The man looked at her as though she were out of her mind and shouted, "What? ⑬Put her out on a night like this? Are you crazy?"

"Why? ⑭She'll be all right in the barn, won't she?"

⑮The man was furious. "Well, I don't want a cat in the house," he said. ⑯"But that doesn't mean putting her out in the rain. ⑰Look, she's trembling like a leaf!"

⑱Trembling was right. ⑲I was trying to keep from laughing out loud.

⑳I got onto the man's shoulder while he was reading the newspaper and stayed there. ㉑Suddenly he put the paper down, yawned, stretched, and remarked, "Bedtime, I guess. Come on, Kitty." ㉒Nothing was said about the barn. All of us went upstairs to bed.

㉓That's the way I entered my house.

このセクションの内容

男性は雨が降るかもしれないと言って、猫を（A.　　　　　）に入れた。次の夜には、猫は家の中で女性の（B.　　　　　）の上にいた。その夜、雷雨にもかかわらず女性が猫を外に出すように言うと、男性は猫をあわれんで激怒した。その後、猫は彼の（C.　　　　　）の上で過ごし、2人と猫はベッドに入った。こうして猫はこの家に入り込んだのだった。

① He came back into the barn looking confused, picked me up out of the box, and said, "What the hell are you after, Kitty?"

▶ looking confusedは「困惑した様子で」。

▶ What the hell ～？は「いったい全体～」（≒ What on earth ～？）。

▶ be after ～は「～がほしい、～を求めている」（≒ want ～）。

✍ 次の英文を日本語に直しなさい。

This is the kind of dress that she has been after.

____

② His wife must have been waiting at the door for him, for I heard her say, "Darling, what on earth have you been doing?

▶ must have been V-ingは「～していたに違いない」。

▶ for I heard her sayは「彼女が～を言うのを聞いたので」。forは接続詞。〈hear + O + *do*〉で「Oが～するのを聞く」。

▶ what on earth ～は「いったい全体～」（≒ what in the world ～）。

例 *What on earth* made you decide to quit your job?
≒ *What in the world* made you decide to quit your job?
「いったいどうして仕事を辞めると決めたのですか」

③ You've been ages," and his reply, "I thought maybe it might be going to rain.

▶ You've been agesは「あなたはずいぶん長くかかっている」。agesはa long timeを誇張した表現。

▶ mightは〈可能性・推量〉を表し、「～かもしれない」の意味。

▶ thought、maybe、mightなどのあいまいな表現から、男性が答えに窮していることがわかる。

④ She can stay there."

▶ 猫をitではなくsheと呼んでいることが、男性の心変わりを示している。

▶ thereはthe barnを指す。

⑤ Me stay there!

▶ MeはIの代用。「私は（すぐに）家に行くつもりだけどね！」と、男性の発言を嘲笑している。

⑥ That was a good one!

▶ Thatは、She can stay there.という男性の発言を指す。

▶ 皮肉を込めた表現で、「それはおもしろい冗談だ」の意味。

⑦ I laughed myself to sleep.

▶ laugh *oneself* to ～は「笑いすぎて～（の状態）になる」。*cf.* cry *oneself* to sleep「泣きつかれて寝てしまう」

✍ 次の英文を日本語に直しなさい。

I couldn't stop laughing myself to tears.

____

⑧ Of course, after that it didn't take long at all, and the very next night I thought it was time to take him.

▶ after thatのthatは、納屋での男性と猫のやり取りを指す。

▶ it didn't take long at allは「長くはまったくかからなかった」。

▶ the very next nightは「まさにその翌日の夜」。

▶ it is time to *do*は「～するとき[時期]だ」。

⑨ I was sitting on the woman's lap interfering with her sewing and the man was reading his newspaper as usual.

▶ interfering with ～は「～のじゃまをしながら」、sewingは「縫いもの」。

▶ as usualは「いつものように」。

⑩ Just then there was a flash of lightning and a crashing of thunder and it began to rain hard.

▶ Just thenは「ちょうどその時」。

▶ a flash of lightningは「稲妻の閃光」、a crashing of thunderは「落雷」。

⑪ Some time later the thunder and lightning went away, but it kept on raining and the woman said, "Will you put the cat out?"

▶ Some time laterは「しばらくして」。

▶ keep on V-ingは「～し続ける」。

⑫ The man looked at her as though she were out of her mind and shouted, "What?

▶ as though ～は「まるで～かのように」（≒ as if ～）。

▶ she were out of her mindは仮定法過去。be out of *one's* mindは「正気を失っている」（≒ be crazy）。

✍ 英文を完成させなさい。

そんな高価な車を買うなんて、彼は正気を失っているに違いない。

He must be (　　　) (　　　) his mind to buy such an expensive car.

このセクションの内容 の答え→ A. 納屋　B. ひざ　C. 肩

⑬ Put her out on a night like this?

▶ a night like thisとは、雷雨の夜のこと。

⑭ She'll be all right in the barn, won't she?"

▶ will be all rightは「大丈夫だろう」。

▶～, won't she?は付加疑問で「～ですよね」の意味。

⑮ The man was furious.

▶ furiousは「ひどく怒って」。⑭の文の女性の発言に怒っている。

⑯ "But that doesn't mean putting her out in the rain.

▶ thatは直前の文I don't want a cat in the houseを指している。

⑰ Look, she's trembling like a leaf!"

▶ trembleは「(恐怖などで)震える」、like a leafは「木の葉のように」。

⑱ Trembling was right.

▶「震えていることには違いなかった」または「確かに震えてはいた」という意味。

⑲ I was trying to keep from laughing out loud.

▶ keep from V-ingは「～しないようにする、～するのをこらえる」(≒ avoid V-ing)。

✍ 次の英文を日本語に直しなさい。

He gave up eating snacks in order to keep from gaining weight.

▶ laugh out loudは「声を出して笑う」。

⑳ I got onto the man's shoulder while he was reading the newspaper and stayed there.

▶ gotとstayedが並列関係になる。get onto ～は「～の上に乗る」。

▶ thereは男性の肩の上を指す。

㉑ Suddenly he put the paper down, yawned, stretched, and remarked, "Bedtime, I guess.

▶ yawnは「あくびをする」、stretchは「伸びをする」。

▶ remarkは「(意見など)を述べる」。

㉒ Nothing was said about the barn.

▶ Nothingが主語の受け身の文。「納屋に(入れておくことに)ついて何も言わなかった」ということ。

㉓ That's the way I entered my house.

▶ That's the way ～は「このようにして～」(≒ That's how ～)。

▶ entered my houseとは、「家猫になった」ということ。

確認問題

語彙

1 次の文の意味が通るように、右から単語を選んで（ ）内に補いなさい。

interfere
spoil
fetch
tremble

(1) Try not to (　　　) the opportunity.

(2) Her lips began to (　　　) and she burst out crying.

(3) Knowing he was busy, they tried not to (　　　) with his work.

2 次の各組で下線部の発音がほかと異なるものを１つずつ選び、記号で答えなさい。

(1) ア crazy　イ fasten　ウ flashlight　エ affluence

(2) ア miserable　イ piteously　ウ resist　エ lightning

(3) ア yawn　イ awkward　ウ claw　エ bellow

文法・表現

1 日本語に合うように、（ ）内に適切な語を入れなさい。

(1) 私たちはすぐにパーティーの準備にとりかかった。
We (　　　) (　　　) immediately preparing the party.

(2) マイクは決断をまったく急いではいなかった。
Mike was not (　　　) any (　　　) to make a decision.

(3) いったい全体、彼らはそこで何をしているのだろう。
(　　　) on (　　　) are they doing there?

(4) 加藤先生はいつものように、即座にすべての質問に答えた。
Ms. Kato answered all the questions (　　　) and (　　　), as usual.

(5) もっと好意的な態度だったら、彼の気持ちを和らげることができたのに。
A friendlier attitude (　　　) (　　　) (　　　) him up.

(6) 宝くじに当たったあと、彼は興奮して正気を失っていた。
After winning the lottery, he was (　　　) of his (　　　) with excitement.

2 日本語に合うように、（ ）内の語句を並べかえなさい。

(1) 彼は何も知らないかのように、そのことについてたずねました。
He asked me about that (knew / he / as / nothing / though).
He asked me about that ______________________________.

(2) 難民たちは何日も水しか口にしていなかったに違いない。
(off / have / living / the refugees / been / must) only water for days.
__________________________________ only water for days.

(3) 彼のぼうしを見たとき、私は声を上げて笑うのをがまんできなかった。
I (out / keep / loud / laughing / couldn't / from) when I saw his hat.
I __________________________________ when I saw his hat.

(4) サリーは上司に取り入るために、その仕事をするのを申し出た。
Sally offered to (to / to / the tasks / her boss / do / make / up).
Sally offered to __________________________________.

総合

次の文を読んで、あとの問いに答えなさい。

He unfastened me and put me down. I kept on yelling as he went off, and of course, as I knew he would, he turned around and turned on his flashlight to see whether I was following him, (①) of course I was. He picked me up, saying, "Kitty, stay there!" I anchored myself to his shirt again. We kept going through this routine. He said, "Don't kid yourself, Kitty," and marched off with me, but this time he took me to the barn, (②) he rummaged about until he found an old cardboard box, into (③) he dumped me. He said, "There! You can stay there, and ④( ) heaven's ( ) keep quiet!" Then he walked off again but couldn't resist turning around and putting the light on to see if I was going to follow him again. This time I didn't. ⑤I just sat there looking at him, (showing / my head / with / the box / above), and he stood looking at me. And so I gave him the Silent Miaow. When I give ⑥the Silent Miaow I open my mouth as if I am going to miaow. But no sounds come out. I look so sad that people give me anything I ask for.

問1 (①)(②)(③)に適する語を下から選んで入れなさい。ただし、同じ語を2回使ってもかまわない。
〔that which where what〕

問2 下線部④が「お願いだから」という意味になるように、( )に適する語を入れなさい。

問3 下線部⑤の( )内の語句を並べかえて、英文を完成させなさい。

問4 下線部⑥はどのようなことに役立つか、日本語で説明しなさい。

Story 2 Mute in an English-only World

教科書pp.166〜167 *ll*.1〜25 I

①When I read of the trouble in Palisades Park, New Jersey, over the proliferation of Korean-language signs along its main commercial strip, I unexpectedly sympathized with the frustrations, resentments, and fears of the longtime residents. ②They clearly felt alienated and even unwelcome in a vital part of their community. ③The town, like seven others in New Jersey, has passed laws requiring that half of any commercial sign in a foreign language be in English.

④Now I certainly would never tolerate any exclusionary ideas about who could rightfully settle and belong in the town. ⑤But having been raised in a Korean immigrant family, I saw every day the exacting price and power of language, especially with my mother, who was an outsider in an English-only world. ⑥In the first years we lived in America, my mother could speak only the most basic English, and she often encountered great difficulty whenever she went out.

⑦We lived in New Rochelle, New York, in the early seventies, and most of the local businesses were run by the descendants of immigrants who, generations ago, had come to the suburbs from New York City. ⑧Proudly dotting Main Street and North Avenue were Italian pastry and cheese shops, Jewish tailors and cleaners, and Polish and German butchers and bakers. ⑨If my mother's marketing couldn't wait until the weekend, when my father had free time, she would often hold off until I came home from school to buy the groceries.

このセクションの内容

「私」は、パリセーズパークの韓国語の（A.　　　　　）の激増による、長年の住民の怒りや疎外感に同情している。（B.　　　　　）系移民の家庭で育った「私」は、アメリカで暮らし始めた最初の数年間、母が英語だけの世界で大変な苦労をするのを見てきた。母は基本的な英語しか話せなかったので、（C.　　　　　）に行くにも、父の時間が空く週末まで待てないときは、「私」が学校から帰るまで待っていた。

背景　ニュージャージー州パリセーズパークでは、1980年代後半に韓国系の移民が急増し、街はハングルの看板であふれていた。ハングルの看板は韓国系移民だけしか理解できず、英語を使う古くからの住民の反感を買っていた。1994年に自治体は、商店の看板に英語の併記と、さらに英語が看板の半分を占めるように義務づけた。この義務化には、反対派の韓国系の商店主らと賛成派の古くからの住民の間で議論が起こった。本編は、韓国系アメリカ人作家のChang-Rae Leeがこの騒動についてニューヨークタイムズ紙に寄稿したものである。

① When I read of the trouble in Palisades Park, New Jersey, over the proliferation of Korean-language signs along its main commercial strip, I unexpectedly sympathized with the frustrations, resentments, and fears of the longtime residents.

▶ read of ～は「～のことを読んで知る」。

▶ Palisades Park, New Jersey「ニュージャージー州パリセーズパーク」は韓国系移民の多い地区として知られている。

▶ (trouble) over ～は「～についての(問題)、～をめぐる(問題)」。

▶ the proliferation of Korean-language signsは「韓国語の看板の激増」。

▶ itsはPalisades Parkを指す。commercial stripは「繁華街」。

▶ sympathize with ～は「～に同情する」、frustrationは「いらだち」、resentmentは「怒り、憤り」。

▶ longtime residents「長年の住民」とは、主に白人で英語を使い、韓国語が理解できない人々のことを指す。

② They clearly felt alienated and even unwelcome in a vital part of their community.

▶ Theyは①の文のthe longtime residentsを指す。

▶ feel alienatedは「疎外されていると感じる」(≒ feel like not belonging)。*cf.* alien「〔形容詞〕異質な」、「〔名詞〕外国人、異星人」

▶ in a vital part of ～は「～の重要[不可欠]な部分で」。

③ The town, like seven others in New Jersey, has passed laws requiring that half of any commercial sign in a foreign language be in English.

▶ pass lawsは「法律を可決する」。

▶ requiring ～はlawsを修飾する現在分詞で、laws requiring that ～で「～ということを要求する[義務づける]法律」の意味。

▶ that以下は仮定法現在で、動詞は原形になる(イギリスでは〈should＋動詞の原形〉が使われることが多い)。仮定法現在は、提案や要求を表す文の

このセクションの内容 の答え→　A. 看板　B. 韓国　C. 買い物

that節内で使われる。

例 It is *necessary* that smoking indoors *be* prohibited.
「屋内での喫煙は禁止される必要がある」

✍ 次の英文を日本語に直しなさい。

The doctor advised her that she stay in bed for a few more days.

____

④ Now I certainly would never tolerate any exclusionary ideas about who could rightfully settle and belong in the town.

▶ Nowは「さて」、certainlyは「確かに、間違いなく」。

▶ would never tolerate ～は「決して～を容認するつもりはない」。wouldは現在の〈意志〉を表す。

▶ exclusionary ideasは「(異文化や異民族に対する) 排他的な考え」。

▶ who以下はaboutの目的語で、「町に定住する正当な資格が誰にあるか」の意味。rightfullyは「正当に」、belongは「(所属する) 資格がある」。

✍ 次の英文を完成させなさい。

何が目標の達成の助けになるか、話し合いましょう。

Let's talk about (　　　) (　　　) help us achieve our goals.

⑤ But having been raised in a Korean immigrant family, I saw every day the exacting price and power of language, especially with my mother, who was an outsider in an English-only world.

▶ having been raisedは完了形の受け身の分詞構文。「(韓国人移民の家庭で) 育てられたので」(理由) の意味。

✍ 次の英文を日本語に直しなさい。

Having been written in a language I didn't know, I was at a loss.

______________________________、私はとまどった。

▶ the exacting price and power of languageは「言語の厳しい代償と権力」。移民として暮らすためには、土地の言語 (ここでは英語) の習得が不可欠であり、言語が生活する上で決定的な力を持つということ。

▶ especially with ～は「特に～に対して」。

▶ who以下はmy motherを補足説明している。outsiderは「よそ者、部外者」。

⑥ In the first years we lived in America, my mother could speak only the most basic English, and she often encountered great difficulty whenever she went out.

▶ In the first years we lived in ～は「私たちが～に住んでいた最初の数年間に」。weの前に関係副詞のwhenが省略されている。

▶ encounterは「(困難や予期せぬことなど)に遭遇する」。

▶ whenever ～は「～するときはいつも、～するたびに」。

✍ 次の英文を日本語に直しなさい。

I feel relaxed whenever I walk in this park.

____

⑦ **We lived in New Rochelle, New York, in the early seventies, and most of the local businesses were run by the descendants of immigrants who, generations ago, had come to the suburbs from New York City.**

▶ in the early seventiesは「70年[1970年]代初頭に」。

▶ were run by ～は受け身で、「～によって経営されていた」。

▶ the descendants of immigrantsは「移民の子孫」。

▶ whoは主格の関係代名詞で、immigrantsを修飾する。

▶ had comeは過去完了で、1970年代に筆者とその家族がニューロシェルに住んでいたころよりもさらに(何世代も)前のことを表す。

⑧ **Proudly dotting Main Street and North Avenue were Italian pastry and cheese shops, Jewish tailors and cleaners, and Polish and German butchers and bakers.**

▶ Italian ～ bakersが主語で、その様子(述部)が文頭に倒置されている。

✍ 次の英文を日本語に直しなさい。

Displayed on the wall were the artist's famous paintings.

____

▶ Proudly dotting ～は「～に誇らしげに点在している」。dotは他動詞で「～に点在している」の意味。

▶ tailorは「仕立て職人」、butcherは「精肉店」。

⑨ **If my mother's marketing couldn't wait until the weekend, when my father had free time, she would often hold off until I came home from school to buy the groceries.**

▶ marketingは「買い物」(≒ shopping)。

▶ when my father had free timeはthe weekendがどのような時か補足説明している(非制限用法の関係副詞節)。「その時(＝週末)は父の時間が空いていたのだが」の意味。

▶ would often *do*は「(よく)～したものだ」の意味で、過去の習慣を表す。

▶ hold offは「待つ、後回しにする」(≒ wait)。ここでは、「私」が学校から帰宅するまで、買い物に出かけずに待っていたということ。

▶ to buy the groceriesは「食料雑貨品を買うために」。

教科書pp.167〜168 *ll*.26〜54 Ⅱ

①Though I was only six or seven years old, she insisted that I go out shopping with her and my younger sister. ②I mostly loathed the task, partly because it meant I couldn't spend the afternoon off playing catch with my friends but also because I knew our errands would inevitably lead to an awkward scene, and that I would have to speak up to help my mother.

③I was just learning the language myself, but I was a quick study, as children are with new tongues. ④I had spent kindergarten in almost complete silence, hearing only the high nasality of my teacher and comprehending the little but cranky wails and cries of my classmates. ⑤But soon, seemingly mere months later, I had already become a terrible ham and mimic, and I would crack up my father with impressions of teachers, his friends, and even himself. ⑥My mother scolded me for aping his speech, and the one time I attempted to make light of hers I got a roundhouse smack on my bottom.

For her, the English language was not very funny. ⑦It usually meant trouble and a good dose of shame, and sometimes real hurt. ⑧Although she had a good reading knowledge of the language from university classes in South Korea, she had never practiced actual conversation. So in America she used English flash cards and phrase books and watched television with us kids. ⑨And she faithfully carried a pocket workbook illustrated with stick-figure people and compound sentences to be filled in.

⑩But none of it seemed to do her much good. ⑪Staying mostly at home to care for us, she didn't have many chances to try out sundry words and phrases. ⑫When she did, say, at the window of the post office, her readied speech would stall, freeze, sometimes altogether collapse.

このセクションの内容

「私」は6、7歳で母の（A.　　　　）に付き合い、母に代わって話をした。「私」の英語の上達は早かった。一方、母は（B.　　　　）の練習をしたことがなく、練習帳は持っていたものの役に立たなかった。母はたいてい家にいたため、単語やフレーズを試す（C.　　　　）が多くなかった。

① Though I was only six or seven years old, she insisted that I go out shopping with her and my younger sister.

▶ sheは筆者の母親を指す。

▶ insist that ～は「～を要求する[言い張る]」。

② I mostly loathed the task, partly because it meant I couldn't spend the afternoon off playing catch with my friends but also because I knew our errands would inevitably lead to an awkward scene, and that I would have to speak up to help my mother.

▶ mostlyは「たいていは」、loatheは「～をひどく嫌う」(≒ hate)。

▶ the taskとは、母親と一緒に買い物に行くこと。

▶ 買い物を嫌う理由が、partly because ～ but also because ...「一部には～という理由で、しかしまた…という理由で」と２種類述べられている。

▶ spend ～ off V-ingは「…して～をのんびり過ごす」(≒ spend ～ leisurely V-ing)、play catchは「キャッチボールをする」。

✍ 次の英文を日本語に直しなさい。

She usually spends her evenings off reading books.

____

▶ but also because以下は、knew (that) ～ and that ...の形で、knewの目的語にあたる節が２つ続いている。

▶ errandは「使い走り、任務」、inevitablyは「必然的に」、lead to ～は「～につながる、～という結果になる」。

▶ なぜ母親との買い物がan awkward scene「気まずい状況」になるのかは、and that以下で述べられている。speak upは「大声で話す」。

▶ ２つ目の理由は、英語が話せない母親との買い物は、彼女の代わりに「私」が店員と大声で話さなければならず、それが必然的に気まずい状況になるとわかっていたから。

③ I was just learning the language myself, but I was a quick study, as children are with new tongues.

▶ be just V-ingは「まさに～しているところだ」。the languageは英語のこと。

▶ be a quick studyは「学習[暗記]が早い」(≒ learn very quickly)。

▶ as children areは「子どもが(そうである)ように」。areのあとにquick studiesが省略されている。with new tonguesは「新しい言語に関して」。

④ I had spent kindergarten in almost complete silence, hearing only the high nasality of my teacher and comprehending the little but cranky wails and cries of my classmates.

このセクションの内容 の答え→ A. 買い物 B. (英)会話 C. 機会

▶ had spent kindergarten「幼稚園（の時期）を過ごした」は過去完了で、「私」が6、7歳のころよりも前のことを表す。

▶ in almost complete silenceは「ほとんど何も話さずに」。

▶ hearing ～とcomprehending ～は〈付帯状況〉の分詞構文。comprehendは「～を十分に理解する」。

▶ high nasalityは「高い鼻音[鼻声]」、the little but cranky wails and criesは「小さいが不機嫌そうな泣き叫ぶ声」（≒ the little but irritable whining and crying）。

⑤ But soon, seemingly mere months later, I had already become a terrible ham and mimic, and I would crack up my father with impressions of teachers, his friends, and even himself.

▶ seeminglyは「どうやら～」。seemingly mere months laterは「どうやらほんの数か月後に」の意味で、直前のsoonについて補足説明をしている。

▶ become a terrible ham and mimicは「ひどく大げさにふるまったり、ものまねをしたりするようになる」。hamは「演技過剰の役者」、mimicは「ものまねをする人」。

▶ would *do*は「～したものだ」（過去の習慣）、crack up ～は「～を大笑いさせる」（≒ make ～ laugh a lot）。

✍ 次の英文を日本語に直しなさい。

She told a joke that cracked up her friends.

____

▶ with ～は「～で」（手段）。with impressions of ～で「～のものまねで」。hisとhimselfはmy fatherを指す。

⑥ My mother scolded me for aping his speech, and the one time I attempted to make light of hers I got a roundhouse smack on my bottom.

▶ scold ～ for ...は「～を…（の理由）でしかる」。

▶ apeは動詞で「～のものまね[猿まね]をする」の意味。

▶ speechは「話し方」。hisは「私」の父親のこと。

▶ the one time ～は「一度だけ～のときには」の意味で、hersまでが副詞節になる。

▶ attempt to *do*は「～しようとする」、make light of ～は「～をからかう、～を軽視する」（≒ joke about ～）、hersはher speechのこと。

▶ roundhouse smackは「大きな平手打ち」。*cf.* roundhouse kick「回しげり」

⑦ It usually meant trouble and a good dose of shame, and sometimes real hurt.

▶ a good dose of ～は「かなりの量の～」(≒ plenty of ～)、real hurtは「本当の傷」。

⑧ Although she had a good reading knowledge of the language from university classes in South Korea, she had never practiced actual conversation.

▶ from university classesは「大学の授業で得た」の意味で、knowledgeの出所を表す。

▶ had never practicedは過去完了で「私」の幼少時代よりも前のことを表す。actual conversationは「実際の会話」。

⑨ And she faithfully carried a pocket workbook illustrated with stick-figure people and compound sentences to be filled in.

▶ faithfullyは「忠実に、欠かさずに」。

▶ a pocket workbook illustrated with ～は「～で説明された小型の練習帳」。illustratedはa pocket workbookを修飾する過去分詞。

▶ stick-figure peopleは「棒人間(手足や胴体が線で描かれた人)」、compound sentences to be filled inは「書き込み式の[空所になった]重文」。

⑩ But none of it seemed to do her much good.

▶ none of itのitは、⑨の文のa pocket workbookを指す。「それ(＝練習帳)に載っているどんなものも～ない」という意味。

▶ do ～ goodは「～の役に立つ」(≒ benefit ～)。

✍ 英文を完成させなさい。

野菜を食べると肌によいでしょう。

Eating vegetables will (　　　) your skin (　　　).

⑪ Staying mostly at home to care for us, she didn't have many chances to try out sundry words and phrases.

▶ Staying ～は分詞構文で「～にいるので」(理由)の意味。

▶ care for ～は「～の世話をする」。

▶ many chances to *do*は「～する多くの機会」、try out ～は「～を試してみる、～を(試しに)使ってみる」、sundryは「さまざまな」(≒ various)。

⑫ When she did, say, at the window of the post office, her readied speech would stall, freeze, sometimes altogether collapse.

▶ didは⑪の文のtried out sundry words and phrasesを指す。

▶ 挿入されているsayは、「例えば」の意味。

▶ stall, freeze, sometimes altogether collapseは「行き詰まり、凍りつき、ときには完全に崩壊する」。

教科書pp.168〜170 *ll*.55〜80 Ⅲ

①One day was unusually harrowing. ②We ventured downtown in the new Ford Country Squire my father had bought her, an enormous station wagon that seemed as long as an ocean liner. ③We were shopping for a special meal for guests visiting that weekend, and my mother had heard that a particular butcher carried fresh oxtails, which she needed for a traditional soup.

④We'd never been inside the shop, but my mother would pause before its window, which was always lined with whole hams, crown roasts, and ropes of plump handmade sausages. ⑤She greatly esteemed the bounty with her eyes, and my sister and I did also, but despite our craving cries she'd turn us away and instead buy the packaged links at the Finast supermarket, where she felt comfortable looking them over and could easily spot the price. ⑥And, of course, not have to talk.

⑦But that day she was resolved. ⑧The butcher store was crowded, and as we stepped inside, the door jingled a welcome. No one seemed to notice. ⑨We waited for some time, and people who had entered after us were now being served. ⑩Finally an old woman nudged my mother and waved a little ticket, which we hadn't taken. ⑪We patiently waited again, until one of the beefy men behind the glass display hollered our number.

⑫My mother pulled us forward and began searching the cases, but the oxtails were nowhere to be found. ⑬The man, his big arms crossed, sharply said, "Come on, lady, whaddya want?" ⑭This unnerved her, and she somehow blurted the Korean word for oxtail, *soggori*.

このセクションの内容

週末に来客をもてなすために、「私」と妹と母は車で繁華街へ行き、(A.　　　　) なオックステールを買うことにした。母は精肉店に入り、順番待ちの (B.　　　　) の番号が呼ばれると、進み出てケースの中を探した。しかしオックステールは見当たらず、店員に何がほしいのかと英語でたずねられると、母は動揺して思わず (C.　　　　) で答えてしまった。

① One day was unusually harrowing.

▶ unusuallyは「いつになく」、harrowingは「悲惨な」（≒ painful）。

② We ventured downtown in the new Ford Country Squire my father had bought her, an enormous station wagon that seemed as long as an ocean liner.

▶ ventureは「思い切って～へ行く」。

▶ Ford Country Squireはフォード・モーター社の自動車の車種の名前。

▶ my father had bought herはthe new Ford Country Squireを修飾する節。had boughtはventuredよりも過去を表す。

▶ an enormous以下は、Ford Country Squireの補足説明。

▶ thatは主格の関係代名詞。as long as an ocean linerは「遠洋定期船[オーシャンライナー]と同じくらい長い」。

③ We were shopping for a special meal for guests visiting that weekend, and my mother had heard that a particular butcher carried fresh oxtails, which she needed for a traditional soup.

▶ guests visiting that weekendは「その週末に訪れる訪問客」。visitingは現在分詞。

▶ had heard that ～は過去完了で「（その時すでに）～を聞いて知っていた」の意味。

▶ carryは「（商品など）を扱っている」、fresh oxtailは「新鮮なオックステール」。オックステール（または牛テール）は牛のしっぽ部分の肉のこと。

▶ 〈, which〉以下はfresh oxtailsの補足説明。

④ We'd never been inside the shop, but my mother would pause before its window, which was always lined with whole hams, crown roasts, and ropes of plump handmade sausages.

▶ We'd（= We had）never been inside ～は過去完了で「（それまでに）～に入ったことがなかった」。

▶ would pause before its windowは「窓の前で立ち止まることがよくあった」（過去の習慣）。itsはthe shopを指す。

▶ 〈, which〉以下はits windowの補足説明。

▶ be lined with ～は「（道など）に沿って～が並べられている」。

例 The street *was lined with* food stalls.
「通りには食べ物の屋台が軒を連ねていた」

▶ ropes of plump handmade sausagesは「（つるされた）ぷりぷりの手づくりソーセージ」。ソーセージのひとつなぎをa rope of sausageという。

⑤ She greatly esteemed the bounty with her eyes, and my

このセクションの内容 の答え→ A. 新鮮　B. チケット　C. 韓国語

sister and I did also, but despite our craving cries she'd turn us away and instead buy the packaged links at the Finast supermarket, where she felt comfortable looking them over and could easily spot the price.

▶ greatly esteemed ～ with her eyesは「～を目にして大いに称賛した」(≒ looked at ～ longingly)。

▶ bountyは「(食べ物などが) ふんだんにあること」(≒ something provided in large quantities)。

▶ despite our craving criesは「私たちの欲望の[食べたいという]叫びにもかかわらず」。

▶ turn ～ awayは「～を拒絶する、～を追い払う」。

▶ linksは「(ソーセージの) ひとつなぎ」(≒ a chain of long thin sausages)。

▶〈, where〉は非制限用法の関係副詞で、where以下はthe Finast supermarketの補足説明をする。

▶ feel comfortable V-ingは「～して快適に思う[満足する]」、look ～ overは「～を見渡す」、spot the priceは「価格がわかる」。

✍ 次の英文を日本語に直しなさい。

He didn't feel comfortable speaking in front of a large audience.

____

⑥ **And, of course, not have to talk.**

▶ not have to talkは「(英語を) 話す必要がない」(≒ she did not have to talk)。

⑦ **But that day she was resolved.**

▶ that dayは、新車に乗って繁華街へ出かけた日のこと。

▶ resolvedは「決心していた」(≒ she resolved)。ここでは、新鮮なオックステールのある精肉店で買い物をしようと決心していたということ。

⑧ **The butcher store was crowded, and as we stepped inside, the door jingled a welcome.**

▶ as ～は「～すると(同時に)」(≒ when)。

▶ jingle a welcomeは「歓迎の音を立てる」(≒ give a welcoming ring)。

⑨ **We waited for some time, and people who had entered after us were now being served.**

▶ who ～ usはpeopleを先行詞とする関係代名詞節。

▶ had enteredは過去完了で、were now being servedより前の動作を表す。

▶ be servedは「(客として) 対応される」。

⑩ **Finally an old woman nudged my mother and waved a little**

ticket, which we hadn't taken.

▶ nudgeは「(人)を軽くつつく」。

▶ waved a little ticketは「小さなチケットを振った」。年配の女性が「私」の母に、順番待ちにはこのチケットが必要だと教えている。

▶〈, which〉以下はa little ticketの補足説明。チケットを取っていなかったので、呼ばれなかったということ。

⑪ **We patiently waited again, until one of the beefy men behind the glass display hollered our number.**

▶ one of the beefy men behind the glass displayは「ガラスの陳列棚の向こうにいる太った男性(店員)の一人」。beefyは「でっぷり太った、たくましい」(≒ big or muscular)。

▶ hollerは「～を叫ぶ」(≒ shout loudly)。

⑫ **My mother pulled us forward and began searching the cases, but the oxtails were nowhere to be found.**

▶ pull ～ forwardは「～を前に引っ張っていく」。

▶ be nowhere to be foundは「どこにも見つからない」。be to *do*は〈予定〉〈可能〉〈義務〉などを表す。

✍ 英文を完成させなさい。

空には星が一つも見えなかった。

Not a star was (　　　) (　　　) (　　　) in the sky.

⑬ **The man, his big arms crossed, sharply said, "Come on, lady, whaddya want?"**

▶ 挿入句のhis big arms crossed「大きな腕を組んで」は〈付帯状況〉を表し、hisの前にwithが省略されている。

✍ 英文を完成させなさい。

私の父は目を閉じて音楽を聞いていた。

My father, his (　　　) (　　　), was listening to music.

▶ Come onは「さて、さあ」と客の注文を促している。

▶ whaddya wantはwhat do you wantのなまった音声。

⑭ **This unnerved her, and she somehow blurted the Korean word for oxtail, *soggori*.**

▶ Thisは⑬の文の、店員のことばを指す。

▶ unnerveは「～をおびえ[動揺]させる」(≒ frighten)。

▶ somehowは「どういうわけか」、blurtは「～を思わず口に出す」(≒ say something suddenly and without thinking)。

教科書pp.170〜172 *ll*.81〜116 Ⅳ

①The butcher looked as if my mother had put something sour in his mouth, and he glanced back at the lighted board and called the next number.

②Before I knew it, she had rushed us outside and back in the wagon, which she had double-parked because of the crowd. ③She was furious, almost vibrating with fear and grief, and I could see she was about to cry.

④She wanted to go back inside, but now the driver of the car we were blocking wanted to pull out. ⑤She was shooing us away. ⑥My mother, who had just earned her driver's license, started furiously working the pedals. ⑦But in her haste she must have flooded the engine, for it wouldn't turn over. The driver started honking and then another car began honking as well, and soon it seemed the entire street was shrieking at us.

⑧In the following years, my mother grew steadily more comfortable with English. ⑨In Korean she could be fiery, stern, deeply funny, and ironic, in English just slightly less so. ⑩If she was never quite fluent, she gained enough confidence to make herself clearly known to anyone, and particularly to me.

⑪Five years ago she died of cancer, and some months after we buried her, I found myself in the driveway of my father's house, washing her sedan. ⑫I liked taking care of her things; it made me feel close to her. ⑬While I was cleaning out the glove compartment, I found her pocket English workbook, the one with the silly illustrations. I hadn't seen it in nearly twenty years. ⑭The yellowed pages were brittle and dog-eared. ⑮She had fashioned a plain paper wrapping for it, and I wondered whether she meant to protect the book or hide it.

⑯I don't doubt that she would have appreciated doing the family shopping on the new Broad Avenue of Palisades Park. ⑰But I like to think, too, that she would have understood those who now complain about the Korean-only signs.

⑱I wonder what these same people would have done if they had seen my mother studying her English workbook—or lost in a store. Would they have nodded gently at her? ⑲Would they have lent a kind word?

このセクションの内容

精肉店の店員は、韓国語を話した母を見て対応を止め、次の（A.　　　　　）を呼んだ。動揺した母は「私」と妹を店から出し、その後も車のエンジンがかからないトラブルで悲惨な目にあった。次第に英語に慣れていった母も、（B.　　　　　）に亡くなった。約20年ぶりに母の（C.　　　　　）を見つけた「私」は、母と今のパリセーズパークの人々に思いを巡らせている。

① **The butcher looked as if my mother had put something sour in his mouth, and he glanced back at the lighted board and called the next number.**

▶ as if 〜は「まるで〜かのように」。as if my mother had put something sour in his mouthで「母が彼（＝店員）の口に何かすっぱいものを入れてしまったかのように」。

▶ glance (back) at 〜は「〜をちらっと（再び）見る」。

② **Before I knew it, she had rushed us outside and back in the wagon, which she had double-parked because of the crowd.**

▶ Before I knew itは「知らぬ間に、気がつくと」。

▶ rushは「〜を急がせる」。had rushed us outside and back in the wagonで「私たち（＝私と妹）をせかして店の外に出し、ワゴンの中に戻らせた」。

▶〈, which〉以下はthe wagonの補足説明。

▶ double-parkedは「二重［並列］駐車する」（≒ illegally park a car next to another）。

③ **She was furious, almost vibrating with fear and grief, and I could see she was about to cry.**

▶ almost vibrating 〜は〈付帯状況〉の分詞構文で「ほとんど震えながら」。

▶ be about to *do*は「（まさに）〜しようとしている」。

④ **She wanted to go back inside, but now the driver of the car we were blocking wanted to pull out.**

▶ go back insideは精肉店の店内に戻ること。

▶ the car we were blockingは「私たち（の車）が妨害していた車」。

▶ pull outは「（車などが）外に出る」（≒ start moving onto the road）。

⑤ **She was shooing us away.**

▶ shoo 〜 awayは「〜を追い払う」（≒ make 〜 go away）。

⑥ **My mother, who had just earned her driver's license, started furiously working the pedals.**

▶〈, who〉以下はMy motherの補足説明。earn a driver's licenseは「運転免許証を取得する」。

▶ furiouslyは「猛烈に」、start working the pedalsは「ペダルを踏み始める」。

⑦ But in her haste she must have flooded the engine, for it wouldn't turn over.

▶ in *one's* hasteは「急いでいる、あわてている」(≒ in *one's* hurry)。

▶ must have *done*は「～したに違いない」(推量)。

▶ flood the engineは「エンジン(のスパーク)を濡れさせる」(≒ fill the engine with so much fuel that it will not start)。日本語で「エンジンかぶり」または「スパークかぶり」と言われ、エンジンがかからなくなる。

▶ for ～は「というのも～」、wouldn't *do*は「どうしても～しようとしなかった」、turn overは「(エンジンなどが)始動する」(≒ start)。

⑧ In the following years, my mother grew steadily more comfortable with English.

▶ grow comfortable with ～は「～に自信がつく、～に慣れてくる」。

⑨ In Korean she could be fiery, stern, deeply funny, and ironic, in English just slightly less so.

▶ fiery, stern, deeply funny, and ironicは「激しく、厳しく、とてもおかしく、皮肉っぽい」。

▶ in Englishの前にbutが省略されている。just slightly less soは「それがわずかに弱まる」。soは直前のfiery, stern, deeply funny, and ironicを指す。

⑩ If she was never quite fluent, she gained enough confidence to make herself clearly known to anyone, and particularly to me.

▶ If ～はここではEven if ～「たとえ～でも」の意味。

▶ enough confidence to *do*は「～するための十分な自信」。

▶ make *oneself* known to ～は「～に自分のことを知って[わかって]もらえる」(≒ make *oneself* understood by ～)。

✍ 次の英文を日本語に直しなさい。

The neighbors tried to make themselves known to each other.

____

⑪ Five years ago she died of cancer, and some months after we buried her, I found myself in the driveway of my father's house, washing her sedan.

▶ die of ～は「～で死ぬ」。

▶ find *oneself* in ～は「～にいる」、drivewayは「私道」。

▶ washingはmyselfを修飾する現在分詞。

このセクションの内容 の答え→ A. 番号 B. 5年前 C. 練習帳[ワークブック]

⑫ I liked taking care of her things; it made me feel close to her.

▶ itは直前の「母の物（＝遺品）を手入れすること」を指す。

⑬ While I was cleaning out the glove compartment, I found her pocket English workbook, the one with the silly illustrations.

▶ clean out ～は「（内部を）掃除する［片づける］」。

▶ the one ～はher pocket English workbookの補足説明（同格）。

⑭ The yellowed pages were brittle and dog-eared.

▶ yellowed pagesは「（古くなって）黄ばんだページ」、brittleは「もろい」（≒ fragile）、dog-earedは「ページの隅が折れた、使い古された」（≒ used so much that the corners are damaged）。

⑮ She had fashioned a plain paper wrapping for it, and I wondered whether she meant to protect the book or hide it.

▶ fashionは「（手や道具で）～をつくる」、plain paper wrappingは「無地の紙の包装」。itはher pocket English workbookを指す。

▶ wonder whether ～ or ...は「～かまたは…だろうかと思う」。

⑯ I don't doubt that she would have appreciated doing the family shopping on the new Broad Avenue of Palisades Park.

▶ don't doubt that ～は「～だと疑わない、～に違いない」。

▶ would have *done*は仮定法過去完了で「～しただろう」の意味。母が生きていればという仮定の意味が含まれている。

▶ appreciate V-ingは「～することを楽しむ」。

▶ the new Broad Avenueは、1994年に問題になっている大通りで、韓国語の看板が増えて様変わりしたため、newを加えている。

⑰ But I like to think, too, that she would have understood those who now complain about the Korean-only signs.

▶ 言葉がわからずに苦しんだ母なら、韓国語だけしか書かれていない看板に文句をつける人々を理解しただろうという文。

⑱ I wonder what these same people would have done if they had seen my mother studying her English workbook—or lost in a store.

▶ these same peopleは⑰の文のthose who以下の人々を指す。

▶（韓国語が理解できずに疎外感を覚えている）住民は、生前の母の様子を見てどうするだろうかという文。

⑲ Would they have lent a kind word?

▶ lend a kind wordは「優しいことばをかける」（≒ speak kindly）。

確認問題

語彙

1 次の文の意味が通るように、右から単語を選んで（　）内に補いなさい。

(1) This could be a difficult (　　　) for kids.
(2) Any (　　　) of this town can join the event.
(3) He is a (　　　) of a famous painter from the 19th century.

resident impression errand descendant

2 第２音節にアクセント（強勢）のある語を２つ選び、記号で答えなさい。

ア　tol-er-ate　　イ　i-ron-ic　　ウ　im-mi-grant
エ　com-pre-hend　　オ　gro-cer-y　　カ　re-sent-ment

文法・表現

1 日本語に合うように、（　）内に適切な語を入れなさい。

(1) 私たちは10日間の休暇を沖縄に滞在して過ごした。
We (　　　) ten days (　　　) staying in Okinawa.
(2) 彼はよく姉のクモ嫌いをからかう。
He often (　　　) (　　　) of his sister's fear of spiders.
(3) そのウェブサイトの情報はまったく役に立たなかった。
The information on the website didn't (　　　) me any (　　　) at all.
(4) 彼はあわてて傘を持たずに出かけた。
(　　　) his (　　　), he went out without an umbrella.
(5) 英語を話さない人々は、地域社会から疎外されていると感じている。
People who don't speak English (　　　) (　　　) from the community.
(6) その時、私は駐車場から車を出そうとしていた。
I was trying to (　　　) (　　　) of the parking lot then.

2 日本語に合うように、（　）内の語句を並べかえなさい。

(1) 恥ずかしがらずに、自分のことを他人に知ってもらうようにしなさい。
Don't be shy, and (to / to / known / make / try / others / yourself).
Don't be shy, and ______________________________.
(2) 健康でいるためにはたくさん笑う必要があります。
You need (to / of / stay / dose / healthy / laughter / a good).
You need ______________________________.

(3) コメディアンのダンスで、観衆は大笑いした。
The comedian's (the audience / up / dance / cracked).
The comedian's ________________________________.

(4) 彼は私を慰めるために、優しいことばをかけてくれた。
(me / make / word / lent / to / he / a kind) feel better.
________________________________ feel better.

総合

次の文を読んで、あとの問いに答えなさい。

We'd never been inside the shop, but my mother would pause before its window, which was always lined with whole hams, crown roasts, and ropes of plump handmade sausages. She greatly (①) the bounty with her eyes, and my sister and I did also, but despite our craving cries she'd turn us away and instead buy the packaged links at ②the Finast supermarket, where she felt comfortable looking them over and could easily spot the price. And, of course, not have to talk.

But that day she was (③). The butcher store was crowded, and as we stepped inside, the door jingled a welcome. No one seemed to notice. We waited for some time, and people who had entered after us were now being served. Finally ④an old woman nudged my mother and waved a little ticket, which we hadn't taken. We patiently waited again, until one of the beefy men behind the glass display hollered our number.

⑤My mother pulled us forward and began searching the cases, but (to / nowhere / were / found / the oxtails / be). The man, his big arms crossed, sharply said, "Come on, lady, whaddya want?" This unnerved her, and she somehow blurted the Korean word for oxtail, *soggori*.

問1 (①)(③)に適する語を下から選んで入れなさい。
〔unwelcomed resolved loathed esteemed〕

問2 下線部②の場所についての次の説明を完成させなさい。
「私」の母にとって、包装されたソーセージを見渡すことができ、(　　　)が簡単にわかり、(　　　)必要がない場所。

問3 下線部④について、老婦人は「私」の母に何を教えたのか、日本語で説明しなさい。

問4 下線部⑤の( )内の語句を並べかえて、英文を完成させなさい。

解答

Lesson 1

▶ Section 1

⑦ differ from, another
⑨ Some, others don't

▶ Section 2

⑦ trained, to
⑧ in how

▶ Section 3

⑦ 一人暮らしが困難な
⑪ in, couple
⑭ あなたは意見と事実を区別することができますか。

▶ Section 4

⑥ requires, to
⑦ less likely
⑩ 成功者[成功する人間]になろうとするのではなく
⑫ be gone[absent/away]

確認問題

《語彙》

1 (1) vocabulary
(2) quantity
(3) realm
(4) landscape

2 イ、エ、オ

《文法・表現》

1 (1) differs[varies] from
(2) Some, others[some]
(3) start[begin] with
(4) in the, distance

2 (1) Some languages don't
(2) the way you

3 (1) in how we think about
(2) I asked you what season you like the best
(3) be less likely to be rainy
(4) is that you never give up

《総合》

問1 in
問2 ウ
問3 言語による色のスペクトラムの分類方法の違いは、重要な結果をもたらす。
問4 明るい青[*goluboy*]と暗い青[*siniy*]という言語における区別。
問5 色が変わったこと[色の変化]にすばやく気付くから。

Lesson 2

▶ Section 1

④ independently of
⑫ across

▶ Section 2

② which[that] is
⑩ as if
⑫ 私の観点では

▶ Section 3

⑬ cares for[looks after]
⑭ 助けが必要な[困っている]人々を助けることに喜びを感じた

▶ Section 4

③ in, supply

確認問題

《語彙》

1 (1) servants
(2) possibly
(3) intention

2 (1) × (2) × (3) ○ (4) ○

《文法・表現》

1 (1) took place
(2) as if
(3) work independently

(4) sense that
(5) draw out
(6) tangled[caught] up

2 (1) the way
(2) point, view
(3) all

3 (1) not a pet but rather a part of our family
(2) What's interesting about this movie is that
(3) found Madoka's speech to be excellent

《総合》

問1 ① growth
⑤ companionship

問2 介護者が極度に不足しているという問題

問3 ③ designed
④ easing

問4 only does it give comfort to the elderly

問5 ひょっとしたら、岡田氏の弱いロボットを応用できる可能性が最もあるのは、まさにこの分野においてかもしれない。

Lesson 3

▶Section 1

③ cope[deal] with
⑪ お金が十分にあったら、私はあのピアノを買うことができただろうに。

▶Section 2

① nor do
⑥ contributed to
⑩ 誰にとっても重要な問題だ

▶Section 3

③ 自分の人生を楽しめるかどうかはあなた次第だ。
⑮ 彼はその新聞が報道することなら何でも疑うことなく受け入れがちだ。
⑰ critical of

▶Section 4

⑤ Going[Proceeding] with
⑦ 交通渋滞に巻き込まれるのを巧みに回避した
⑧ より長生きする傾向がある

確認問題

《語彙》

1 (1) obtain
(2) rumor
(3) disagree

2 (1) エ (2) ウ (3) ウ (4) ア

《文法・表現》

1 (1) result of
(2) makes, for
(3) nor did

2 (1) tend, without
(2) caught[tangled] up
(3) gut level
(4) critical of

3 (1) It is a matter of the greatest importance
(2) are more likely to get angry when
(3) let their only daughter do whatever she wanted
(4) thinking of getting Tom to lend me

《総合》

問1 フェイクニュースを規制するための1つの方法は、ソーシャルメディアのサイトが自分たち自身を監視することだ。

問2 フェイクニュースに気付いて、それを広めるのをやめること

問3 be[feel] ashamed[embarrassed]

問4 The only thing I know for sure is

Lesson 4

▶ I

③ その事故がどのようにして起こったかを知った

⑦ By, time

▶ II

① set out[themselves]

⑤ 方向がわからなくなった

⑨ 私はどこへ向かっているのかわからなくなった。

⑬ gave way

⑭ no longer[more]

▶ III

① 目覚めると、私は彼女が家を出て行ったのだとわかった。

⑩ no reason

▶ IV

⑧ 匹敵するサックス奏者だ

⑫ committed[dedicated/devoted] to

確認問題

《語彙》

1 (1) prominent
(2) artificial
(3) rudimentary

2 ウ、エ、カ

《文法・表現》

1 (1) By, time
(2) become[get/be] disoriented
(3) drawing on
(4) no longer
(5) lost track

2 (1) There is no reason that she should
(2) woke up to find that it had
(3) think that the higher the income
(4) some of which were over 10,000 feet
(5) anger at him gave way to sympathy

《総合》

問1 切断手術をした人が、生物学上の[本物の]脚をもつ人々と同等の速さと労力で歩くこと。

問2 場所にもっと速く到着することを望む人々
長距離を歩く際に余力を残しておくことを望む人々

問3 イ

問4 (損傷を受ける前の)元の脊髄

問5 where technology not only helps eliminate disability but

Lesson 5

▶ I

① variety[range] of

④ とても進歩した

▶ II

⑤ fact is

⑨ 試験はすでに終わっているのに

▶ III

④ miss out

⑩ 私はテレビゲームをして時間を無駄にしないように言われた。

▶ IV

④ long way

⑧ コンテストで優勝した[1位をとった]のは

確認問題

《語彙》

1 (1) embarrassment
(2) accomplishment
(3) resist
(4) terribly

2 (1) イ
(2) ウ

(3) イ

《文法・表現》

1 (1) before you

(2) is, sight

(3) fact is

(4) at[in] hand

(5) last minute

(6) day, day

2 (1) Why would I go out when it

(2) go a long way toward making

(3) anytime you want to talk about

(4) I want nothing to do with
[I want to do nothing with]

《総合》

問1 ① miss

③ hit

⑤ keep

問2 knowing the deadline was drawing near

問3 1日の大半を、先延ばしをして無駄にしたと感じること。

問4「重要な入口」をうまく通り抜けるというのはつまり、仕事を始めるべきときに、していることは何でもやめるということだ。

問5 何か大変なこと[仕事]/何か楽しいこと

Lesson 6

▶ I

④ 彼らは貧困の問題に取り組んでいる。

⑧ 別の見方では、農業は環境にダメージを与える。

⑩ expected to

▶ II

③ partly because

⑤ 料理に関しては

⑩ referred to as

▶ III

④ たくさん練習すればするほど、緊張しないでしょう。

⑤ turned into

⑦ on, rise[increase]

▶ IV

① 10代の間で勢いづき始めている

⑦ 来週から実施される

⑨ set, of

確認問題

《語彙》

1 (1) unable

(2) disposable

(3) inevitable

2 (1) ○

(2) ×

(3) ○

(4) ×

《文法・表現》

1 (1) goal of

(2) expected to

(3) side, coin

(4) followed suit

(5) on the

2 (1) The sooner you get your homework done

(2) against cybercrimes will come into effect

(3) It was expected that the movement would gain ground

(4) associated with deforestation are being discussed

《総合》

問1 イ

問2 家電製品の寿命が短くなっていること。

問3 古いテレビは、たとえまだ申し分なく使用できるとしても、時代遅れのものとして交換される。

問4 故障で購入から5年以内に交換の

必要があった大型の家電製品の割合が、2004年の3.5パーセントから2012年には8.3パーセントに増加したという問題。

問5 製造業者が売り上げを伸ばすために製品の寿命を意図的に短くする戦略。

Lesson 7

▶ I

③ 彼は若いころ、昆虫採集に魅力を感じていた。
⑥ 彼女は事故の知らせを聞いてショックを受けた。
⑨ no choice but

▶ II

③ とても重要なものになるだろう
⑥ bring himself
⑦ of no
⑧ 私が記事のためにインタビューをした(人々の)ような人々

▶ III

② 3人に絞り込んだ
③ time writing
⑤ faced with
⑨ 彼らのほとんどはボードゲームを楽しんだ

▶ IV

① 現在進行中だ
⑥ 彼は新しいビジネスの機会を得るのに役立つ人脈をつくった。
⑨ provides[supplies], with
⑫ thrown[sent] into

▶ V

③ チームワークは、目標の達成に重要な役割を果たす。
⑥ 解決の仕方がわからなかった
⑭ think for[by]

▶ VI

① 気候変動が人間の活動によって引き起こされていると確信している
③ deprived us of
④ All[What], could do
⑤ パーティーに誰かを招待するのはあなた次第だ。

確認問題

《語彙》

1 (1) majority
(2) initiated
(3) resolution
(4) sympathized

2 エ、オ

《文法・表現》

1 (1) be of
(2) no, but to
(3) faced with
(4) All, sudden, found herself
(5) up to you

2 (1) convinced[sure/certain] that
(2) provided[supplied], with
(3) bring herself

3 (1) All we can do is to help them stand
(2) were deprived of a house to live in

《総合》

問1 ① he had been transferred to the police force
④ I know what I'm going to do

問2 これまであまりにも多くの人が、守らない約束を彼にしてきたから。

問3 マイケルの信頼を得ること / マイケルが学校に戻ることを許可するように、彼の上官を説得すること

問4 (1) ○
(2) ×
(3) ×

Lesson 8

▶ I

⑧ あなたはなぜ友人にそのような言葉を言ったのですか。

⑱ as, case of

▶ II

③ as it looked

④ restored, to

⑬ 彼はプレゼンテーションを写真やグラフで補った。

⑯ must have

⑲ あなたの助言がなければ、私は事故を避けることができなかっただろう。

▶ III

⑦ 音楽の驚くべきことは

▶ IV

⑤ あなたの連絡先の情報を主催者に伝えてください。

⑦ are being

⑩ 自分自身の勤務時間を選ぶことができる

⑪ 彼女の技能は重要だった[役立った]

確認問題

《語彙》

1 (1) impressive
(2) restoration
(3) analysis
(4) endanger
(5) deterioration
(6) possibility

2 (1) ○
(2) ○
(3) ×
(4) ×

《文法・表現》

1 (1) was[felt] delighted
(2) right off
(3) in, case
(4) available[accessible] to, public
(5) on display
(6) supplements, with

2 (1) What made
(2) Without
(3) must have lost

3 (1) What's amazing about this car is that
(2) The term "tablet" is used to refer to

《総合》

問1 any limit to what you can do

問2 ② pass
④ restore

問3 Much of the world's great art

問4 instrumental

問5 芸術作品へのアクセス[芸術作品に触れること]が増えるほど、(ますます)異文化に対する敬意が強まる。

Lesson 9

▶ I

⑤ 私はスクリーンから目を離すことができなかった

⑥ take up[start learning]

⑦ まだ彼らの慣習の中に生き続けている

▶ II

② おもしろいとわかった

⑦ 私の家族で何世代も受け継がれてきた

⑨ dress up

▶ III

⑤ out, blue

⑦ 彼らが何を言っても、あなたはあきらめるべきではない。

⑪ 濡れた地面が今朝雨が降ったことを意味するのは明らかだ。

▶ IV

② 市の中心部では手に入れるのが難しい

④ passed to

▶V

① 住むことができると考えられている
② パイロットは嵐に合わせて飛行ルートを調整しなければならなかった。
⑦ これらの植物は熱帯地方で生育する。
⑬ reluctant[unwilling] to
⑮ 私たちは今、インターネットの黄金時代を経験している。

確認問題

《語彙》

1 (1) definition
(2) appearance
(3) evolutionary
(4) instinctive
(5) migration
(6) exclusive

2 (1) ×
(2) ×
(3) ○
(4) ×

《文法・表現》

1 (1) much like
(2) live on[keep living]
(3) dressed up
(4) year, year
(5) out of, blue
(6) obvious[clear] explanation [thing]

2 (1) take my eyes
(2) Whatever happens
(3) reluctant[unwilling] to

3 (1) decided to take up knitting
(2) The technique has been passed down to
(3) the experiment turned out to be a great success

《総合》

問1 ハンガーで巣づくりをすること。
問2 ② come
③ settle
問3 Just as lobtail feeding began with one humpback whale and then was passed on
問4 現在、ハンガーの巣がとても多いので、それらが問題になってきている。

Lesson 10

▶I

④ differently from
⑤ 洪水は町の多くの[数十の]家を破壊した。
⑥ 住宅の需要も(同様に)増える

▶II

② 目的は犬が新しいおもちゃを気に入るかどうか
④ twice as much
⑤ either, or
⑨ slapped[slammed/banged], down
⑪ 生徒[学生]は本を読む時間がだんだん少なくなって[減って]いる。

▶III

③ spent, weeks
⑪ 黙っている人の２倍の知識を得る
⑫ It, who[that]
⑬ 助けることを優先したい
⑭ 音が大きすぎない限り

▶IV

① 彼らは先例のない[空前の]経済成長を経験した。
③ of reach
⑤ every reason
⑥ concerned about[concerned with/serious about]
⑦ 気温が下がるにつれて
⑨ さまざまな産業に影響を与えている[さまざまな産業で感じられている]
⑫ matter of

▶ **V**

② out, control
⑦ 自然災害の影響を受けた家族を助け出した

確認問題

《語彙》

1 (1) economic
(2) honesty
(3) celebration
(4) pursuit

2 (1) ×
(2) ○
(3) ○
(4) ×

《文法・表現》

1 (1) reason to
(2) In the end[event/result]
(3) put[place], above[before] [prioritize, over]
(4) long as
(5) out, reach
(6) less and less

2 (1) worked in favor of our team
(2) have applied themselves to developing new vaccines
(3) geniuses see things differently from ordinary people
(4) are concerned about the pollution of drinking water

《総合》

問1 seems that the situation is out of control
問2 of
問3 研究者たちは、ビデオを見たあとで人々がどれだけ喜んで見知らぬ人を助けるかを調べた。
問4 子どもの貧困のビデオを見た裕福な人々が、ちょうど貧しい人々と同じくらい寛大に、そして喜んで見知らぬ人を助けるようになったこと。
問5 ⑤ compassion
⑥ challenge

Story 1

▶ **I**

② 船を乗っ取り、宝物を奪った
③ grew, to be[become]
⑭ said[thought] to herself
⑱ 彼は娘をまるで幼い少女のようにかわいがる。

▶ **II**

⑨ will be coming[arriving]
⑯ 生徒たちは先生に取り入ろうとした

▶ **III**

② この薬があれば彼女の命は助かったのに。
⑤ 私は彼女の態度を軟化させようとした
⑪ 思い違いをすべきではない
⑭ with tears running[streaming/going/falling/dropping]

▶ **IV**

① これが彼女のほしがってきた[求めてきた]種類のドレスだ。
⑦ 私は笑いすぎて涙が出るのを止められなかった。
⑫ out of
⑲ 彼は体重を増やさないようにするために、軽食をとるのをやめた。

確認問題

《語彙》

1 (1) spoil
(2) tremble
(3) interfere

2 (1) ア
(2) エ
(3) エ

《文法・表現》

1 (1) set about[set out/set off/start out]
(2) in, hurry[haste/rush]
(3) What, earth
(4) then, there[there, then]
(5) could have softened
(6) out, mind[senses/wits]

2 (1) as though he knew nothing
(2) The refugees must have been living off
(3) couldn't keep from laughing out loud
(4) do the tasks to make up to her boss

《総合》

問1 ① which
② where
③ which

問2 for, sake

問3 with my head showing above the box

問4 自分の求めるものを何でも人から与えてもらうことに役立つ。

Story 2

▶ I

③ 医者は彼女にもう数日寝ているように助言した。
④ what will[can]
⑤ 知らない言語で書かれていたので
⑥ この公園を歩くときはいつも、私はリラックスした気分になる。
⑧ 壁に展示されていたのは、その芸術家の有名な絵画だった。

▶ II

② 彼女はたいてい夜は読書をしてのんびり過ごす。
⑤ 彼女は友人たちを大笑いさせる冗談を言った。
⑩ do, good

▶ III

⑤ 彼は大勢の聴衆の前で話すのを心地よく思わなかった。
⑫ to be seen
⑬ eyes closed

▶ IV

⑩ 隣人たちは、お互いのことを知ってもらおうとした。

確認問題

《語彙》

1 (1) errand
(2) resident
(3) descendant

2 イ、カ

《文法・表現》

1 (1) spent, off
(2) makes light[fun]
(3) do, good
(4) In, haste[hurry]
(5) feel alienated[excluded]
(6) pull out

2 (1) try to make yourself known to others
(2) a good dose of laughter to stay healthy
(3) dance cracked up the audience [dance cracked the audience up]
(4) He lent a kind word to make me

《総合》

問1 ① esteemed
③ resolved

問2 価格[値段] ／ (英語を)話す

問3 買い物をするには(順番待ちの)チケットを取る必要があること。

問4 the oxtails were nowhere to be found

Acknowledgments

Lesson 1 Adapted from "How language shapes the way we think," Ted talks by Lera Boroditsky, November 2017

Lesson 5 Adapted from "Why Procrastinators Procrastinate" and "How to Beat Procrastination," Wait But Why by Tim Urban

Lesson 10 Adapted from "Does Money Make You Mean?" by Paul Piff

Story 1 Adapted from *The Silent Miaow* by Paul W. Gallico Copyright © 1964 by Paul W. Gallico and Suzanne Szasz. Copyright 1964 by Mathemata AG. Copyright renewed 1992 by Virginia Gallico and Suzanne Szasz. English and Japanese reprint arranged with Aitken Alexander Associates, London through Tuttle-Mori Agency Inc., Tokyo

Story 2 Adapted from "Mute in an English-only World" by Chang-Rae Lee © The New York Times. Distributed by The New York Times Licensing Group.